SHAPING
KRUGER

**Animal behaviour, ecology and management
in Africa's premier game park**

Mitch Reardon

For my African family, Lindsay, Reza, Nina, Miari, Max and David
And for Olivia, my beautiful Singaporean granddaughter

Published by Struik Nature
(an imprint of Penguin Random House (Pty) Ltd)
Reg. No. 1953/000441/07
The Estuaries No 4, Oxbow Crescent, Century Avenue, Century City, 7441
PO Box 1144, Cape Town, 8000 South Africa

Visit **www.randomstruik.co.za** and join the Struik Nature Club
for updates, news, events and special offers.

First published 2012

10 9 8 7 6 5 4

Publisher: Pippa Parker
Managing Editor: Helen de Villiers
Editor: Lesley Hay-Whitton
Project Manager: Colette Alves
Design director: Janice Evans
Designer: Louise Topping
Cartographer: Martin Endemann
Proofreader and indexer: Emsie du Plessis

Picture credits (front cover): Gerald Hinde; insets: Walter Jubber

Reproduction by Hirt and Carter Cape (Pty) Ltd
Printed and bound by Toppan Leefung Printing Ltd

ISBN 978 1 43170 245 9 (PRINT)
ISBN 978 1 77584 017 6 (EPUB)
ISBN 978 1 77584 016 9 (PDF)

To download a comprehensive bibliography, go to **www.randomstruik.co.za/krugerbiblio**

Acknowledgements

I am indebted to Professor Norman Owen-Smith, a friend and A-rated scientist in the School
of Animal, Plant and Environmental Sciences at the University of the Witwatersrand, who
taught me a great deal about the ecology and behaviour of the Kruger's large mammals while
patiently fact-checking the first draft of the manuscript. I would also very much like to thank
Dr Harriet Davies-Mostert and Jessica Watermeyer who made many helpful comments regarding the
Cheetah and Wild Dog chapters. They are, of course, in no way responsible for any errors that may
remain. I am grateful to Yolan Friedmann, Grant Beverley and André Botha from the Endangered
Wildlife Trust for help and instruction during my field research, and to Kelly Marnewick, for fact-
checking the Cheetah chapter and supplying much needed fieldwork photographs. And, finally,
special thanks to my publisher, Pippa Parker, and my editor, Lesley Hay-Whitton, for providing a
happy combination of good fellowship and professionalism. And to the editorial and design team
at Random House Struik: Colette Alves, Louise Topping and Helen de Villiers, for the stream of
creative ideas and plain hard work.

Contents

Introduction

Nature conceals her mystery by means of her
essential grandeur, not by her cunning.

Albert Einstein, 1930

One crisp winter morning, I stood on the crest of Nkumbe Escarpment in southeast-central Kruger National Park, and gazed westward across weathered, straw-yellow grassy plains furrowed by a drainage line's winding green course. There was barely a sound or sight to remind me of the immediate century; it was like peering into the past. I could see for miles, but not far enough to spot the nearest building or road. Except for where I stood, the few traces of humans were poignantly fleeting. It was an image of old Africa distilled.

Because of the grip wild country has on the imagination, we feel drawn to this rigorous landscape and its primordial paradox, its blend of claw and thorn and subtle beauty. You can almost envisage that era when Earthly patterns and relationships existed solely between the land, the weather and the animals, when nature worked with all its parts. But that impression of a missing human link could not be further from the truth. As the stories you are about to read make explicit, people and their works, good and ill, are very much at the forefront of the Kruger Park saga.

There's another contradiction at play in these rugged, primeval expanses. With its potent allure, it's not surprising that to the untrained eye this mighty savanna appears ancient and enduring. However, appearances can be misleading. Savannas are Africa's newest environment. They arose around 25 million years ago when a dry phase swept across the entire continent, shrinking rainforests and ushering in an energy-rich, dynamic mix of woodlands, thickets and grassy plains. Nourished by seasonal rains and with year-round solar energy pumping through the food chain, this intensely physical landscape became a place of inordinate biological riches. Africa's savannas still support the largest herds of herbivores on the planet, side by side with a mix of herbivore-eating carnivores. This profusion, this density of life, contributes to a natural unruliness. Studies have shown that savannas are far from constant; instead they are forever changing, but these fluctuations are a part of ecosystem[1] functioning. At one extreme there are long-term oscillations, for example in climate and fauna and flora. We

Looking west from the crest of Nkumbe Escarpment.

Savannas are Africa's newest environment.

see only small parts of these in our lifetime. There are also short-term changes – drought and deluge, fire, nutrient flow and the impact of browsing and grazing – which manifest themselves in fits and starts. Intact ecosystems are generally resilient, with a capacity to absorb stresses and disturbances. How these biological systems operated before the influence of post-industrial humans is near impossible to guess, but what we do know is that there is no original condition to which we can hope to return, just as attempting to maintain the existing state is an ecological oxymoron; it's also unrealistic for a dynamic ecosystem such as the Kruger's. Change is inevitable; indeed, it is natural.

Grooming sessions help bond baboon society while freeing individuals of parasites.

The African savanna was also the place where some seven million years ago the evolutionary lines of apes and proto-humans diverged, with the descendants of the latter eventually gaining the upper hand, with all that meant to the other animals as soon as he got his hands on them. In the beginning, however, African animals co-evolved with members of our lineage. Africa still harbours many of the megafauna[2] that roamed much of the Earth in the last geologic period, but which have largely been exterminated elsewhere; this is largely due to the fact that for millions of years a prehistoric arms race ensued as animals honed their attack and avoidance strategies in lockstep with our early ancestors' improving hunting prowess. The naïve big beasts in the Americas and Australia, by contrast, first encountered humans just tens of thousands of years ago, by which time we were already fully modern, highly intelligent, organised and wielding lethal weapons. Entire species were hunted to extinction before they had time to beware of these new technological predators. Now we have arrived at the point where biologists calculate that *Homo sapiens'* uncontrolled population growth and depletion of resources threatens 50 per cent of the Earth's fauna and flora with extinction within a hundred years. Everything is affected: mammals, birds, insects, fish and plants. Our role as an exterminator species is shifting into an apocalyptic trajectory.

An awareness of what was being lost first stirred in the industrialising nations during the late 19th century. Although to many the protection of wild animals seemed an outlandish idea, South Africa became an early proponent of preserving parts of its biological heritage. Much of the country's wildlife had already been extirpated and the land converted to ranching or agriculture, but in 1898 the government set aside a chunk of rain-deprived wilderness between the Crocodile and Sabie rivers in the Transvaal Lowveld and called it the Sabi Game Reserve. Unchecked hunting had already wiped out Sabi's elephants and white rhinos but small numbers of other big game held on, thanks in part to the presence of what some colonial conservationists liked to refer to as the best damn wildlife wardens in Africa: the tsetse fly – carrier of sleeping sickness – and the anopheles mosquito – carrier of malaria – though the tsetse disappeared after the rinderpest[3] pandemic of 1896 nearly exterminated its cloven-hoofed hosts, particularly buffaloes, kudus and warthogs.

Sabi Game Reserve's first official permanent game warden set up camp in 1902, and for a man in love with wilderness it was a grand place to be and a grand existence. James Stevenson-Hamilton was 35 years old at the time, a tough-minded British ex-cavalry officer and aristocrat from the landed gentry. Before long he would become a ferocious guardian of this wild place. Like the African world

A warthog's tusks grow constantly, so this old boar's mighty ivories attest to a long-lived life.

he came to inhabit, Stevenson-Hamilton was filled with complexities and ambiguities. He evinced inner emotional intensity and outward formal coolness tending to aloofness. He admired order and discipline and could be a martinet; the black subsistence farmers he evicted from the Sabi Game Reserve gave him the African name Skukuza, 'he who wipes clean', which should not be mistaken for a compliment. Though short in stature, he conveyed the impression of contained power within a larger-than-life persona. His vision, ambition and impatience of others who did not share his view garnered him as many critics as it did admirers. Yet there was something almost poignant in Stevenson-Hamilton's avidity for his cause. He was an environmentalist ahead of his time, one of those solitary, pioneering naturalists who have all but vanished into history. For him, a patrol through the bush was akin to stepping into the library of life.

Driven by curiosity and provoked by wonder, this most scrupulous of observers used all his senses; he was a 'participant-observer' in the language of modern field sciences. Nothing escaped his eye; he wrote it all down with a hard-headed compulsion to describe everything he encountered with scientific rigour and cautious conclusions. A cross-section of that careful research, knowledge and understanding is threaded through this book. After 44 years of service he left the Kruger Park as his life's legacy to the nation. He and his wife, Hilda, chose Shirimantanga koppie (Stevenson-Hamilton's favourite retreat, this imposing granite outcrop south of Skukuza rest camp offers expansive views across the southern bushveld) as their final resting place. It's a fitting shrine to a remarkable man.

> **Like the African world he came to inhabit, Stevenson-Hamilton was filled with complexities and ambiguities.**

In 1926, with the ink dry and the reality of South Africa's first national park a matter of law, the stage was set for the Kruger to become one of the world's leading stewards of biological diversity. Although this book concentrates on the big end of the mammal spectrum – the so-called charismatic quadrupeds that attract tourists from across the world – the park also supports a startling profusion of other wild creatures. Among these are teeming invertebrates, which crude measurements suggest have as much impact as the large mammals; it has been estimated that about 50 per cent of South Africa's insect

Lichen-decorated boulder at Shirimantanga koppie, James Stevenson-Hamilton's final resting place.

diversity is conserved in the Kruger's four per cent share of the country. There are also 505 breeding and non-breeding bird species, 118 reptile species, 35 amphibian species and 50 indigenous freshwater fish species. The Kruger's 148 mammal species (of a total of 350 species for the whole of southern Africa) include 18 listed in the *Red Data Book*[4]. There are also 2 000 or so plant taxa[5], of which more than 200 are true trees, together with some 235 species of grass and a thousand forb[6] species.

But these days it's not enough for scientists and managers simply to monitor a list of species – the Kruger's wild creatures are more than merely a haphazard collection of life forms in a species-rich ecosystem. Species are indicators of the health of the natural systems that support them; the more species living in an ecosystem, the healthier and more productive it is. Consequently, park management must be able to interpret the processes that allow species to survive in a changing environment. And though ecosystems vary over time and space, they must be conserved as a complex and interactive whole. Reductionist science[7] is good for solving single issues but ultimately what is needed is a big-picture scenario that connects the dots and delivers a holistic overview – that's the essence of the science of ecology.

> **Consequently, park management must be able to interpret the processes that allow species to survive in a changing environment.**

A century ago conservation seemed simpler. The main issue was whether or not wildlife could survive commercial and trophy hunting. Now we have come to realise that ecosystems are so complex that the large number of interactions occurring within them means their behaviour cannot be described by a few simple rules. Most visitors' initial image of the Kruger's ecology is one dominated by the life-and-death struggle between predators and their prey. But the welfare of this system may be dependent upon an equally aggressive predator: transmitted diseases. Or the fickle arrival of seasonal rainfall. Or the intensity and timing of veld fires. The intricate and dynamic relationships between animals and their environment and the time scale over which

these events take place are inextricably linked to the
functional component of biodiversity[8]. It is only where
we are able to conserve the web of relationships that
make up intact ecosystems that all these interactions
can be accommodated.

In 1950 a research unit staffed by scientists of various
disciplines was established at Skukuza and, ever since,
zoologists, biologists, entomologists, ornithologists,
ecologists, archaeologists, technicians and technical
facilities have changed the way the Kruger is managed.
Conservation biology is a new and inexact science. Since
the Kruger's pioneer wildlife biologists had no textbook

A mating pair of elegant grasshoppers. Kruger has an extraordinary diversity of invertebrate species.

to consult to learn the consequences or propriety of interfering with nature's processes,
mistakes were made. Just a few decades ago most mainstream ecologists in the applied
fields of grazing land and wildlife management viewed savannas as stable ecosystems
where plants and animals were in an equilibrium determined primarily by soil type and
rainfall. Ecological theory held that plant production stabilised at a fixed 'climax' state
and that herbivore populations stabilised at levels determined by their habitat's ability
to support them in the long term. This was referred to as the veld's 'carrying capacity'. I
remember being told by a district ranger back in the 1970s that the Kruger was really just
a two million-hectare farm and needed to be managed as such. This was in keeping with
a concept that has its roots in livestock farming. In practice it involves keeping animal
numbers at well below their food supplies' ability to support them, so as to ensure healthy
herds and plant communities only lightly affected by herbivores. Back then it all seemed
to make elegant good sense.

Tending the Kruger as a wildland farm was all part of a science-based style of wildlife
guardianship, in which carefully planned grazing and browsing impacts were as important
a land management tool as fire. This period of interventionist management came to
be known as the command-and-control era. In an
attempt to impose order, at different times predators
were destroyed; elephants, buffaloes, hippos, impalas
and wildebeest were culled to maintain predetermined
population levels; and wild fires were tamed and
prescribed rotational burning was introduced. Ungulate[9] migrations were severed when
a veterinary fence (intended to keep wild animals from transmitting diseases to cattle)
was built along the Kruger's western boundary and again later when an electrified security
fence went up on the eastern border. The building of nearly 300 permanent waterholes –
268 boreholes at 230 sites plus 36 earthen and 33 concrete dams – became a top priority to
offset savage droughts that earlier had devastated wildlife populations. The development of
safe game-capture techniques made it possible to translocate wild animals between parks,
including the hugely successful reintroduction of white and black rhinos into the Kruger.

Yet, despite intensive and time-consuming input, arriving at viable solutions was
not always easy. The Kruger's old hands-on style of management represents a cautionary

This period of interventionist management came to be known as the command-and-control era.

Sunset over the Sabie River, and a hippo rouses itself for a night's on-shore grazing.

tale in that it has shown how bad humans are at trying to replicate nature's subtleties. It was one thing to respond to nature's long-term cycles and events, quite another to control them. Critics complained that culling wildlife in a national park was akin to playing God and that many conservation decisions were based on perceptions rather than knowledge. Was culling in the Kruger an ecological necessity or is the system capable of managing itself? Could elephant population growth trigger ecological suicide – ecocide – by destroying the environmental resources their species and many others depend on? Over the last couple of decades I began questioning my own reflexive support for programmes such as culling, which in hindsight seemed as much a state of mind as a policy. Some misconceptions are repeated so often that they become self-perpetuating. For instance, many members of the public 'know' that the Kruger's ecological carrying capacity for elephants is 7 000, although that figure was never declared policy nor based on much scientific evidence.

Now a new generation of scientists has taken up the challenge, determined to learn from past mistakes. They have had to execute U-turns on old policies regarding all three principal drivers of the Kruger's bushveld: fire, water and elephant. A nearly 50-year-old fire policy was dropped after it was realised that a fixed rotational fire regime, whereby blocks were burned at regular intervals, had homogenised wildlife habitat; it has now been replaced by a more variable system. It was also belatedly discovered that the relatively straightforward action of installing a new water point cast a broad ecological shadow, which resulted in a whole cascade of environmental side effects that changed the newly exposed area. Today you can see many of the abandoned bores and dams from the well-intentioned Water for Wildlife programme, which had the unintended effect of distorting wildlife movements and undermining the natural competitive advantage enjoyed by less water-dependent species, such as the brown hyaena. Elephant culling has been suspended, pending review. It's also now accepted that corrective action by conservationists, which can mask that of natural processes, should be reduced to a minimum. In a spirit of shared learning, policy makers now integrate interdisciplinary studies into protected area management plans in which science, monitoring and management are linked in an adaptive 'learning by doing' system. If scientists have models of how species and landscape interact, they can better predict the impact of climate change or other disruptive forces.

Although some scientists and rangers have written popular accounts of their work, many more have not, and often the latest research initiatives appear only in obscure scholarly journals. In *Shaping Kruger* I have attempted to bring together some of these important studies in an accessible way and arrange their stories in a historical context. You cannot make reliable conservation decisions without knowing the history – the natural history – of a place. So the narrative casts occasional backward glances into the little-understood ecology of pre-colonial southern Africa and is informed by the recollections of trailblazing hunter-explorers and the country's first conservationists.

We sometimes sidetrack to visit other African parks, for there is much to learn from their experiences. But my main aim is to give readers an insight into the lives of some of the animals that significantly contribute to the workings of the Kruger's ecosystems, and to do so by synthesising the results of decades of ground-breaking research into single species, predator–prey relationships, mammal distribution and browsing and grazing interactions. It's this kind of knowledge that those who manage game parks want scientists to provide, because our understanding of these matters is far from complete. And that's the thing about the Kruger: there's still so much more to learn that you always leave wanting to come back.

Now a new generation of scientists has taken up the challenge, determined to learn from past mistakes.

---

1   An ecosystem is here defined as the collection of living and non-living elements that exist and function as a unit.
2   Megafauna is a term used to refer to large-bodied mammals weighing more than 45 kilograms.
3   Rinderpest is a highly infectious bovine typhus introduced with Indian cattle into Eritrea, which swept the length of Africa and reached the Kruger area at the end of the 19th century.
4   The IUCN Red List of Threatened Species (also known as the IUCN Red List or Red Data List), founded in 1963, is the world's most comprehensive inventory of the global conservation status of biological species. The International Union for Conservation of Nature (IUCN) is the world's main authority on the conservation status of species. A series of Regional Red Lists are produced by countries or organisations, which assess the risk of extinction to species within a political management unit. The IUCN Red List is set upon precise criteria to evaluate the extinction risk of thousands of species and subspecies. These criteria are relevant to all species and all regions of the world. The aim is to convey the urgency of conservation issues to the public and policy makers, as well as help the international community to try to reduce species extinction.
5   Taxa (plural form of taxon) are groupings of organisms given a formal taxonomic name, such as family, genus, species, subspecies, race.
6   Forbs are any herbs (non-woody plants) that are not grass or grass-like.
7   Reductionism in science says that a complex system can be explained by reduction to its fundamental parts. Some argue that inappropriate use of reductionism limits our understanding of complex systems. A contrast to the reductionist approach is holism, the idea that things can have properties as a whole that are not explainable from the sum of their parts.
8   Biodiversity (short for biological diversity) is an expression of the variability of life, comprising genetic diversity, species diversity and ecosystem diversity.
9   Ungulates are mammals that walk on the tips of their toes, which characteristically bear hooves.

1

The role of the elephant

What is the right way to treat
beings such as elephants?
What is their proper share of
land and resources?
Why bother to keep them
around in the first place?
It depends upon whom you ask.

Douglas H. Chadwick, *The Fate
of the Elephant*, 1992

There is nothing that reduces us to our proper dimensions more rapidly and completely than spending long periods in the company of elephants. There is something special about them. It is not just their size, although theirs is a mighty life force. Perhaps it is their fabled wisdom and sagacity. Elephants have a highly convoluted brain, which like ours has a well-developed temporal lobe that endows them with an awareness of self and empathy for others. They also have a large hippocampus and cerebral cortex, parts of the brain associated with memory and the power of recognition. Memory is the cement that holds elephant society together. Adults can differentiate between as many as 200 individuals, some of whom they may see only occasionally. In times of drought, the herd matriarch dredges from her store of knowledge the best routes to take to exploit remote sources of food and water, information gathered throughout her life by memorising the paths taken by previous matriarchs. Her mental map pinpoints far-flung clay pans and seasonally fruiting trees linked by ancient trails pounded into the earth by the feet of many generations.

It is easy to become anthropomorphic when dealing with elephants. Little wonder we have such strong empathy for them – they reflect qualities we recognise in ourselves, or perhaps qualities we would wish to see in ourselves. But I wonder: am I ascribing human qualities when I watch youngsters at play within a matriarchal herd, tussling amiably while developing social skills, confidence and strength, and suspect that an almost-human sense of fun lurks inside them? Anyone who has spent time with elephants comes to realise that they evince complex emotions such as solicitousness, mischievousness and happiness.

They look after their ill and elderly and mourn their dead. They communicate using all their senses and have regionally unique languages.

Familial relations are various and fascinating, and emphasise care, concern, loyalty, altruism and huge affection for one another. They look after their ill and elderly and mourn their dead. They communicate using all their senses and have regionally unique languages. A good memory for the purpose of recognition and a sophisticated communication system are qualities shared by only a few of us in the animal world.

On the other hand, elephants possess some attributes quite unlike our own. I was intrigued to learn that, by using infrasound on ultra-low frequencies below the bass threshold of human hearing, they can communicate with other elephants over many kilometres. By making electronic printouts, researchers have discovered a total of over 400 elephant calls, three times the number that can be heard by human ears. With older matriarchs able to recognise the rumbles of at least 100 other elephants, these subliminal vocalisations keep kinship clans bonded as they trade information about resources and dangers and seek partners across pachyderm-scale spaces. The

Field studies are only now beginning to reveal the elephant's pivotal and very complex role in the unique dynamics of savanna ecosystems.

discovery of this previously unheard voice explained to me what till then had appeared to be a kind of elephantine extrasensory perception. On other occasions they can pass messages to one another through the merest twitching of the trunk. All of this only adds to the almost mythical status of this charismatic African icon. So when, in 2005, the South African National Parks (SANParks) called attention to the Kruger's burgeoning elephant population and confirmed that, after a decade-long moratorium, culling elephants would again become a management option, there was a predictable outcry, quickly followed by an acrimonious renewal of the great elephant controversy.

For all its majesty and mystery, the world's mightiest terrestrial animal is the most difficult for modern humankind to live with. In consequence, elephants continue to be the subject of much impassioned debate between differing factions within the conservation arena. No species has drawn more attention from the worldwide community of research scientists; elephant studies date back over half a century. Hundreds of theses, dissertations, books and published articles – of which more than 150 concentrate solely on the elephants of the Kruger Park – are available, all dealing with different aspects of elephant social behaviour, physiology, biology, ecology and management. The intense focus is justified, given the elephant's economic value and propensity for rearranging its habitat, not only for itself but for many other creatures as well. Yet, despite all that is known about them, elephants still remain, on some level, unknowable.

Field studies are only now beginning to reveal the elephant's pivotal and very complex role in the unique dynamics of savanna ecosystems. These megaherbivores[1] are the prime example of a keystone species[2] in that their activities can affect the niches and population levels of a variety of less dominant life forms. Anyone who has watched elephants going about their daily affairs soon realises that there is just no getting around it: their impact on vegetation is as spectacular as their size. In their pursuit of food, elephants transform their environment more than any other creature, except humans. Ecologists recognise that, together with fire and rainfall, these woodland modifiers helped mould the very look of savanna Africa. Up to 50 tonnes of its environment is eaten annually by each adult elephant. Foraging for 18 to 20 hours every day, a six-tonne bull grinds down as much

A protective mother elephant flicks her trunk in warning at a photographer who has ventured too close to her calf.

During Kruger's dry winter months, elephants are particularly partial to nutritious tree bark.

as 180 kilograms of wet mass consisting of grass, succulent herbs, leaves, roots, stems, fruits, flowers and tree bark, using molar teeth the size of house bricks. When pregnant or suckling a calf, a three-tonne cow eats proportionately more than a bull.

As bulk mixed feeders[3], elephants have the advantage of switching between trees and grass, depending on the season. Grass is preferred during the wet season, when it is most palatable and nutritious. In the long dry season, when annual grasses die back and perennials wither and become fibrous (with less than five per cent protein), elephants turn to trees and shrubs that have 12 to 15 per cent protein in their leaves. Using chemical analysis to measure carbon and nitrogen levels in elephant dung, University of Cape Town biologist Jacqui Codron discovered that in both the northern and southern Kruger an elephant's wet-season diet comprises 50 per cent grass, but in the north grass still makes up 40 per cent of their dry-season diet, whereas in the south it drops to 10 per cent. In the mopane tree-dominated north, elephants browse heavily on mopane twigs, but the foliage contains chemicals that inhibit digestive processes, and if enough is eaten it may even be poisonous. Codron believes that the northern elephants load up on poor-quality dry-season grass as an alternative to a potentially toxic diet of too many mopane leaves.

About 60 per cent of the huge amount of vegetation going through that vast cavern of a gut passes undigested. Via their abundant droppings – around 100 kilograms daily – elephants ensure a secure depository for the eggs of dung beetles and other insects and a food source for their developing larvae. By spreading the semi-digested food in their manure during their constant travels, elephants also provide a prodigious seed-dispersal service. Tests have shown that seeds of some sort are present in nine out of 10 elephant-dung heaps. As the smoothly rounded, carbohydrate-rich seeds of the umbrella thorn (*Acacia tortilis*) travel through an elephant's digestive tract, gastric juices soften their tough outer casing and those seeds not destroyed by chewing and digestion pass out unharmed. As many as 12 000 acacia seeds have been counted in just one ball of manure. The elephant benefits by eating the nutritious pods and the acacia benefits by having its seeds dispersed and fertilised. When the rains come, those seeds are ready to sprout immediately, whereas seeds in pods must weather for a long period before water can penetrate. Acacia seeds in elephant dung have a germination success rate of up to 75 per cent, compared with only 12 per cent for seeds taken from the pod; this means that changes in elephant numbers affect both micro- and macro-organisms linked to their food web.

As many as 12 000 acacia seeds have been counted in just one ball of manure.

A big bull at full stretch. As succulent browse becomes increasingly scarce towards the end of the dry season, elephants go to ever greater lengths to reach it.

Dependence on such powerful browsers for the dispersal of its seeds can, however, be dangerous for the parent tree. The sweet, fleshy, vitamin C-rich marula fruit so loved by Kruger's elephants (and by many other animals, including humans) is a case in point. Elephants feed not only on the fruit but also on the foliage and bark, which may damage or even kill the tree. Only female marula trees produce fruit, but evolution has not provided them with stronger branches than males – instead, the selective pressure of browsing may favour female trees with good resprouting ability.

The subject of marula fruit begs the question: do elephants really get tipsy by gorging on large quantities, as decades of anecdotes in travelogues and the popular press would have us believe? After all, fallen marula fruit can naturally ferment to an ethanol content of around three per cent after three or four days and is the base for the popular Amarula liqueur. A 2006 study by biologists Steve Morris, David Humphreys and Dan Reynolds from the University of Bristol discounts the legend as myth. 'Intoxication would minimally require that the elephant avoids drinking water, consumes a diet of only marula fruit at a rate of at least 400 per cent normal maximum food intake and with a mean alcohol content of at least three per cent,' they report. One theory posited by the researchers – that the elephants' apparently drunken behaviour may result from eating marula bark, which harbours beetle pupae traditionally used to poison arrow tips – has been discounted because elephants do not eat bark in summer when they seek out the fruit. Nor have the researchers eliminated the possibility that elephants may be much more sensitive to small amounts of alcohol than humans. Perhaps the issue is still unresolved.

Elephants also open up thickets and break down, trample and feed on tall woody grasses in a process known as facilitation, whereby one species provides niches for other species. Their role as a habitat modifier is urgently required to help re-establish the natural grazing succession in Mozambique's Gorongosa National Park. After more than 20 years of indiscriminate hunting, the 350 000-hectare park is being rehabilitated by the non-profit, United States-based Gregory C. Carr Foundation. One of its priorities is the reintroduction of elephants to reduce the enormous quantity of unproductive three-metre-tall thatching grass that is too high for more selective grazers to access. Elephants play a pioneering role in transforming tall grasslands into young regenerating grass shoots that are eagerly sought after by buffaloes and zebras. These intermediate grazers mow the grass down further, attracting wildebeest and impalas. In September 2008, SANParks veterinarian Markus Hofmeyr and his game-capture team helped speed up restoration by translocating six bull elephants 1 300 kilometres from the southern Kruger to Gorongosa.

Acacias are favourite elephant fare but the huge herbivores compensate for their heavy predation by providing a prodigious seed-dispersal service.

It is readily apparent that elephants facilitate ecological processes. But, insist those charged with managing the Kruger's biodiversity, too many elephants may have adverse consequences, not only for a host of other species, but ultimately for the elephants themselves. In enclosed and protected parks like the Kruger, the elephant population increases rapidly, doubling every decade or so to levels that are, it is argued, artificially and unsustainably high. At these densities[4], elephant-induced habitat change could adversely affect other species and potentially lead to large-scale elephant mortalities. Those advocating a minimal intervention approach point out that die-offs would ultimately regulate elephant populations, unless reproductive rates slowed earlier as a result of females' poor condition.

Proponents of holding elephant numbers at a desirable level point to events that occurred in East Africa in the 1960s as an example of what these giants are capable of doing in a congested environment. In Kenya, as the human population rapidly expanded, elephant range countrywide was cut from 70 per cent in 1929 to only 17 per cent by 1959, creating what became known as 'the elephant compression problem'. Formerly free-ranging elephants crowded into parks and reserves, and in several their feeding pressure helped transform savanna woodlands into grasslands. Tsavo National Park became a classic example of the

Elephants play a pioneering role in transforming tall grasslands into young regenerating grass shoots that are eagerly sought after by buffaloes and zebras.

compression hypothesis as its elephant population soared to an unsustainable 36 000 in the late 1960s. Concentrated in the arid 20 000-square-kilometre park – about the same size as the Kruger – the great herds began dismantling large tracts of the closed commiphora thorn scrub in inverse proportion to the distance from water, reducing it from an average of 90 mature commiphora shrubs per hectare in 1970 to five per hectare four years later.

As the elephants' food supply dwindled, an already critical situation turned desperate when a severe drought struck in 1971. The consequences were horrifying. According to park warden David Sheldrick, 9 000 elephants succumbed to nutritional anaemia, disease and heat stress, but wildlife consultant Ian Parker, a keen observer of events in Tsavo, put the total at closer to 15 000[5]. Tsavo was one of East Africa's last black rhino strongholds but the loss of the bush thickets that rhinos relied on for cover exposed them to poaching, which wiped them out. Another casualty was Tsavo's baobabs. Starving elephants used their tusks to gouge huge, fibrous strips of the soft, pithy wood from the baobabs' trunks, eventually bringing the weakened trees crashing down. By 1974, less than 20 years after the first reports of elephant damage, Tsavo's baobabs had been virtually eliminated. It was at this time that the first salvos between pro- and anti-culling factions were exchanged in newspapers and journals across Africa and beyond. That debate ended in East Africa after the region's elephants were nearly annihilated in an unrelenting poaching epidemic.

As the elephants' food supply dwindled, an already critical situation turned desperate when a severe drought struck in 1971.

Over time there has been a re-evaluation of what happened in Tsavo. It was known that the park had

Wedging himself between conveniently placed trees, an elephant simultaneously rubs fore and aft to remove parasites picked up in the veld and trapped during his mud bath.

alternated between open savanna and closed thorn scrub as elephant populations episodically waxed and waned in the late 19th century, and again in the late 20th century in the wake of intense ivory hunting. Exploring environmental variation over a much longer time frame, paleo-ecologist Lindsey Gillson analysed fossil pollen and charcoal collected from soils and sediments to shed light on how Tsavo's tree cover has changed over the past 1 400 years. Think of Tsavo as a mosaic comprising many patches of diverse vegetation, Gillson suggests, with tree density in each patch changing between woodland and grassland in a fire- and herbivore-affected process that may take several hundred years. Grazing species prosper when grasslands dominate, whereas browsers thrive when trees regenerate. The ecological significance of Tsavo's most recent disturbance cannot be judged without this macro-scale picture of trends and interactions within its ecosystem, she contends. The park may have looked sere and blasted in the short term but it was a lot more resilient than a lot of people anticipated. Contrary to dire predictions that elephant-wrought changes would turn Tsavo into a desert, riverine woodlands have regenerated, a sure sign that widespread irreversible damage did not occur. As Africa's most extreme example of habitat transformation, Tsavo makes a case for waiting and documenting what happens and then learning from it, rather than imposing some preconceived notion of an ideal elephant density before anyone can be sure what the ideal is. After all, not much can be learned about a park's systems' dynamics if elephant populations are kept at artificially low levels by culling.

After all, not much can be learned about a park's systems' dynamics if elephant populations are kept at artificially low levels by culling.

Undoubtedly elephants do remove tall, mature trees from the canopy. Even at low densities these ecosystem engineers leave their mark on the vegetation, but as long as they are free to wander they only temporarily disturb the habitats they use. But what happens when elephants fill up the whole landscape and there are no empty spaces left? Freedom to wander may have worked when elephants were at low densities with lots of unoccupied areas to move to, but ultimately habitable space in even so vast a place as Africa is finite.

So, what limited elephant numbers in prehistoric times? It has been speculated that perhaps there never was equilibrium between trees and elephants, but that instead a stable limit cycle existed in which elephants multiplied until nutritional deficiencies caused by a degraded habitat triggered die-offs and reduced fertility, allowing the vegetation to recover, whereupon elephant numbers began increasing again.

Another premise proposes that the oscillations between savanna vegetation and elephants resulted from varying levels of human predation and that the Kruger's current elephant population represents a return to pre-ivory trade abundance. Elephants and humans co-evolved in Africa and for most of that time 'ecological man' has been a predator of elephants. Although archaeological evidence in the Kruger region documents only sporadic elephant hunting by Stone Age cultures, that changed as people became more technologically sophisticated. When ivory attained its status as a precious commodity, it underpinned trade within sub-Saharan Africa and between Africa and its neighbours long before European colonialism.

In South Africa, commercial relations between the Limpopo Valley trading centre of Mapungubwe and Arab traders from Kilwa, Sofala and other Indian Ocean trading ports flourished in the 12th and 13th centuries. Traders travelled up the Limpopo River to barter glass beads and ceramics for gold, ivory, slaves and pelts (for instance leopard). Slivers recovered from ivory-working sites indicate that, although some ivory was used locally for personal adornment, it is probable that most was destined for export markets. In the late 15th century the Portuguese subjugated the east coast ports and by the 1780s bustling Delagoa Bay (modern Maputo) was exporting nearly 50 000 kilograms of ivory annually, mainly to the insatiable Indian and Chinese markets (until the Industrial Revolution Europe's demand remained moderate).

This was a raw, chaotic frontier society in which the white colonialists were still trying to figure out a way to survive and turn a profit. In this unfettered, formative stage there were few restraints and no questions were asked. The pioneers' attitude towards wilderness was hostile and utilitarian, the perfect milieu for the professional ivory hunter. Local tribes were eager to cash in on the 'white gold' rush. At times Europeans employed hundreds of skilled African hunters armed with rifles, who were able to operate in summer because of their partial immunity to malaria and on foot in the tsetse-fly belts where horses could not go. Inexorably the commercial-scale killing of elephants spread southwards to the very tip of Africa. A parade quickens as it goes downhill and by the mid-19th century the ivory rush was hurtling towards its climax. The English sport hunter William Cornwallis Harris recorded large herds of elephants around the Magaliesberg in the 1830s, but 20 years later when the artist Thomas Baines arrived they no longer existed. It was estimated that in 1855 more than 90 000 kilograms of ivory was exported from the independent, Boer-ruled territory known as the Transvaal, near the end of a commercial elephant hunting era that had begun almost 800 years earlier.

> The pioneers' attitude towards wilderness was hostile and utilitarian, the perfect milieu for the professional ivory hunter.

Where they are available, historical benchmarks provide an invaluable insight into elephant abundance in a particular place and what the vegetation looked like a century or more ago. Botswana's Chobe river front is a case in point. In 1877, the legendary British hunter, explorer, naturalist and bestselling author Frederick Courteney Selous and his party discovered as 'we continued our journey westwards along the southern bank of the Chobe ... that a dense continuous jungle, interspersed with large forest trees, came down in most parts to the water. This jungle-covered land rises in some places abruptly, in others in a gentle slope, leaving along the shore a margin of open ground (from 10 to 100 yards broad), covered with short grass, and formed, no doubt, by alluvial deposit. As we proceeded traces of the presence of elephants and buffaloes became more and more frequent, we kept a sharp lookout for fresh spoor.'

Where Selous encountered only traces of elephants, nowadays this part of northern Botswana hosts the largest contiguous elephant concentration in Africa, some 150 000, with dry-season densities of three to 12 elephants per square kilometre along the

Linyanti and Chobe rivers. This great variance in elephant numbers has led to huge, albeit localised, ecosystem changes. The scenic acacia-dominated riverine woodlands have gone and been replaced by shrub vegetation. This has raised anxiety among conservation managers and tourists alike regarding the elephants' potential to harm biodiversity by degrading the ecosystem. However, an in-depth research project launched in 1998 by the Department of Wildlife and National Parks in cooperation with Norwegian universities found little evidence of adverse ecological effects. On the contrary, it reported that the heavily elephant-impacted areas close to Chobe River had the highest biodiversity and were favoured by animals ranging from insects to guinea fowls, antelopes and lions. Fewer canopy specialist bird species were found than at less affected sites but there was no loss of bird diversity as there were larger numbers of generalist species[6]. A 2007 survey of the distinctive-looking Chobe bushbuck, for which particular concerns had been expressed, showed that their numbers had fluctuated with changes in woody vegetation density. Their population was low around 1900, peaked in the 1960s as the recovering elephant population made extra food available to smaller browsers by lowering the vegetation, and then declined to the 1990s as competition for food intensified. The population has since stabilised in shrubland unpalatable to elephants. All of these findings have led many scientists to conclude that Chobe's riverine woodlands were a 'transient artefact' resulting from low elephant numbers due to centuries of overhunting and that the return of the giants is restoring the vegetation to what it was before their reduction.

This great variance in elephant numbers has led to huge, albeit localised, ecosystem changes. The scenic acacia-dominated riverine woodlands have gone and been replaced by shrub vegetation.

Trees destroyed by elephants in a riverine forest: destruction or simply habitat modification? Attitudes are changing but the question remains a hot issue.

In what would become the Kruger Park, another English hunter, Frederick Vaughan Kirby, recalled: 'As lately as five years ago [circa 1890] there were elephants on the Timbavati [River], a herd of over fifty being encountered by some Boer hunters: they came from the extensive reed-beds at the junction of the Letaba and Olifants rivers and some still exist in the dense bush on the Libombo [sic] slopes.' When, in 1902, James Stevenson-Hamilton arrived as first resident warden of the Sabi Game Reserve, he found that 'the only indications of elephants were a few tracks in the neighbourhood of the Olifants Gorge. During the early part of the [Anglo-Boer] War a small herd had existed between the Olifants and Letaba Rivers, but after several had been shot, the rest had migrated to the east of the Lebombo, and no more were reported in the Reserve until about 1905, when I began to hear of stray ones near the Olifants-Letaba junction.'

As in Chobe, 'the absence of elephants for over a century probably favoured the establishment of Kruger's woodlands,' says Norman Owen-Smith, a research professor in African ecology at the University of the Witwatersrand and an expert in the ecology of large mammals and their impacts on vegetation in African savanna ecosystems. But more recently, with bush encroachment identified as one of contemporary Kruger's most pressing environmental problems, 'the conversion of extensive areas from savanna woodland to open parkland or even grassland through elephant impacts need not be detrimental', he argues[7]. That process was set in motion in the first decade of the 20th century as elephants filtered back to reclaim their place among the Kruger's megafauna.

'I think that these were the first elephants seen in the Game Reserve.'

In his delightful book *Memories of a Game Ranger* Harry Wolhuter – tall, gaunt, low-key and unpretentious, he was Sabi Reserve's first game ranger – remembers early one morning 'as I rode down towards the Olifants I saw what I at first took to be two huge rocks away out in the sandy bed of the river. It struck me as strange that I had not previously noticed these rocks, as I had passed that very spot many times; and then, as I watched, one of the rocks moved distinctly, and with a tremendous thrill it dawned on me that of course in reality they were elephants! I think that these were the first elephants seen in the Game Reserve.'

Five years later, in 1908, recolonisation through natural growth and international refugees arriving from Mozambique had more than doubled the size of the elephant population to 25. In that year, 'during the season of the marula fruit – about March – solitary bulls were noted by the rangers nearly as far south as Satara,' Stevenson-Hamilton reported.

By 1920 they were spreading up the Tende River and were fairly numerous along the Letaba. It was not, however, until in 1926 the wedge of country extending north of the Olifants River to the Letaba was incorporated within the Kruger National Park that the elephants were left completely undisturbed in this, their favourite country ... In 1938 there were several considerable breeding herds along the Olifants and Letaba Rivers, and others of smaller dimensions right up to the northern boundary of the Park ... Elephant hunting across the Portuguese frontier brought in a good many refugees, and altogether there could not have been less than 400 of the animals present in the Park in the above-mentioned year.

By 1957 there were 1 000. In 1964, with persecuted elephants thronging in from Mozambique and Zimbabwe (then known as Rhodesia), there were well over 2 000, though it is probable that these early ground surveys were gross underestimates. In 1967 the first complete aerial survey counted 6 500 elephants. The figure was a shock to the park's wildlife managers – far higher than the 1964 count of 2 400 would have led them to expect. Biologists working in the Kruger had already voiced concern about the effect elephants were having on vegetation. The latest count persuaded management to activate a decision taken at a 1965 symposium that had focused on the 'overprotection' of wildlife populations in parks. It recommended that in Kruger seven species – elephant, buffalo, hippo, giraffe, wildebeest, zebra and impala – be controlled by culling.

In 1967 the first complete aerial survey counted 6 500 elephants in Kruger.

The decision to cull was in keeping with the prevailing philosophy that adhered to a 'balance of nature' concept, which sought to protect the habitat's steady state. To do so required that elephant numbers be maintained below a ceiling of 7 000, or roughly one elephant per square mile (four elephants per 10 square kilometres), 'if the total destruction of the vulnerable areas near water is not to result', although this warning came after rainfall had remained well below average for five successive years. Elephant numbers were later capped at between 6 000 and 8 000, which was also the density at which they had been observed to disperse from favoured habitats to populate other areas. Eventually the culling of species other than elephants was discontinued when it was realised that most herbivore populations grow and decline with the 20-year cycles of wet and dry weather that characterise the region. Elephants, however, are largely unaffected by short-term climatic cycles. Their large size means they have a low metabolic rate per unit of body mass, which enables them to obtain adequate nutrition even from nutrient-poor plants. So the Kruger's annual elephant cull continued until 1994, by which time 16 027 elephants had been removed.

The momentous political changes roiling South Africa in 1994 helped create a platform within the country's conservation establishment for airing new ways of thinking. The culling of elephants had for years raised the ire of a whole battalion of animal welfare groups both locally and internationally, and now they again vociferously questioned the science and ethical morality behind lethally managing elephants. This outcry, together with the realisation by SANParks that their entire elephant policy required review, prompted a suspension of the cull. One particularly rewarding plus for Kruger visitors, which evolved soon after the killing stopped, was the change in attitude of breeding herds towards motor vehicles. Where once defensive mothers would have hurried their calves away or acted aggressively, they quickly realised that they were no longer in harm's way and now docilely go about their business undisturbed by a gridlock of admirers.

By this stage it had also become apparent that, other than slowing the rate of elephant impact on trees, culling had not achieved its major objectives. Indeed, culling was self-reinforcing as it held the population density at a level where reproduction is greatest. It was also observed that after a cull, elephants moved in from surrounding areas to such an extent that their numbers actually increased locally. Moreover, it is now known that bull elephants topple and uproot trees three to five times more frequently than females, so blanket culls that included family groups did not always target the problem. Big trees were extensively damaged and felled even when culling kept elephant density at a low six elephants per 10 square kilometres. As culling had not prevented the loss of these trees, how few elephants would be needed to halt woodland decline?

Although aerial photographs do show a marked decline in trees taller than five metres over much of the park, this loss cannot be attributed solely to elephants. The spectacle of a big bull pushing over a tree presents an image of such overwhelming potency that these mountains of muscle are often the only cause considered when investigating vegetation change. But equally significant is the role played by hungry impalas and other browsers in preventing seedlings from developing into mature trees (see Chapter 2, page 40). 'The problem is not the inevitable mortality among big trees,' says Norman Owen-Smith, who has supervised studies on the vegetation impacts of elephants in the Kruger and northern Botswana, 'but rather the lack of recruitment from smaller size classes to replace them.' Fire may have had an even more pernicious effect than browsing in holding back tree recruitment[8]. Most savanna plants are adapted to fire, many even depending on it to germinate their seeds, but fires can also inhibit young trees from developing into large trees. Many do not get much beyond the infant stage but they are not infants. Closer examination reveals that their stout root-systems have much more growth below ground than above and are covered with scars of former aerial parts that have been burnt back. Seedlings caught in the grass layer were harmed by the repeated fires that scorched the Kruger in past decades and remained non-reproductive. It is hoped that the adoption of a new fire policy in 2002 by park management will release vulnerable seedlings from this 'fire trap' and encourage recruitment.

Once recruited into the mature population, a tree should be safe from fires, but this is where elephants come back into the picture. By debarking trees, elephants expose the soft heartwood to veld fires and wood-borers. These scars tend to get bigger with successive burns and the trees eventually become structurally weakened and collapse.

> **Although aerial photographs do show a marked decline in trees taller than five metres over much of the park, this loss cannot be attributed solely to elephants.**

Tree bark has high levels of calcium and is an elephant favourite, particularly towards the end of the dry season when certain acacias and other species are moving sugars stored in the roots in preparation for flowering and leaf production. In 1993/94, a bonanza of intact trees became available to the Kruger's elephants, with the removal of the park's western boundary fence, which had separated it from more than 400 000 hectares of privately owned game reserves, now part of the Greater Kruger National Park ecosystem. No sooner did the fence come down than there was a dramatic influx of elephants into the private parks. In the 62 706-hectare Sabi Sand Private Game Reserve there had never been more than 73 elephants during the dry winter months, but by 1998 that figure had jumped to 429 and by 2007 to over 3 000. This virgin territory's previously unharvested bark must be a powerful inducement to lure so many elephants away from their regular home ranges. According to ecologist Kay Hiscocks who, tragically, was killed by an elephant in 2004 while working at Sabi Sand, nutrient levels are the clue, as bark-stripping decreases rapidly after the first spring rains when pans fill and elephants hurry back to the Kruger's resurging grasslands.

In some parts of the Kruger the impact of elephants, fire and other browsers has resulted in big trees being replaced by dense shrub cover. Over time this may have a serious knock-on effect, as some 40 per cent of the Kruger's bird species are dependent on tall trees for some part of their life. In particular, concerns have been expressed regarding raptors and storks that require big trees for nesting. A study by Swaziland University's Ara Monadjem and David Garcelon in the Hlane-Mlawula protected area in northeastern Swaziland revealed that no vulture nests were found in a fenced section where elephants

Placing the tip of one's trunk in a companion's mouth is considered a friendly gesture in elephant society.

had been introduced some years previously but were fairly common outside, coming right up to the perimeter fence. Vulture nesting density in areas without elephants in Swaziland and near Kimberley in South Africa was 100 nests per 100 square kilometres whereas the Kruger has only around 10 nests per 100 square kilometres. 'Elephants in safe havens are as much a threat to vultures as poison, persecution and power lines if they are not managed,' insists André Botha, head of the Endangered Wildlife Trust's Birds of Prey Working Group, who is monitoring raptor nests in the Kruger. 'Elephants are not endangered but all large raptors are listed as threatened with extinction in the Red Data bird list for southern Africa. Many of South Africa's birds of prey depend on Kruger as a safe place to breed,' he adds, 'but if their nesting trees are lost it's like taking the dam away from a duck.'

Although conservation managers in the Kruger have embraced the 'flux of nature' concept and heterogeneity – understood as the degree of difference among a set of things – they remain anxious that at this stage they do not know enough about the biodiversity consequences of elephant impacts. In the 17 years since culling stopped, the Kruger's elephant population has doubled to over 15 000 and continues to increase at the maximum rate of six per cent annually, with no sign of slowing down. 'If left as is, Kruger's elephant numbers would probably reach 20 000 in five years and in ten years there could be 30 000,' says Kevin Rogers, an ecology professor at the University of Witwatersrand, who has undertaken research in the Kruger for the last 20 years. 'If carrying capacity is defined in terms of food only, Kruger could theoretically accommodate up to 60 000 elephants but the carrying capacity at which biodiversity is maintained will be much lower than that.' Some ecologists worry that even the mighty Kruger may be too small for these fluctuations to take place naturally. They feel that action may be needed before critical components of biodiversity are lost and that something needs to be done sooner rather than later to head off irreversible situations. That squarely puts back on the table the issue of whether the Kruger is large or diverse enough to allow the impact on vegetation of the world's biggest vegetarian to go unchecked.

In particular, concerns have been expressed regarding raptors and storks that require big trees for nesting.

all Walter Jubber

Creative non-lethal strategies – far less controversial although not always entirely without controversy – are being tested to curb high elephant densities, but even here there are difficulties. Translocation is often cited as a humane alternative to culling, now that even intact families and large bulls can be moved. Indeed, it has become a common tool in elephant management, and over 75 South African national, provincial and private parks have elephants that originally came from the Kruger. But already 80 per cent of those parks have reached or surpassed the number of elephants they feel they can support. It is the lack of suitable new reserves that is proving the greatest limitation to using translocation as a means of controlling the Kruger's elephant population size.

Reducing elephant birth rates has an appeal that many people can empathise with. One promising method, immuno-contraception, involves immunising cows with a foreign protein, which activates their immune system to produce antibodies that prevent conception. It has been proved safe, reversible and non-hormonal, without side effects or change in the treated cow's social status, and is safe during pregnancy and with no adverse consequences for calf rearing. A new one-shot vaccine has been developed that lasts for at least a year and, as the vaccine is delivered by darting, there is no need to stress the target animals by immobilising them. However, because an estimated 4 000 adult female elephants would need to be darted repeatedly to keep Kruger's population constant over time, contraception poses hideous logistical problems as well as incurring the prohibitive and recurring costs of helicopter flights and veterinary expertise. On the other hand, it could well be a solution in smaller parks, although ethical concerns have been raised due to the level of interference in natural processes such as social structure within the herd and genetics.

Another strategy involves increasing the amount of available space. In the past, it is thought that around 10 to 15 per cent of the Kruger's elephants moved east in June on well-worn trails into Mozambique, returning as waterholes dried up. That exodus came to a sudden halt in 1976 when a high-security fence was erected along the Kruger's entire eastern boundary. So, when in 2002 a 15-kilometre section of the border fence that separates the Kruger from Mozambique's new million-hectare

Up to a year old, a baby elephant can fit beneath its mother's belly, which is useful when seeking shelter from the midday sun.

Limpopo National Park (LNP) was removed as a first step in creating the proposed Great Limpopo Transfrontier Park, there were high expectations that the ancestral migratory routes could be renewed.

LNP was left denuded of elephants in the 1990s, in the wake of Mozambique's protracted civil war. Not surprisingly, given their learning abilities, elephants seem to have a precise sense of how safe they are in a given set of surroundings, so when 25 were translocated to LNP, most immediately headed straight back to the safety of the Kruger. Over the next two years a further 86 were moved into a 30 000-hectare enclosure where they have settled so successfully that elephants are now moving into LNP on their own initiative, apparently responding to an 'all clear' from those already there. The migration of elephants into Mozambique will relieve some of the pressure on the Kruger, but LNP is much smaller than Kruger, with less suitable elephant habitat and can hold only about 3 000 elephants before they start adversely affecting their new environs.

Ultimately, the biodiversity outcome of increased elephant numbers in the Kruger will depend more on the seasonal distribution of the population than on its size. Because elephants are heavily dependent on water – they need to drink every 48 hours and bulls can down up to 200 litres a day – their foraging range is limited to about 15 kilometres from water. Naturally free-roaming elephants generally move between distinct wet- and dry-season home ranges, congregating near perennial rivers during the dry season, which in areas devoid of water during the dry season gives vegetation time to regenerate. Unfortunately, the Kruger's extensive network of dams and boreholes interfered with this process. A 2003 study investigating surface water constraints on herbivore foraging found that 92 per cent of the total area of the Kruger was within five kilometres of some type of water source during the dry season.

Deciding when and how to intervene in wildlife ecology is a tricky business and resolving the role of the elephant is a particularly daunting conundrum.

When permanent waterholes are too close together, elephants have no need to move in search of water. In the Kruger that has resulted in wet- and dry-season ranges overlapping in the case of breeding herds. Without a shifting mosaic of high and low elephant-feeding pressure, ever-expanding patches of heavily browsed vegetation occur. Spreading elephant impacts evenly across the landscape has tended to homogenise woody vegetation and in the process disrupted plant and animal diversity. It is hoped that the closure of 184 of the park's 325 boreholes since 1996 will help limit damage to susceptible trees such as marulas and baobabs that grow mainly in upland areas. Another crux issue pertaining to waterhole closures is whether the stress of moving to and from water could reduce reproductive rates – particularly calf survival – sufficiently to halt further population increase.

Deciding when and how to intervene in wildlife ecology is a tricky business and resolving the role of the elephant is a particularly daunting conundrum. Norman Owen-Smith maintains that, contrary to public perception, scientists in the Kruger have reached a high degree of consensus on the ecological basis of how to respond to growing elephant numbers. 'Management's aim should be to safeguard threatened components of biodiversity or species while allowing natural processes to proceed little hindered within the context of the fenced park, even if they lead to vegetation states somewhat different from those that were prevalent within the memory of park visitors.'

---

1 A megaherbivore is a plant-eater that exceeds 1 000 kilograms in weight.

2 A keystone species is one upon which many other species in an ecosystem depend, the loss of which could cause a cascade of local extinctions.

3 Bulk mixed feeders are fairly indiscriminate consumers of large amounts and a large variety of plants and use many different parts of those plants.

4 Density is the number of individuals in a given area.

5 Published figures for the total number of Tsavo elephants that died of malnutrition – but not including those later poached – vary from 'at least 6 000, or 15 per cent of the population' to 15 000.

6 A generalist species is able to thrive in a wide variety of environmental conditions and can make use of a variety of different resources.

7 In Kruger's mopane tree-dominated northern half, the conversion of woodlands into open grasslands is unlikely due to the ability of mopane to regenerate by coppice regrowth. Ecologist Frank Fraser Darling, while working in Zambia's Luangwa Valley in the 1960s, noted that, although mopane trees were browsed back to two metres in height by elephants, this made excellent browse conditions available for other animals. A few years later, John Hanks, who also studied elephant impacts in Luangwa, observed that 'under the particular climatic conditions pertaining [to the valley] the decline of tree cover has not so far resulted in luxurious stands of grass; instead, under the severe feeding pressure, the grasses have been rapidly grazed down to ground level and areas of soil, many square kilometres in extent, bared to sheet erosion'.

8 The term 'recruitment' can be defined as survival of young plants and animals from birth to a life stage less vulnerable to environmental change.

2 The ubiquitous **impala**

There is no more beautiful
and fascinating sight than
that of a troop of impala ...
really on the move and
jumping in earnest ... You
have forgotten to shoot;
but they have left you
something better than a
trophy, something which time
will only glorify – a picture
that in daylight or in dark will
fill your mind whenever you
hear the name Impala.

Percy Fitzpatrick,
Jock of the Bushveld, 1907

O ften dismissed as too common to care about by visitors to the Kruger intent on spotting the more glamorous big cats – 'Just another impala!' – this lithe, leggy creature is better appreciated by wildlife professionals who consider it the perfect antelope. They see the impala for what it is – all that an antelope is supposed to be. With its sleek, shiny bright rufous coat, paling to delicate fawn along the flanks and becoming pure white below; strategic black-and-white markings that seem to exist for aesthetic reasons only (but of course do not); long, slender legs; luminous velvet-black eyes (the name 'antelope' derives from a Greek word meaning 'bright eyes') and the male's elegant lyre-shaped horns, among the finest looking in Africa, an impala decorates its environment and in its own delicate way dominates it as well.

Despite efforts to classify it with the gazelle, kob and most recently hartebeest, the impala belongs in a tribe of its own, the Aepycerotini. Fossil evidence has shown that modern impalas have remained practically unchanged since the Miocene, 6.5 million years ago. That is a powerful endorsement for the impala's original design, particularly when contrasted with the closely related hartebeest and wildebeest, which have split into new species at least 18 times since they evolved from the impala or a springbok-like common ancestor around eight million years ago.

The impala's body form, which resembles that of many other antelopes, would seem to qualify it as the archetypal antelope, but impalas also display qualities not found in any other antelope. One of their most distinctive anatomical specialisations is a scent gland just above the hoof on each hind leg that contains an oily compound. Covered by tufts of conspicuous black hair, these fetlock glands release a puff of chemical pheromone when activated by a high kick. This is thought to lay a scent trail and allow herd members to stay together when pursued by a predator and later to regroup.

At different times of the year impalas have as many as five distinct social groupings.

The impala's intricate but at the same time highly flexible social organisation also has characteristics all of its own. At different times of the year impalas have as many as five distinct social groupings. Three main organisations are found during the wet season – territorial males with and without breeding females, bachelor herds of non-territorial adult and juvenile

An impala ram determines a rival's status by sniffing the scent gland on his forehead.

*The old bush tale of the 'sultan'
impala ram and his harem of
females has given way under
scientific scrutiny to reveal a
far more complex relationship
between the sexes.*

males, and breeding herds of females and juveniles including young
males less than four years old. During the dry season, males can be
found together or mixed with female herds. Impala rams are strictly
territorial when it counts – only they have the opportunity to mate
– but the very existence of territoriality was once doubted because
of the rapid turnover of territorial males in the breeding season and the suspension of
territorial behaviour in the dry season, when impalas are often found in mixed herds.

For the impalas of the Kruger Park, a crowded social calendar begins towards the
end of the rainy season, in February, when food is plentiful. Bucks over four years old,
now in peak condition and ready to challenge a territorial male, leave their bachelor
herds. A challenger gives notice of his intentions by raising his tail, yawning, flicking
his tongue and lowering his head. The rivals next engage in ritualised displays such as
parallel walking and head bowing, facing each other head-on, advancing and retreating
without actually touching. This presents an opportunity for one to back down. If neither
gives way, then battle is joined and horns clash as they joust. Back and forth they push,
with the spirals and ridges on their horns acting as a safety device, preventing the horns
from slipping during head-wrestling. Usually only superficial wounds are inflicted but
that is not for lack of trying – they really do their best to stick each other with their
rapier-sharp horns. The surprisingly few instances of critical injury or death are partly
due to the protection provided by a shield of thickened skin that covers a ram's head,
shoulders, upper neck and part of his back. Ewes lack this dermal shield, which indicates
its role in inter-male conflict. Researchers at Letaba Ranch abutting the Kruger's western

boundary examined 491 impalas that had died of natural causes and found that only one per cent had been killed in fights. In the great majority of clashes, one contestant breaks off and flees, leaving the victor holding his head high in the proud posture.

By April most territorial males have staked out a four- to eight-hectare resource-rich patch to hold and defend. Their real estate provides them with breeding opportunities until the females move onto a neighbour's territory. Almost all matings are limited to territorial males, with a study in Zimbabwe showing that four males accounted for 78 per cent of matings in one year and 66 per cent in another. The intensely competitive rams advertise their territories by raising their tail and flashing the white underside while uttering explosive barking roars followed by deep guttural grunts that can be heard for over a kilometre. Roaring lasts for about two months and at the height of the rut a territorial ram may roar nearly 200 times an hour. All this roaring and herding of females helps advance oestrus in ewes and synchronise ovulation. Synchronised mating leads to synchronised births, with most fawns born within a two- or three-week period seven months later, in mid-November in the Kruger, which coincides with a green flush of new grass. Mass births have the advantage of swamping predators so that far fewer impalas are taken at their most vulnerable age. After the rut the males' territorial urge wanes and they regroup into bachelor groups or join breeding herds. Some rams have a brief resurgence in territorial activity when a secondary rut occurs in September, which accounts for the 'out-of-season' fawns seen by April visitors to the Kruger. Why this happens is not fully understood but it is significant that the number of April births in southeastern Zimbabwe was greater than usual for two years after the mega-drought of 1992, which was so punishing that at its bitter nadir impalas had spontaneous abortions.

A challenger gives notice of his intentions by raising his tail, yawning, flicking his tongue and lowering his head.

A relaxed rhino ignores young impala bucks tentatively jousting as a prelude to establishing a future place in the male hierarchy.

Any examination of the southern impalas' lifestyle and ecology reveals that they have become a phenomenally successful species, if success is measured in terms of survival and abundance. Favoured for game farming and hunting, in the past 30 years more than 250 000 impalas have been relocated to private reserves and ranches; add that to natural dispersion and it makes the impala the only indigenous mammal in South Africa to have increased its numbers and broadened its range over the last century. The edge impalas have over many other creatures is due largely to their unusually varied food supply. By switching food on a seasonal basis – primarily grazing in the wet season,

A mother impala and her young lamb emerge from the thicket where they have remained in seclusion since the birth two weeks earlier.

with browsing a fallback option when the availability of green grass is limited by rainfall – impalas take from the best of both worlds. Their home range includes a variety of vegetation types, enabling them to reach high densities with a sedentary lifestyle.

In the Sabi Game Reserve's early days, the ecotones[1] along the Sabie and Crocodile rivers, where acacia thickets and gallery forests meet open bushveld, were traditionally the impalas' main stronghold. The two southern perennial rivers were highly favoured habitat because they abundantly supplied the impalas' most important daily needs – diversity of vegetation, proximity to drinking places and shade trees. Impalas prefer food rich in protein, which they find in succulent growing grass when it is available. Though generalist mixed feeders, they are grazers by choice and are especially attracted to recently burnt areas where grasses and forbs are sprouting.

A 2003 study in the Kruger using chemical analysis to examine carbon and nitrogen levels in impala dung and hair samples found that in the rainy season impala diets comprise 90 per cent grass. However, when average monthly rainfall drops below 30 millimetres for two consecutive months and grass becomes less digestible, they switch to 65 per cent browsing. In the dry season they nibble greater quantities of green foliage and protein-rich seedpods, plus forbs, shoots and pioneer herbs[2] unpalatable to other animals. Fallen leaves, particularly from tamboti trees, contribute substantially to food eaten during the dry months.

The same study found that male and female impalas have different diets, with males grazing more than females. It also discovered marked differences between impala diets in the Kruger's northern and southern regions. Hair data showed that grass forms 82 per cent of an impala's overall diet in the southern marula-knobthorn and bushwillow woodlands but only 44 per cent in the mopane-dominated north.

It is also now recognised that impalas are able to thrive in over-utilised habitat, as a result of which localised overgrazed areas are now regarded as an integral part of the natural mosaic.

Although these days impalas outnumber all of the Kruger's other herbivores put together, that was not always the case. How they achieved their ascendancy in many ways mirrors the momentous history of the Kruger itself. It is a story that begins in the 19th century with the destruction of much of the Lowveld's wildlife. Although seemingly immune to the rinderpest plague that swept through the region in 1896, impalas were not spared the hunting holocaust in the 30 years leading up to the 20th century. The massacre reached its zenith in 1892 during the construction of the Selati railway line that was intended to run from Delagoa Bay to the Selati River Gold Field near Leydsdorp. The hastily floated Selati Railway Company laid 80 kilometres of track from Komatipoort to the Sabie River before going bankrupt. Workers' rations were supplied by men with guns, and trucks piled high mostly with impala carcasses were dispatched down the line almost daily. Despite being fortified by venison and truckloads of liquor, many workers died from malaria and in disputes among themselves. The most enduring epitaph of the ill-conceived enterprise is Sabie Bridge, completed in 1912, which still stands within sight of Skukuza.

Although these days impalas outnumber all of the Kruger's other herbivores put together, that was not always the case.

James Stevenson-Hamilton paid tribute to the impala's 'regenerative power' during a reconnaissance expedition in 1902. He set out from his temporary base at Crocodile Bridge with his career-long colleague Harry Wolhuter. They followed the Biyamiti River almost to its source, then continued north to the Sabie River and finally reached Sabie Bridge. During the trip the men saw lions (they shot several near the Sabie River), leopards, cheetahs and large packs of wild dogs as well as waterbuck, wildebeest and other antelopes. Stevenson-Hamilton made special mention of the big impala herds: 'the bush was red with them', he enthused. The two men then took a leisurely return journey on a trolley pushed by relays of labourers down the now-abandoned Selati line, which had become, in effect, the warden's private railway.

In that same year Stevenson-Hamilton estimated that the Sabi Game Reserve held a paltry five giraffes, five tsessebes, eight buffaloes, 12 sables, 15 hippos, 35 kudus, 40 wildebeest, 100 waterbuck and good numbers of impalas, reedbucks, steenbok and common duikers. The Sabie and Crocodile rivers were highly favoured impala habitat but changes in less-favoured habitats that would profoundly advantage impalas were already under way, so much so that Stevenson-Hamilton was soon to observe: 'Impala are increasing in a manner truly marvellous and spreading far beyond the limits to which they formerly confined themselves.' By 1918 wildlife numbers generally had rebounded spectacularly. There were an estimated 6 800 impalas in the Sabi-Singwitsi (Singwitsi is the old spelling for Shingwedzi) game reserves, together with around 6 500 waterbuck, 5 000 wildebeest, 1 500 sable antelopes, 3 000 zebras plus 25 elephants, 200 hippos, 250 giraffes and 250 buffaloes. Before the 1920s there were no impalas west of Orpen Gate in what are today the private Timbavati and Klaserie game reserves; now they are easily the most prolific mammal there. By 1968, the Kruger's impala population had rocketed to nearly 100 000. Throughout the 1970s their numbers continued growing, and they reached peak abundance in 1985, with an average census total between 1980 and 1993 of 116 000. The jet fuel for their population explosion was provided by bush encroachment, and later permanent artificial waterholes helped speed up the process.

'At Pretoriuskop I saw no impala for about thirty-five years,' recalled Harry Wolhuter, who witnessed first-hand the impala proliferation saga.

'Even the oldest natives who lived near the Kop stated that there were never any impala there within their memory, while now these beautiful and graceful antelopes are quite numerous in this area. When I first became acquainted with Pretoriuskop the surrounding veld was quite open in nature, not unlike the High-Veld, only dotted about with a few Umkuhlu (Cape Mahogany) trees, wild figs, marulas, etc., with no smaller trees and shrubs. Nowadays it can almost be described as bush country: the result of 'Bush Encroachment' … I am of the opinion that the gradually denser nature of the country is due to the absence, through control nowadays, of the great grass fires which used to sweep the bush in former years, taking terrible toll of smaller trees and scrub.'

The 'great grass fires' Wolhuter referred to were set by shepherds every year in autumn to provide fresh winter pasturage. Since 1880 these Highveld trekboers had had a lease arrangement to graze sheep west of the Nsikazi River – the park's present western boundary – in what was part of the Sabi Reserve from 1903 to 1923. Later, after successfully agitating for extended grazing rights, the entire Pretoriuskop station was included as winter grazing for some 9 000 sheep from 1912 until 1926. It was the graziers' pastoral burning that kept Pretoriuskop's grasslands open and park-like.

Favoured by impalas and warthogs, locally overgrazed and trampled areas such as this one are now recognised as a legitimate habitat type.

When the Kruger was proclaimed South Africa's first national park in 1926, the farmers were evicted and their fires – considered excessive and harmful to the grazing lands – were discontinued. Until 1947 fire management was confined to occasional and limited burns to provide wildlife with green winter grazing. Although not well understood at the time, it is now known that fire directly enhances grass production and inhibits the spread of woody plants by destroying tree seedlings and stunting immature plants. Fire also encourages the spread of more palatable grasses at the expense of coarser species. In the absence of fire, however, savanna grasses actually physically change. Nutritious perennials such as red grass (*Themeda triandra*) – which store starchy food reserves underground in rhizomes or bulb-like corms and so are well equipped to survive fire and drought – grow tall and robust under a fire regime, but without fire become slender and wiry and flower less profusely or get crowded out by species previously suppressed by fire. By 1943, three years before his retirement, a concerned James Stevenson-Hamilton was already reporting encroachment by unpalatable tall grasses.

It was by now becoming inescapably clear to park management that fire is a major driver of savanna ecosystems and that the no-burning policy was having seriously detrimental effects.

Between 1948 and 1956, the new warden, Jan Andries Beyers Sandenbergh, established firebreaks to help suppress wildfires and outlawed all controlled burns because of what he regarded as their adverse effect. 'Fire in wild country is bad' underscored conventional wisdom in most of Europeanised Africa at the time. Without fire to rejuvenate the grasses and retard woody growth, Pretoriuskop's open grasslands were invaded by tall, unpalatable thatch grass (*Hyparrhenia dissoluta*) and woody species such as sicklebush (*Dichrostachys cinerea*) and silver cluster-leaf (*Terminalia sericea*). This insidious encroachment ultimately rendered the habitat unsuitable for the big herds of zebras and wildebeest, as well as the tsessebes, sables, roans, oribis, eland, waterbuck, ostriches and cheetahs that had thrived here, while impala and kudu numbers steadily rose. It was by now becoming inescapably clear to park management that fire is a major driver of savanna ecosystems and that the no-burning policy was having seriously detrimental effects.

As Harry Wolhuter discovered, it is astonishing how quickly fire, or the lack of it, can modify savanna habitat. Small wonder, as it was on Africa's savannas that the world's oldest relationship between people and fire developed; the two co-evolved like the bonded strands of a DNA molecule. Indeed, Africa is often referred to as a 'fire continent'. No other human technology has influenced the continent's land ethic for so long and so pervasively. We cannot be sure when our hominid ancestors first incinerated their surroundings to improve their prospects for hunting, but it may have been as long ago as 1.8 to 1.6 million years. Ever since, people have reshaped the landscape. The Bushmen (or San) – Stone Age hunter-gatherers from an animal-dominated past whose luminous art adorns over a hundred rock shelters throughout the Kruger – used savanna burning to attract the herbivores they stalked. Traditions dating back to the 15th century suggest that Iron Age communities in the Kruger region burnt the veld annually at the end of the dry season, to clear land for cultivation and to stimulate fresh grass growth for domestic stock. It is a custom still practised in homelands adjoining the park.

A steenbok browses forbs sprouting after a recent 'mosaic' burn that has promoted fresh forage while leaving patches of unburnt tall grass for shelter.

There remain, however, quite a few visitors to the Kruger who vehemently oppose a policy of deliberately set blazes. Their objections are mainly aesthetic – the ugliness of the charred landscape in the aftermath of tinder-dry grass transformed by shooting flames and glowing embers – and concern that wildlife might get trapped in the conflagration. Although fire may suggest death and devastation, savanna ecosystems have come to depend on fire for their very existence. Fire assists savannas to renew and reinvigorate themselves by removing litter that accumulates at ground level, thus allowing the soil to reach temperatures suitable for seed germination and by removing old dead grass that prevents sunlight from reaching new leaves.

There is historic evidence that the Kruger's landscape has changed dramatically in the last 70 years or so, with a progressive increase in woody vegetation cover and a reduction in open savanna. 'I first remember Tshokwane, which is now surrounded by fairly dense secondary forest, to have been relatively open country,' Stevenson-Hamilton recalled in the 1940s. 'The same could be said of most other parts of the Park away from the immediate vicinity of the large rivers.' When burning was reinstituted in the Kruger in the 1950s, a series of experiments confirmed that fire is crucial to the balance of grass and trees – in most cases, blocks that were never burnt developed into dense woodlands.

The Kruger's burning policy has evolved over the years as fire ecologists came to understand fire's role in the ecosystem better. In 2002 a new policy was adopted that aims to spread fires throughout the dry season rather than restrict them to after the first rains in spring, so as to break up the fuel load and create a mosaic of burnt and unburnt patches. This should assist in preventing hot, high-intensity dry-season fires from becoming unmanageable and do less damage to the seedlings of trees like knobthorns and marulas. Also, early burns sometimes induce a green flush during the dry season. Some burns, however, are intended to knock back bush encroachment species, so the new fire regime includes hot fires and follow-up cool burns that will

By feeding on trees less than a metre high, impalas are largely responsible for the slow growth rates in saplings of this size.

kill plants such as sicklebush and gives grasses a chance to flourish. It is anticipated this will emulate or reinstate burning patterns that shaped this savanna for centuries before the colonial era and hopefully re-establish the Kruger's endangered open savanna.

Early hominids and their human descendants have set fires for well over a million years, to the point that Africa's savannas have evolved to depend on regular burns.

Fire has a profound and obvious impact on savanna dynamics, but browsers like impalas also have a substantial but much less obvious modifying effect on woodlands. By feeding on trees less than a metre high, impalas are largely responsible for the slow growth rates in saplings of this size. Although we do not automatically think of the dainty impala as a landscape engineer, perhaps the concept is not so strange when we take into account the species' high-density population. In common with elephants, impalas have a considerable impact on their habitat and are able to change it to suit their requirements, by maintaining the vegetation in an actively growing and palatable state.

It is only since the late 1970s that it has become apparent just how much of an impact impalas have on their habitat. The elephant-induced reduction of riverine woodland cover on the alluvial plains along the Chobe River in northern Botswana from 90 per cent in 1962 to 30 per cent by 1998 was accompanied by an impala population explosion that went from nine impalas per 100 square kilometres in 1962 to 6 400 impalas per 100 square kilometres 36 years later. Their soaring numbers were a direct result of elephants breaking down the woodlands to a much lower, more accessible height for impalas, which tend to browse below one metre. Research by Lucas Rutina and Jose Miguel from the Agricultural University of Norway confirmed that both elephants and impalas were critical factors in structuring the ecosystem along the Chobe river front. When seedling predators such as impalas exceed 20 animals per square kilometre, regeneration of woody species is significantly reduced. Now that Chobe's woodlands have all but disappeared, their re-establishment would require drastic reductions of impalas and elephants, which is impractical on a landscape scale and would only lock in an artificial equilibrium between plants and plant predators.

Today these woodlands are characterised by even-aged stands of trees, dating from the times when impala populations were low.

Rutina and Miguel's conclusions support the hypothesis that tall closed-canopy woodlands originate during episodic windows of opportunity for seedling survival. How such windows can occur was demonstrated in northern Tanzania's Lake Manyara National Park in 1977 and again in 1983 when outbreaks of anthrax greatly reduced local impala populations. With the primary removers of acacia seedlings gone, the acacia woodlands were able to regenerate. Today these woodlands are characterised by even-aged stands of trees, dating from the times when impala populations were low.

As far back as 70 years ago, the Kruger's explosively expanding impala population and its potentially adverse impact on the environment had caught the attention of the park warden. Although no fan of wild dogs, Stevenson-Hamilton nonetheless stressed that 'they still fill a useful place in Nature's economy, and the Kruger National Park certainly would be better for a considerably larger number than exists at the time of writing [1945], to keep the prodigious and growing numbers of impala from increasing to their own ultimate specific detriment'.

By the 1960s, park biologist and later SANParks' chief director, Uys de Villiers (Tol) Pienaar, was reporting that 'if it is borne in mind that impala never roam over a large area or far from water, then it is soon clear that the only overcrowded area in the Park, where considerable mortalities occur annually due to starvation in the winter months, is where excessive numbers of impala occur. Reference is here made to the stretch along the Crocodile River on the Crocodile Bridge section. Impala represent more than 80 per cent of the herbivore community in this area, and they constitute approximately 45 to 55 per cent of the community in practically all other areas.' A similar situation existed along the Crocodile River in the Malelane section – where a high number of impala deaths was due to wild dogs preying on impalas weakened by hunger – and along the Sabie River between Lower Sabie and Skukuza. At the time, Pienaar calculated that there were 10 000 impalas per 100 square kilometres along the river. In the north of the park, impalas in the Pafuri area were thought to be responsible for exacerbating denuded conditions brought on by the 1958 floods and subsequent silting.

Pienaar was also concerned by the direct competition that prevailed each dry season along the Sabie River between impalas and less numerous browsers such as bushbuck and duikers. 'The browse line is higher than that of bushbuck ewes and duiker, especially, and before impala suffer any shortage of food, a situation of acute food shortage may be created for the lesser browsers,' he observed. 'Numerous deaths among bushbuck and duiker have been recorded along the Sabie and Crocodile rivers this year [1965]. It is possibly just this phenomenon that is responsible for the relatively low population density of bushbuck and duiker where impala occur in large numbers.'

Impalas also starve when they exceed their range's dry-season carrying capacity. Indeed, this sedentary species' population numbers can vary considerably. While investigating leopard predation on impalas, leopard researcher Ted Bailey recorded impala population trends at his Sabie River study site. Between 1973 and 1975 he documented a decline from 143 to 56 impalas per square kilometre. He attributed the precipitous crash to a die-off directly caused by starvation as well as indirectly by increased predation and disease owing to the impalas' poor condition. When stressed by food shortages, impalas are susceptible to diseases and many die of pneumonia brought on by the damp and cold following the season's first heavy rains.

During the 1960s, management policies in the Kruger were strongly influenced by two major events: the introduction of annual aerial counts, which gave a more accurate profile of wildlife numbers and trends, and the onset of a drought that lasted the entire decade. Large concentrations of animals crowding isolated waterholes resulted in progressively larger areas of over-utilised habitat. The pressure of these and other forces culminated in a decision to cull a predetermined number of elephants, buffaloes, hippos, zebras, wildebeest and impalas.

The impala cull commenced in 1966. Loosely based on their yearly recruitment, an annual culling rate of 10 per cent of the population was prescribed for the Sabie River east of Skukuza and the Crocodile River between Malelane and Dzuweni stream. Later the Sweni-Nwanetsi area, Tshokwane and other heavily populated areas along the Sabie and Crocodile rivers were also included. A total of 18 236 impalas were shot between 1966 and the cull's conclusion in 1974. Conditions had changed – a high rainfall phase during the 1970s brought about a sudden surge in grass and other plant growth and precipitated a steep decline in species like zebra and wildebeest that had prospered during the drought. Now impalas were needed as a buffer to alleviate predator pressure on wildebeest and zebras. In the end, the cull had little effect on overall impala densities – that has always been determined by variations in rainfall and alternating abundance and want.

Impalas also starve when they exceed their range's dry-season carrying capacity.

As the most numerous antelope in the Kruger, impalas are naturally viewed as fast food by an array of predators, including crocodiles and pythons, while fawns are small enough to be carried off by martial eagles. Records of 49 453 carcasses found by the Kruger's section rangers and other field staff in the 46 years between 1954 and 2000 may sound like a mass of data, but in the expert hands of Norman Owen-Smith and Gus Mills it tells a superb tale of what goes on in the wilds. The many insights include a comparative breakdown of the prey killed by the five largest mammalian carnivore species in the Kruger and adjoining game reserves. It revealed that impalas are numerically the most frequently recorded prey of lions – they comprised 20 per cent of the actual 23 829 lion kills identified in the carcass study (although that was corrected to 39 per cent to compensate for the under-recording of smaller species). By following lions over many nights in the Kruger's southeastern region, researchers Gus Mills and Harry Biggs noted that impalas accounted for 29 per cent of the 111 observed lion kills. A study by research zoologist and later Senior Research Officer with the National Parks Board, Butch Smuts, in the Kruger's Central District in 1975 found that, despite their teeming presence, impalas accounted for just 28 per cent of lion kills. These figures correspond with those recorded at neighbouring MalaMala where impalas made up 38 per cent of the 2 129 lion kills sighted. However, wildebeest, zebras and buffaloes are the lions' principal prey species in terms of the weight of meat eaten each year. Impalas and similar-sized species together comprise just 14 per cent of the total amount of meat eaten by the park's 1 800 lions.

Impalas comprise around three-quarters of all kills made by Kruger's cheetahs.

Lions prefer bigger pickings. Weighing around 40 kilograms, impalas come in under the lion's favoured prey size range of 60 to 250 kilograms but are the prey species of choice for leopards, cheetahs and wild dogs, all of which weigh much the same as an impala. An examination of the diets of the Kruger's other major predators based on data collected during the above-mentioned analysis found that leopards kill more impalas in the Kruger than any other predator, with impalas making up 76 per cent of all found leopard kills. At MalaMala, impalas constituted 48 per cent of 1 452 observed leopard kills, with duikers and steenbok coming in at 24 per cent. In the Kruger, the small cheetah population of roughly 200 contributed only four per cent of carcasses found, with impalas making up 77 per cent. Impalas were selected in 65.5 per cent of the 321 cheetah kills observed at MalaMala. Impalas comprised 88 per cent of wild dog kills in the carcass study and 67.5 per cent of observed wild dog kills at MalaMala, with steenbok and duikers comprising 22 per cent. Wild dog packs in the Kruger typically capture two or more impalas a day, varying their diet with steenbok, duikers, young kudus and waterbuck. Five years of mortality data recorded at Letaba Ranch reveal that wild dogs had the second-highest impala capture rate (22 per cent) after leopards. Impala-sized prey forms more than 50 per cent of the Kruger hyaena's diet. Hyaenas can run down adult impalas and they take large numbers of fawns. Fawns come in for a lot of predatory attention in general, with fully half of newborns lost, especially to jackals.

It is most probable that predation pressure accounts for the male/female imbalance in impala populations. Ted Bailey found that at birth sex ratios appeared to be even, but by the second year there were just 60 males for every 100 females and by the third year that had dropped to 40 males per 100 females. Young males become vulnerable during the rut when they are driven from their natal clans by territorial rams and forced to occupy marginal thickets where leopards wait in ambush. Bailey found that 63 per cent of males predated by leopards were less than two years old, whereas ewes less than two years old made up only 19 per cent of females killed by leopards. Adult females were more likely to be caught by a leopard than juvenile females, probably because they retire to secluded thickets – leopard country – during lambing. Of 10 000 Kruger impalas sampled in 1969 by biologist Neil Fairall, 33 per cent were less than one year old, 22 per cent were one to two years old and 45 per cent were over two years old. Mean life expectancy was 2.6 years and few were older than 10 years.

It is most probable that predation pressure accounts for the male/female imbalance in impala populations.

With so many enemies it was an evolutionary imperative for impalas to develop a whole range of anti-predator behaviours. Of necessity they lead very careful lives. A hunting leopard knows every inch of its territory and exactly where impalas are likely to spend the night. To minimise a leopard's hunting opportunities, impalas choose open resting places at night where they mostly ruminate while lying down, although few of them actually sleep. Avoidance of dense cover is another crucial strategy, especially during the wet season, although in the dry season, after leaves have fallen and grasses dried out, they are more inclined to venture into thickets to feed.

Because they spend so much time in bushy habitat, impalas are always alert to possible danger. Potential trouble spots such as dense reed beds are carefully avoided and they will often use tourist and firebreak roads to pass through thick vegetation. Waterholes surrounded by heavy foliage are seldom used. Rather than walk through riverine undergrowth to reach clear river water, impalas continue drinking muddy, stagnant water at seasonal pools in open, short-grass terrain. It is not until surrounding waterholes dry up that they reluctantly drink at rivers, and then it might take hours for them to approach the water's edge. When they are drinking – usually in the late morning when predators are least active – their heads are raised every few seconds, as if anticipating danger, and often the slightest disturbance is enough to panic them into flight.

Gregariousness is another impala anti-predator stratagem. Ted Bailey noted that herd size declined in dense cover and increased in open habitats during the wet season. Keeping company with baboons, vervets and bushbuck adds to their many-eyes-

and-ears early-warning system, although there is a serious danger in associating with baboons during the lambing season when adult male baboons will sometimes catch and eat baby impalas. An impala will nervously raise its head when grazing to survey the surroundings, or suddenly look up after lowering its head to feed or hold its head still to detect movements. When a predator is spotted, impalas adopt an alert posture, alarm-snort and foot-stamp. They also exhibit flight intention by a sudden upward head movement, with neck stretched forward, although they seldom flee from a visible big cat. Instead, with heads held stiffly up and flanks twitching, the staring herd attempts to keep it in view while maintaining a suitable flight distance. By drawing attention to a lion, leopard or cheetah, they spoil any chance it may have of an ambush and continue escorting it until it is no longer a threat.

When a pack of hunting African wild dogs lopes into view, impalas often use an intriguing defence strategy called stotting or pronking. With backs arched, they run, using stiff-legged leaps with all four feet off the ground. Wild dogs are coursing predators[3] that depend on stamina to run down prey, so by demonstrating its fitness in this way an impala signals that it will be difficult to catch and that an easier target should be selected. Research on wild dog hunting behaviour in the Serengeti revealed that this 'pursuit deterrence' tactic works. Wild dogs invariably singled out animals with a significantly lower stott rate (stotts per minute) while avoiding higher rate stotters. When they pursued those stotting at high rates their hunting success was lower.

When a predator is spotted, impalas adopt an alert posture, alarm-snort and foot-stamp.

These impalas drink at a muddy seasonal waterhole rather than risk ambush by walking through thick cover to reach a clear river flowing nearby.

When attacked by a predator that stalks within pouncing range, a herd of impalas reacts by exploding in all directions simultaneously. It is a sight as astonishing as it is splendid. Their athleticism is breathtaking – spectacular high jumps three metres into the air and 10-metre-long jumps in a single running bound. The intention is to confuse the predator and break its concentration.

A big cat's vision is not as coordinated as a human's and may be disrupted by such antics. I have seen the display on several occasions but my most indelible memory is of one mid-morning at Rabelais Dam (now closed) in the central Kruger. The land was in drought and large herds of zebras, wildebeest and impalas gathered to drink. I noticed an impala ewe quietly emerge from the scrub with one of those April babies close to her side and watched through binoculars as she introduced her newborn to its clan. Suddenly the impala herd blew apart, detonating, so it seemed, into a world without gravity. Then they were gone. As the dust haze cleared I found myself looking directly into the eyes of a leopard that unblinkingly returned my stare. Its tail was curled over its back, the dead fawn hung from its jaws. Then it turned and strode into the bush, followed by a pair of howling jackals.

As the dust haze cleared I found myself looking directly into the eyes of a leopard that unblinkingly returned my stare. Its tail was curled over its back, the dead fawn hung from its jaws.

Impalas are not only leading actors in the Kruger's daily dramas but are also principal players in the park's vast and complex ecosystem. They may be everywhere but that is no reason to overlook them – indeed, their very profusion is what makes them so interesting. Their sheer numbers mean impalas act as savanna architects by modifying the vegetation structure. They are also an indicator species[4], reflecting the direction the savanna is going, and it is almost always going in one direction or another. A recent example is the occurrence of impalas in central Kruger's high grassveld, which may indicate pasture deterioration due to encroachment by thickets of sticky thorn (*Acacia borleae*). So, next time you see a herd of impalas in the riverside shade, pull over and watch awhile with fresh eyes as, twitching at flies, new scents and suspect shadows, they pass a few unremarkable minutes in their otherwise remarkable lives.

---

1 An ecotone is the transition area between two adjacent but different plant communities, such as forest and grassland.
2 Pioneer plants are those that colonise disturbed areas or raw mineral soils and improve the habitat, making it easier for succeeding, more complex plants, to grow there.
3 Coursers, such as wild dogs, hyaenas and wolves, chase their prey down, whereas lions, leopards and tigers are stalk-and-charge predators.
4 An indicator species is one that is so closely associated with an ecosystem that its presence or absence is indicative of the health of the ecosystem. It can also offer early warning signs of ecological stresses.

3 The mingled destinies of zebras and wildebeest

There is no animal so frequently met with in the Low Country [Lowveld] as the quaint omnipresent blue wildebeest ... But for the astonishing numbers in which they existed a few years ago, they must long ere this have become extinct, few animals being more eagerly sought after by the itinerant hide-hunter than these.

Frederick Vaughan Kirby, *In Haunts of Wild Game,* 1896

There was a time when the Lowveld had its own smaller version of that most spectacular of animal land movements, the annual migration of wildebeest and plains zebras. Historically the Lowveld ecological unit extended from the Mozambique coastal plain in the east to the Drakensberg escarpment in the west, although it no longer functions as an intact unit due to fences, international borders and other man-made intrusions[1]. Much of this wild country was interwoven by well-defined migratory paths that in the wake of spring thunderstorms beckoned family groups of zebras and long single-file columns of wildebeest towards greening pastures and rain water trapped in ephemeral pans. When winter returned, the shallow pans evaporated and the zebras and wildebeest were once again compelled to trek, this time to the plains adjoining permanently flowing rivers.

Acting like a massive natural mowing machine, the herds – unhindered by fences – practised a natural form of grassland management. After grazing down one area they would move to another, leaving behind trampled mulch that retained moisture and permitted light penetration, which in turn stimulated grass growth during the following season of rest. Recent insights into ecological systems have revealed that the best basal cover[2] and veld conditions occur under high-impact grazing when feeding, excreting and the trampling down of moribund grass tufts, shrubs and tree seedlings by many animals promote the growth of healthy grazing lawns of young, nutritious shoots. In this way wildebeest, in particular, acted as ecological landscapers, in that they modified the vegetation structure by maintaining open grasslands that may otherwise have been dominated by woody vegetation. In so doing they helped shape Africa's archetypal energy-rich savannas and the dynamic interplay between woodlands and grasslands.

Acting like a massive natural mowing machine, the herds – unhindered by fences – practised a natural form of grassland management.

'It is always remarkable to note how after the first rains, the more migratory species such as zebra and wildebeest suddenly appear in vast numbers in places where none have been seen for months,' marvelled James Stevenson-Hamilton. 'There is, and always has been, a certain migration eastwards annually into Portuguese territory [Mozambique], where the country is relatively fertile, but the greater movement is westwards.'

Zebras and wildebeest were born to roam; for them migration is a way of life. Both are almost exclusively grazers and both have evolved to live at high densities on an unstable food supply. At different times of the year zebras may compete with wildebeest for forage or the two like-minded species may share pastures, with the zebras facilitating the wildebeest's grazing by eating down the thicker vegetation, while at other times they have altogether dissimilar requirements. Thus migratory herds

Wildebeest bulls battle for possession of prime territory that is sure to attract cow herds, thus enhancing the victor's chances of mating.

evolved an opportunistic way of life; for them, survival lay in moving from the dry and withered to the wet and green. Such interactions – between wet and dry seasons, between fauna and flora, between the animate and the inanimate – kept the cycles of the natural world in motion.

Migratory herbivores have many advantages over their more sedentary counterparts. Life on the move permits them to get the right amount of energy and nutrients in their diet at critical times of the year. Also, since migration avoids over-exploitation of food resources, there comes with it the great advantage of being able to collect together in much bigger herds. This 'big-herd effect' acts as a very efficient anti-predation strategy. For a beast the colour and size of a wildebeest, hiding is all but impossible. While it may be able to defend itself against smaller predators, a wildebeest's best strategy against its principal enemies, lions and spotted hyaenas, is to meld into an anonymous herd. When a predator is detected, wildebeest close ranks. A dark blue-grey wall of animals is uninviting to a hunter that needs to target an individual. The author and naturalist Peter Matthiessen 'once watched a hyena gaining on a wildebeest that only saved itself by plunging into the heart of the panicked herd; the hyena lost track of its quarry when the herd stampeded'. Big herds on open plains also benefit from mutual alertness and communication of alarm. In woodlands, where visibility greatly contracts, big herds fragment into discrete groups and so lose their anti-predator advantages.

Big-herd protection is particularly valuable for newborn wildebeest which, unlike many other antelope species, do not lie-out[3]. A calf's chances of being picked off are greatly reduced when not only is it shielded by its mother, but it also has other wildebeest attempting to screen mother and offspring from a predator. Migrants further benefit by being able to trek beyond the range of their main predators for part of the year – research in Serengeti has shown that lion numbers there are determined by the availability of prey during the period when the migrations have left their

Zebras and wildebeest were born to roam; for them migration is a way of life.

territories. As a result, migratory herbivores head the animal biomass[4] wherever they occur, as was once the case in the Kruger region, as Vaughan Kirby attested to.

Traditionally the Kruger's western subpopulation of wildebeest and their zebra travelling companions migrated along age-old trails with little variation from year to year. In the dry winter season, thousands of wildebeest and zebras gathered to forage on the rolling plains north of Skukuza and the adjoining MalaMala, Flockfield and Charleston sections in what is today the Sabi Sand Private Game Reserve, always within five to 10 kilometres of the Sabie and Sand rivers' reliable waters. Wildebeest were usually found clumped together in areas of favourable grazing. Rather than feeding on what was available in one area, they chose the area in which to feed; that is, they selected a place where the grass was at the most suitable growth stage. Wildebeest prefer certain grasses over others; they appear to look for short, growing grass that is easily digested and full of nutrients. As the dry season progressed and they were compelled to turn to older, longer grasses, they became more selective, choosing those parts that had the least fibre content. This method of feeding kept the grass cropped and growing in readiness for their return.

Stevenson-Hamilton noted that 'zebra, which in the early part of the winter migrate westwards, about the end of September come to the neighbourhood of Tshokwane in great numbers and their whinnying fills the bush by day and night. Lions, of course, find the spot an ideal hunting ground; every night their great voices swell in chorus among the hills, and sometimes in the early morning they may even be seen.' As the dry season advanced the temperature steadily climbed until the land throbbed with heat and thirst. Then in November cool grey curtains of rain swept the land, rinsing dust from grasses and trees. Almost overnight green shoots poked up from the earth.

Wildebeest had only to see lightning or hear thunder or smell a downpour's earthy aroma to respond immediately. If rain poured down on top of them they would prance about in a kind of ecstatic rain dance like so many excited bucking broncos. Since migrating animals travel to where the grass is green and growing rather than waiting for the rain to come to them, the western herds dispersed after the first drenching spring showers. Wildebeest have a highly developed social sense – one cannot resist doing what all the others are doing. Small groups joined larger congregations and, following the mob, they trudged northwest at a steady pace. Their route took them through what is today Manyeleti Game Reserve to the high-quality short-grass gabbro[5] and clay plains around Orpen and parts of the Timbavati and Klaserie game reserves and westwards to present-day Klaserie village south of Hoedspruit.

Man-made water troughs like this one in central Kruger tend to anchor zebras and wildebeest in areas traditionally visited only seasonally.

A looming rhino presents far less danger to the startled wildebeest calf than does the threat of bush encroachment, a process already well under way in this scene.

This northwest–southeast migration was a purposeful trek and took only a few days. During November the wildebeest cows had gathered on their traditional calving grounds – a month earlier in the better-watered west than in the Kruger where calves are born between early December and mid-January. In a flurry of activity that lasted as little as three weeks, they gave birth to as many as 90 per cent of the western group's annual crop of calves. Such synchronised births act as another effective anti-predator tactic, by overwhelming hunters with a glut of easy pickings that ensures much higher calf survival than if cows delivered year-round.

As summer's exuberance faded and seasonal waterholes dried one by one, the western subpopulation would gradually return southeast towards its winter grazing grounds on the expansive seeplines[6] at Ripape – west of present-day Nhlanguleni picnic site – and Sabi Sand.

A second subpopulation grazed the nutrient-rich sweetveld around Satara on the Central District's eastern side where fertile soils produce good crops of grass in years of relatively high rainfall. These wildebeest and zebras were more sedentary, trekking locally in search of fresh grazing, but did not undertake long migrations and at all times remained within the park's boundaries. A third subpopulation spent the winter months in the south of their range in the neighbourhood of Mlondozi Dam and migrated north in summer to the Lindanda Plains and Sweni River area, with zebras following a different route from wildebeest. The second and third subpopulations were separated from each other by the Sweni River, and from the western subpopulation by dense thickets of Delagoa thorn (*Acacia welwitschii*) that proved an almost impenetrable barrier to the open plains-loving wildebeest.

The beginning of the end for the western subpopulation's annual migration was set in motion in 1923 when almost a million hectares of critically important habitat was excised from the Sabi Game Reserve's western boundary. Much of the expropriated land ended up being used for cattle ranching. 'Prior to the excision of the western portion of the Reserve the game could trek freely and yet remain within the sanctuary,' Stevenson-

Hamilton lamented. 'After this country was shorn away, the animals still continued their long established usual movement but were of course then lost temporarily to the Park.' Ancestral winter and summer pastures used by the wildebeest and zebras living along the western boundary now included large tracts of land both inside and outside the reserve. 'It is unfortunate that the grazing and watering facilities within the Park should be inferior to those of the areas immediately adjoining but one has to remember that the Park is only a wildlife sanctuary because it was deemed useless for any other purpose,' Stevenson-Hamilton sardonically noted.

In 1943, shortly before he retired, Stevenson-Hamilton's annual report alluded to a new threat to the wildebeest herds. They were becoming 'definitely less numerous than they used to be in the eastern and central portions south of the Olifants River ... I am inclined partly to attribute this situation to the spread of the thick bush and the consequent decrease in the amount of open grazing which is becoming increasingly manifest all over the Park.' The savanna landscapes inhabited by wildebeest and zebras are typically a mosaic of grassland and woodland areas so 'the tendency will increasingly be for wildebeest, zebra and other types of migratory game, which are of the purely grazing type, to work further and further westwards', Stevenson-Hamilton warned. 'The western areas still remain comparatively open though much grown up compared with what I recollect of them forty years ago.' It is instructive that a landscape of Tshokwane in 1920 painted by this enthusiastic amateur watercolourist portrays open grassland with only an occasional small tree or shrub, in stark contrast to today's overgrown woody aspect.

> With the grasslands grazed to stubble, desperate animals migrating out of the park became exposed to intense hunting.

The danger to wildlife trekking westwards was highlighted during a succession of severe droughts in 1926–28, 1933–36 and 1944–48. With the grasslands grazed to stubble, desperate animals migrating out of the park became exposed to intense hunting. The new park warden, Jan Andries Beyers Sandenbergh, writing in 1947, ruefully reported: 'The Satara and Tshokwane sections lost a lot of game to the West, and, at the height of the drought, I personally saw thousands of head of large game moving out of the Park to the Sand River to drink. Fortunately, good sportsmen own the properties between the Park and the Sand River, and comparatively little shooting went on. From Buffelshoek [in present-day Manyeleti Game Reserve] up towards the Olifants [River] the story was quite different; thousands of head of game moved out in the direction of Klaserie and hundreds of shottists descended on the game and, had it not been for the police patrols, these herds of game moving in search of water and grazing would have been decimated.'

In 1953 the serving warden, Louis Steyn, alerted the park's National Board of Trustees anew to the consequences of bush encroachment. He spoke of a 'most pertinent and alarming phenomenon which has been in progress for about ten years. This phenomenon is the decrease among the pure grazers, e.g. sable antelope, roan antelope, tsessebe, waterbuck, wildebeest, zebra and reedbuck, in contrast to the increases among browsers, e.g. impala, giraffe and elephant.' Steyn also mentioned that zebras were now in the majority whereas wildebeest had previously been more numerous. It was an ominous portent for the Lowveld's wildebeest population. Ideally suited to open country, wildebeest were now confronted with relentless habitat loss due to spreading bush encroachment. And worse was to come. Although few realised it at the time, the Kruger's wildebeest hovered on the cusp of a catastrophic convergence of crises.

In 1959 the construction of a 520-kilometre-long game-deterrent veterinary fence on the Kruger's western boundary between the Olifants and Sabie rivers was begun, amid considerable opposition from conservationists. Completed in 1961, the fence was intended to keep wildlife safe from illegal hunting, while also protecting cattle ranchers from the spread of foot-and-mouth and any other contagious diseases that wild animals can transmit to domestic stock. But natural migrations and arbitrary borders do not go together. Wildlife is prevented from spreading out in good years or moving to well-watered areas in times of drought. Not only do fences disrupt routes between resource areas, but increased grazing pressure and the consequent loss of combustible material due to the confinement of animals can also reduce the frequency of fires, which often precipitates bush thickening. By their innermost design, the Kruger's wilds were never intended to be measured off and contained – flux is the life beat of their resiliency. The game-proof barrier severed the unity of the central Lowveld from the more western grasslands where higher rainfall and productive soils had provided a dependable source of forage. For all its vastness, the Kruger was now only a fragment of the wildlands its inhabitants had once depended on. It had, in effect, become an ecological island.

The herds instinctively continued trekking west but now found a fence barring their way. Their first response was to crash through, which resulted in the deaths and injury of numerous zebras, wildebeest, giraffes and kudus, to say nothing of the multiple breaks in the fence. Family groups and herds were fragmented and young animals separated from their mothers. Satara's regional ranger, Gus Adendorff, was aghast. 'This

A hunting lioness focuses her attack on a vulnerable zebra foal.

is something that I shall never forget as I witnessed the tragedy of it all,' he recalled. 'I saw wildebeest and zebra massed against the fence, some wanting to come and others wanting to leave. Carnivora were in the pink of condition as they did not have to hunt, simply chasing their prey into the fence. The animals could not comprehend and they congregated at the fence, dying of thirst and hunger and remaining there to rot. The carnivora could not cope with the situation and the stench from the carcasses was terrible. It took the herds a long time to accustom themselves to the fence and I found many giraffe which had died after being trapped between the strands of wire.'

The animals' suffering caused an understandable public outcry. In the same year that the fence was completed, the Veterinary Department was obliged to lower it in a number of places in the Kingfisherspruit area, near Orpen, to allow the milling herds back into the park. While conceding that 'the fencing of the western boundary of the Park had become an urgent necessity because of agricultural and poaching pressure', park biologist Tol Pienaar pointed out that the western border 'is for the most part artificial and had, at the time of proclamation, unfortunately not been demarcated with the object of creating an ecologically self-sufficient game sanctuary'. The boundary fence, Pienaar concluded, 'brought about the realization more than any other single factor that the Kruger Park, despite its extensive area, is incapable of supporting and maintaining a large inherent game population without artificial aid in the form of a network of boreholes and dams and a policy of scientific management'.

Supplementing natural water sources by drilling bore-wells and raising dam walls was not a new idea. Water is the most critical factor influencing wildlife; other than the five perennial rivers, permanent water sources were few and far between when the Kruger was established. As early as 1925, Stevenson-Hamilton encouraged building artificial waterholes to avoid 'having great masses congregated at the end of each dry season in such spots as may be most favourable for food and water, whereas the satisfactory grazing in waterless areas remained untouched'. Between 1955 and 1959 seven dams were built to compensate for when the Sand River was due to be fenced out of the park.

The risk to wildebeest of predation by lions increases exponentially as their open grassland habitat becomes overgrown.

In Kruger a zebra's life is filled with danger, including from poachers' wire snares like this one that bites deeply into the victim's neck.

During 1960 and 1961 the Shimanguaneni Dam, south of Muzandzeni picnic site, was built on the upper reaches of the Sweni River and 11 new boreholes were sunk, in an effort to replace natural pans lost to the fence and to relieve concentrations along the boundary. Early indications suggested that the strategy was working. 'As a result of the building of artificial watering points and controlled burns [to provide fresh grazing] along the Western boundary of the Tshokwane Section, the movements of migrating game (especially blue wildebeest and zebra) were especially interesting,' recorded a ranger's report. 'The general impression is that these artificial control methods definitely influenced the trek rhythms which this year were characterised by a series of restless to and fro movements in contrast with the previous seasonal movements which could be predicted with great regularity.' Just as intended, zebras and wildebeest were lured away from the western boundary and deeper into the park's hinterland.

What had not been foreseen was that the bewildered herds would build up around several artificial waterholes set down in traditional summer pastures in the Kingfisherspruit section and remain there even after they normally would have migrated south for the winter. Thirsty animals milled around the water. Not only was the migration disrupted but the man-made waterholes anchored the herds on grazing land they previously would have used only seasonally. Confined to one area, they embarked on what is known as 'constant nibble', without allowing time for the grass to recover. It is not the number of mouths and trampling hooves at any one stage that impacts the health of grasslands; instead it is the crucial growing, flowering and seeding period afterwards. Adding hardship to the confusion, the building of the fence coincided with below-average rainfall in seven of the nine years between 1961 and 1970.

Only parts of the Central District's total area are suitable habitat for wildebeest and zebras; the rest is waterless, too hilly or too dense. Concerned by the impact their high densities were having on favoured grasslands in the Kingfisherspruit area, park authorities were forced to consider several difficult options to alleviate an increasingly severe overgrazing problem. They first tried driving off the herds by shooting some of the wildebeest and zebras for rations, in the hope that this would compel those that remained behind to follow the others south, but that did not work. Another idea involved mass capture by adding tranquillisers to their drinking water, but that had to be abandoned because a suitable drug could not be found. Ultimately it was decided to fence off the affected area. To the wildlife managers involved in the decision-making process, the need to do something seemed paramount – by congregating in big herds, wildebeest and zebras can significantly contribute to severe localised overgrazing, which may lead to the loss of perennial grasses and dominance by fibrous annual species, with soil erosion as a possible grim end result. Tragically, it also meant that the western herds were now completely locked out of all their traditional summer grazing areas.

Finally, in March 1966, citing the need to halt or at least slow further habitat degradation, park officials authorised culling wildebeest, zebras and impalas until conditions improved. Three problem areas, all within traditional summer grazing grounds, were identified as having excessive numbers of zebras and wildebeest: the Kingfisherspruit area; the Mbhatsana waterhole area in the Nwanetsi section, northeast of Satara; and the Lebombo plains north of Crocodile Bridge.

Based on their annual net population recruitment, the culling rate for wildebeest was set at five per cent of the overall population and for zebras at three per cent. In all, 3 315 wildebeest were shot between 1965 and 1972. Between 1965 and 1974, 3 697 zebras were captured and translocated – foot-and-mouth disease restrictions do not apply to zebras – to game farms, nature reserves and other parts of the Kruger. Zebras that could not be captured alive were shot. Yet, despite the fence, the drought and, so it at first seemed, even the cull, during the 1960s the wildebeest population in the 5 560-square-kilometre Central District remained stable at around 14 000 and zebras at 13 000. Then, beginning in 1969 and continuing into 1970, aerial counts revealed that the number of wildebeest, and to a lesser degree zebras, had declined markedly. At the time the population reversal was attributed to the drought, although in hindsight it became apparent that the cull was more likely the main cause.

But what at first glance appeared to be a sublime natural tableau concealed a biological time bomb.

At last the rains came. In the summer of 1971/2 the drought was suddenly replaced by a very wet cycle, changing events dramatically. The difference between the two extremes had to be seen to be believed: one presented a sere and yellow landscape; the other exuded the green breath of life, with rain-gorged pastures choked by a profusion of tall grasses and bushes and trees in full leaf. But what at first glance appeared to be a sublime natural tableau concealed a biological time bomb.

In response to the rains the herds dispersed to take advantage of the copious pans and streams. Despite the lush conditions, the aerial count that year showed that both wildebeest and zebra numbers had continued to drop, with each reaching the predetermined level of 10 000, at which point culling was supposed to be suspended. However, because of uncertainty as to the reliability of the count it was decided to continue with the cull, albeit at a reduced rate.

At first the drop in wildebeest and zebra numbers was seen as a welcome development in curtailing range deterioration. However no one was prepared for just how precipitous the drop would be. The 1972 census results indicated that the wildebeest in the Central District had plummeted by 52 per cent to 6 750 and zebras by 42 per cent to 7 500. Alarmed park managers immediately called a halt to the wildebeest cull and halved the zebra quota, before discontinuing it two years later. But the declines continued. At first nobody was sure why. Was the western boundary fence the cause? Or was it the change in weather and the possibility that the dense hunting cover provided by the rank vegetation had rendered wildebeest and zebras vulnerable to predators, in particular lions? The latter would account for the unusually high calf and foal mortalities. The search for answers prompted the launch of an intensive investigation that included in its agenda ways to put an end to the population declines.

The changes and trends in vegetation, wildlife numbers and distribution, and their interrelationship in response to rainfall, had been recognised early in the park's history. In annual reports from the 1920s to the 1940s, Stevenson-Hamilton noted that wildebeest 'had died during the rains' between 1916 and 1924 followed by a 'rapid and uninterrupted increase' during a dry phase. There are, he observed, 'annual curves of alternating abundance and want, which affect herbivore and carnivore conversely'. Put crudely, hard times for herbivores equal good times for their predators, and vice versa. As had been the case with the earlier population oscillations, it was apparent that the key component driving the Kruger's ecosystem was rainfall and that the wildebeest and zebra population crashes did not happen *despite* the verdant conditions but *because of* them.

The Kruger's first scientific probe into the problems incurred as a result of heavy rains as opposed to drought was spearheaded in 1975 by Butch Smuts. Fresh from attaining his PhD detailing the growth, reproduction and population dynamics of the Kruger's zebras, the ever-curious field ecologist could now give his full attention to the intricate puzzle of how wildebeest, zebras, climate and predators fitted together. He had already observed the park in the grip of severe drought, with huge herds of animals congregating around the remaining waterholes. 'This is true Africa!' the young scientist had marvelled, thrilled at the spectacle provided by the sheer multitude of wild creatures. 'Little did I realize that what I was witnessing was the end of a dry cycle and that in less than two years above average rainfall would transform the whole park into a lush, green paradise with zebra and wildebeest incapable of coping with grass growth.'

Alarmed park managers immediately called a halt to the wildebeest cull and halved the zebra quota, before discontinuing it two years later.

K. Yoganand

(Left) Translocating captured zebras.
(Above) Researcher Yogi Yoganand and SANParks pilot Charles Thompson attach a GPS collar to a sedated wildebeest.

It did not take Smuts long to confirm that the declines were linked to the big rains. 'The extremely wet conditions … had a deleterious effect on both zebra and wildebeest,' he observed. 'During these months the tremendous increase in grass cover favoured the hunting activities of predators … Although it was realized that these declines were linked to cropping operations, the drought, and marked habitat changes associated with five years of above average rainfall, there was some evidence that large predators, principally the lion, were the proximate cause of the declines.' In support of this interpretation he pointed out that buffaloes, waterbuck and kudus had increased during the wet years while exposed to the same predator abundance.

Smuts also tackled the vexed question of why lion predation had suddenly had such an impact on wildebeest and zebras. It was already known that, wherever wildebeest are abundant in East and southern Africa, they constitute the lion's principal prey while zebras make an important contribution. Of the more than 12 300 lion kills recorded by rangers in the Kruger between 1933 and 1966, wildebeest accounted for 2 900, or almost 25 per cent. Tol Pienaar calculated prey preference indices for the Kruger lion and found that wildebeest were taken in proportions well above

Lions used the long grass surrounding the short grass islands as hunting cover to pick off wildebeest that grazed within charging distance.

their relative abundance. However the predation rates that Smuts encountered were even higher than usual. Ultimately his painstaking research would provide valuable data on this aspect of the predator–prey relationship and make it possible to fit more important pieces into the puzzle.

Some of the answers related to the vegetation changes caused by the unusually high rainfall. The tall grasses had compelled the wildebeest and zebra herds to break down into smaller groups that grazed islands of short grass or ventured into the taller grasses. Lions used the long grass surrounding the short grass islands as hunting cover to pick off wildebeest that grazed within charging distance. Animals entering the sea of tall grasses were stalked unseen by ambush predators. In addition, hyaenas found it easier to locate newborn wildebeest calves in these small groups.

Big cats and other carnivores generally have little impact on prey numbers but, when something stops a prey species migrating, predators start to have a major adverse effect. So, while predation has little impact on the migratory Serengeti wildebeest population, in nearby Ngorongoro Crater, where the wildebeest population is sedentary, predation is their main limiting factor. In the Klaserie Private Nature Reserve, on the Kruger's western boundary, lion predation accounted for 99 per cent of all the wildebeest killed by large predators. Ultimately predation and drought so reduced the Klaserie population that lions were compelled to switch from their preferred prey species, wildebeest and zebras, to the abundant impalas and bigger buffaloes and giraffes. In the Kruger's Central District, records of kills revealed that wildebeest made up over 30 per cent of a lion's diet and zebras almost 20 per cent. That worked out at roughly four wildebeest and two zebras a year per adult lion. For the western wildebeest subpopulation the increased predation proved the terminal point in a series of calamitous events that ultimately overwhelmed them. Their numbers crashed from roughly 6 000 in 1965 to 750 in 1979. Once totalling nearly a third of the entire Kruger wildebeest community, they were reduced to a sedentary herd living on scattered patches of suitable habitat.

By the time Smuts undertook his study in 1975, the proliferation of artificial water supplies in the Kruger's Central District – around 70 boreholes and 25 dams – had resulted in a doubling of the area's lion population, to over 700 in the 42 years since the first borehole was drilled in 1933. At least 12 new prides – or almost 13 lions per 100 square kilometres – had become established in areas where artificial waterholes had been built. Based on the known ratio of one lion to 110 prey animals in the Central District – an extraordinarily high figure when compared with the Serengeti's one lion per 1 000 prey animals – Smuts calculated that the resident lions required about 2 500 wildebeest annually as part of their minimum diet. Since the potential wildebeest recruitment was only about 3 300 calves, this left an excess of only 800 calves if lions were the sole predators. However, hyaenas, leopards, cheetahs and wild dogs also took a percentage, as did accidents and disease. In addition, Smuts discovered that there were four times as many newly independent subadult lions in areas favoured by wildebeest and zebras as there had been two-and-a-half years earlier. This had come about because the many small groups of wildebeest and zebras were spread over a much larger area, which permitted the nomadic subadults to hunt almost anywhere without coming into competition with the resident territorial prides. Although Smuts acknowledged that the situation would in all likelihood come to an end in the next dry cycle when surface water evaporated and herbivores again concentrated around permanent waterholes and on shorter grass, he was concerned that the above-average rains had 'enabled the lion population to remove a large quota of wildebeest and zebra from populations that are no longer able to absorb this rate of predation … Because of this, predator control may be necessary….'

Smuts went on to recommend that 'at least 80 per cent of the lions and spotted hyaenas should be removed from the summer grazing area and this resultant low predator density should be maintained during summer until the wildebeest and zebra populations recover'. An experimental cull of 75 per cent of the lions and hyaenas in a 4 500-square-kilometre section of central Kruger was approved, a decision that set in motion the largest systematic predator cull in the Kruger's history. Between 1974 and 1980, 445 lions and 375 hyaenas were destroyed. The operation was terminated when it was realised that, despite the predator reduction, zebra and wildebeest numbers continued to decline (see Chapter 8, page 130). Both populations subsequently increased from their mid-1970s low to peak abundance during the onset of the next dry cycle in the late 1980s when lions, responding to changing prey vulnerability, shifted their hunting focus from wildebeest and zebras to drought-affected buffaloes, kudus and waterbuck. Between 1980 and 1993 the Kruger's zebra numbers grew to an average of 29 400 and wildebeest to 12 500.

Extended dry periods may have up to 26 per cent less rain than normal years, with grass cover reduced to very low levels over large areas of the Kruger. Strangely enough, plains-loving animals such as zebras and wildebeest increase in number during droughts

Between 1974 and 1980, 445 lions and 375 hyaenas were destroyed.

Over the past century, prime wildebeest range like these open short grass plains in Manyeleti Game Reserve on Kruger's western boundary – once part of the migration route of the western subpopulation of wildebeest – has been lost steadily to bush encroachment in the park itself, and wildebeest don't easily adapt to other habitats.

whereas populations of long-grass feeders, including buffaloes, roans, sables, tsessebes and reedbuck, decrease. Butch Smuts made the point that overgrazed and trampled areas 'do have a certain potential for recovery and one should refrain from placing too much emphasis on the way man sees the habitat but also consider it more seriously from the animals' angle'. Wildebeest do best on short, seemingly 'poorer'-quality grasslands where their foraging holds the grass at a stage where it is nutritious and succulent.

In 1992, wildlife biologists Gus Mills and Tanya Shenk used simulation models based on their direct observations over four years to measure the impact of lion predation on a sedentary wildebeest subpopulation versus semi-migratory zebras in a 235-square-kilometre study area in southeastern Kruger. The results suggested that lion hunting regulated the low-density resident wildebeest but did not seem to have a strong limiting factor on the semi-migratory zebras. One reason was that the lions selected adult wildebeest – many of which were in their prime reproductive years – and calves in relation to their occurrence in the population, whereas they killed more zebra foals than expected and fewer breeding adults, which actually works to the advantage of the overall zebra population's ability to cope with the impact of lion predation. Another important factor was the wildebeest's sedentary behaviour, which made them susceptible to high levels of predation throughout the year. Overall it was found that lion predation in the Kruger affected wildebeest more severely than zebras. Data by Mills and Shenk supported earlier hypotheses, which showed that predators can regulate resident herbivores at low population densities, while such regulation is rare for migratory herds.

Research has also shown that, while plains zebras are able to cope with relatively tall grass or heavily wooded savannas, wildebeest do not easily adapt to habitats other than open short grass plains. Moreover, wildebeest are particularly sensitive to the disruption of migratory routes and often decline in closed ecosystems. Today, except for the Sweni to Mlondozi migration, which is still active, the Kruger's wildebeest subpopulations are either sedentary or vagrant, moving to areas of optimal habitat created by fire and rain, and are much smaller than they were before their western pastures were lost. So, when in June 1993 the perimeter fence between the Kruger and the private reserves was moved 70 kilometres to the west, there was hope that the ecological integrity of the Greater Kruger system could be restored.

Unfortunately the disruptions of the intervening years have led to a succession of changes in the composition and structure of the private reserves' vegetation and consequently the density and distribution patterns of their wildlife. As it turned out, bushveld vegetation is not suited to cattle ranching. Overstocking caused overgrazing and soil erosion, while the proliferation of artificial water points increased localised grazing pressure. Crucially, a lack of systematic burning between the 1940s and 1980s facilitated bush encroachment. Though the boundary fence with the Kruger together with many kilometres of internal fencing is gone, the old migration did not re-establish itself, probably because the private reserves' habitat, which has changed from open savanna to thick woodland, is no longer attractive to wildebeest and zebras.

In the 1960s the wildlife artist and naturalist Charles Astley Maberly thought there were approximately 10 000 wildebeest in the private game reserves. At first they seemed to prosper. In Klaserie, for example, wildebeest increased even though they were enclosed and isolated by the various fences and were also the local lions' favourite prey. Then in 1982/3 the summer rains failed and their population crashed by 94 per cent from 6 560 to 430. Zebras, which had not increased as rapidly, declined 31 per cent from 2 440 to 1 680. They died of starvation when their grazing gave out, although the same drought had little impact on the Kruger's wildebeest and zebras, despite general wildlife mortality reaching 35 per cent. In Klaserie the over-abundance of artificial waterholes had allowed grazers to forage wherever conditions were suitable. When the drought hit they had no reserves to fall back on and game-proof fences ensured that they had nowhere else to go.

Zebras are one of Kruger's lions' favoured prey species but are not as severely affected by predation as are wildebeest.

Further south, in the Sabi Sand Private Game Reserve, the wildebeest situation is equally fraught. When the boundary fence separating the reserve from the Kruger went up in the early 1960s there were an estimated 3 000 wildebeest in Sabi Sand but, trapped between the fences, their numbers crashed soon afterwards due to insufficient grazing and the easy pickings so many panicked wildebeest presented to lions. The population then stabilised at between 600 and 800, depending on the fluctuating rainfall. In 1993 when the fence was relocated the annual aerial census recorded 570 wildebeest but 10 years later the population had mysteriously nose-dived to just 75. There was speculation that Sabi Sand's overgrown habitat prompted some wildebeest to emigrate east into the Kruger, while also encouraging selective predation by lions taking advantage of the woody cover.

Several studies have shown that predators can limit or even extinguish resident prey populations that occur at low densities. With that in mind, Sabi Sand's management decided that measures to safeguard the dwindling wildebeest population would have to go beyond protecting the survivors; they would have to be reinforced by extra wildebeest from elsewhere. Over three years they traded some of their excess white rhinos for 1 800 wildebeest from Swaziland. However, two years after their introduction the new recruits had decreased by 80 per cent, with predation apparently accounting for only 20 per cent of the decline. In order to achieve the reserve's goal of boosting wildebeest numbers to over 500, there are plans to release another 600. But the results are unlikely to be very different. You cannot save a species without first saving its habitat.

Timbavati's wildebeest are so desperate for a patch of open space that the last survivors have taken to gathering on airstrips each evening.

Long-term weather cycles have always occurred in this region and wildebeest numbers have fluctuated with those cycles. Rather, it is the change in the Lowveld's vegetation over time that is the primary cause for this habitat-sensitive species' decrease. The Kruger's 2008 census revealed that wildebeest had declined from 12 000 in 2007 to 8 000. Zebras are down to less than 20 000. Timbavati's wildebeest are so desperate for a patch of open space that the last survivors have taken to gathering on airstrips each evening. That old bush naturalist James Stevenson-Hamilton said it best: 'Each species is plentiful or the reverse within any given area in direct proportion to the suitability of the locality to its special requirements.'

Before habitat change and fences, the passage of the migratory wildebeest and zebra herds had a flow-on effect in maintaining not only plant diversity but also that of associated bird, invertebrate and other mammal species. It was a role that made them both an umbrella species[7] and an indicator species for the health of their ecosystem. To appreciate that is to understand how much has been lost.

---

1   The Lowveld ecological unit was well over 203 000 square kilometres in size and extended from the Drakensberg escarpment in the west to the Mozambique coast in the east and from the northern parts of KwaZulu-Natal in the south to beyond the Limpopo River in the north; the Kruger Park's 19 500 square kilometres represents only a fraction of that.
2   Basal cover is the area of ground covered by basal (new growth) plants.
3   Newborn antelopes are either 'lying-out' babies or they are followers. A follower accompanies its mother when she travels or grazes, without making any attempt to hide when at rest. Followers include wildebeest, buffaloes and tsessebes. The young of lying-out species, including impalas, bushbucks and roan antelopes, seek a place to hide, such as a clump of long grass or depression, and wait motionless until their mothers return to nurse them.
4   Biomass is the total weight or quantity of organisms in a given area. In this book, biomass usually refers to the total weight of a species, herbivore or carnivore, within the Greater Kruger Park.
5   Gabbro is an intrusive igneous rock that forms as slowly cooling magma solidifies within the Earth. In the Lowveld the gabbro plains' impermeable clay-based soils gave rise to high-quantity and high-quality grazing.
6   Seeplines form where poorly drained sandy and clay soils interface. In times of good rainfall they become waterlogged and marshy, making them unsuitable for woody plants but ideal for swards of good-quality grass. In the past, fire, elephants and large herbivore migrations maintained seeplines as open areas.
7   Umbrella species are species selected for making conservation-related decisions, typically because protecting them indirectly protects the many other species that make up the ecological community of its habitat.

4 The riddle of the disappearing roan antelope

In the Kruger National Park there has been an alarming decline in the Roan population from 450 individuals in 1986 to about 25 in 2003 ... The population is in great danger of extinction. This was one of the most secure populations in South Africa but now it is one of the most threatened.

Rob Toms and Salomon Joubert,
'Roan 200 years later',
Science in Africa, 2005

The Kruger's roan antelope population was always small but for the last 25 years it has been perilously low. Because of its rarity, this elegant, horse-sized antelope – its scientific name *Hippotragus equinus* translates as the 'horse-like horned horse' – has long been one of park management's conservation priorities. For the first 60 years after the Kruger's proclamation, roan numbers fluctuated between 150 and 300 depending on the profound effect the region's variable annual rainfall had on grazing. Following a series of high-rainfall years and despite the great El Niño-spawned drought of 1982/3, the roan population count peaked at around 450 in 1986. A few years after the drought, however, roan numbers began dropping progressively through the protracted dry years that followed. Initially wildlife managers were not unduly concerned as all counts are subject to error, but they became increasingly anxious as successive censuses trended lower. As the population spiralled downwards towards its current critically tenuous tally of around 35 free-ranging animals, researchers scrambled to uncover root causes and solutions.

Roans are not the only Kruger antelopes to have experienced drastic population decreases – the future of the roan's more glamorous cousin, the sable antelope, and the tsessebe – the hartebeest look-alike with the glossy purple patches on its thighs and shoulders – also hangs in the balance. Sables are estimated to have plummeted from 2 240 in 1986 to around 300 at present and tsessebes from 1 160 to 250. Eland numbers also tumbled after climbing encouragingly from 300 in 1978 to around 900 by the mid-1980s, when they again fell back to 300. Eland had 'abounded in the Middle-Veld' near modern White River in the 1870s according to pioneer Lowveld farmer Bill Sanderson. In a 1923 report, Sabi Game Reserve's warden, James Stevenson-Hamilton, stated that they 'were beginning to become almost numerous in the north' after being 'heavily recruited from across the frontier [Zimbabwe and Mozambique] since there were few if any in the Reserve up to 1905'. All four antelopes are now at such dangerously low levels that further reductions would make recovery difficult, to say the least. Their disappearance would be a significant loss to the Kruger's biodiversity.

All four antelopes are now at such dangerously low levels that further reductions would make recovery difficult, to say the least.

These locally rare antelope species are concentrated in the northern half of the park. Eland are found, although seldom seen, throughout much of the north, especially the far north. Sables favour mixed mopane woodlands in the western granitic region, while roans and tsessebes occur mainly in shrub mopaneveld on the northeastern basalt[1] plains between Letaba and Punda Maria. The northern Kruger is the park's driest section, with an average rainfall close to the roan, sable and tsessebe's lower tolerance limit, so their recovery, if it comes, will need to be based on a complete understanding of what makes the north what it is.

To appreciate better how a succession of changes within the rare antelopes' ecosystems coalesced to become a conservation catastrophe, it is critical to recognise that every ecosystem has its own special characteristics. To that end, a linked, multi-faceted research and monitoring project under the umbrella of the Northern Plains Programme was developed in 1994 by SANParks' Scientific Services, with the aim of using 'the northern basalt plains and the area north of the Olifants [River] as an intensive study site to examine the ecosystem effects resulting from interactions between the most important system drivers – rainfall, climate, soil fertility, nutrients and herbivores – with management actions such as the provision of additional water, fire and fences'. The intention is to highlight links between rare antelopes, habitat diversity, biodiversity and the way that ecosystems function in this sun-baked land.

Historically, the northern plains' poor-quality habitat and severely limited permanent water supply could support year-round only those large grazers such as roans, sables, tsessebes and eland that occur there at low densities. Indeed, the roan has developed a social structure and organisation that functions best at low densities. Though wildlife artist and naturalist Charles Astley Maberly counted more than 30 in one herd between Punda Maria and Shingwedzi in the 1950s, the Kruger's roan herds more usually comprise between six and 15 females and young, which occupy traditional and exclusive home ranges of 60 to 100 square kilometres. The cows maintain closed social units within the herd via a dominance hierarchy that is reinforced by frequent albeit low intensity aggression, with the oldest female highest and the yearlings lowest. In one Kruger breeding herd the rank order remained unchanged for three years, suggesting that they have little tolerance for newcomers. A single bull accompanies each breeding herd and defends a 300- to 500-metre-wide intolerance zone around the group against incursions by other bulls. So, despite high reproductive potential – fertile cows can bear a calf every year – the ecological limitations imposed by the roan's harsh habitat act to

A dominant roan antelope bull adopts the 'proud' posture, with head held high and ears forward, to intimidate a subordinate, who responds by submissively dropping his head.

space out the herds and restrict carrying capacity within home ranges. This exclusive use of large areas of favoured habitat by a single herd puts significant restrictions on overall numbers.

The intention is to highlight links between rare antelopes, habitat diversity, biodiversity and the way that ecosystems function in this sun-baked land.

As permanent residents, roans, sables and tsessebes are dependent on their home ranges' food resources at the worst time of the year, unlike mobile zebras and wildebeest, which are free to find the best seasonal grazing and so can form much larger herds. The three low-density antelopes have responded to their unforgiving environment by developing into distinct eco-types, able to make the most of the sparse resource base within their narrow ecological niches. They are all dependent on relatively tall grasslands that retain some green leaves during the dry season. Their narrow muzzles have evolved to pluck specific clusters of leaves from grass swards, including largely sourveld areas. Roans feed on a variety of different grass species in different parts of their range at different times of the year, selecting green leaves off the stems of nutritious perennials that may stand as tall as one-and-a-half metres. Tsessebes prefer shorter grass habitats. Sables select from a wide range of medium-height green grasses in savanna woodlands, favouring those species growing under tree canopies and in marshy depressions that retain green leaves longest.

Low-density antelopes also have distinct habitat preferences; their patchy distribution ranges generally occur in landscapes least favoured by the more common grazers. Sable herds are more usually found on granitic substrates than on more fertile basaltic soils and occupy gaps where impalas, wildebeest and, to a lesser degree, zebras are less abundant but are hardly affected by the local abundance of buffaloes, indicating inconsistent relationships with potential grazing competitors. Suitable roan and tsessebe habitat on the 2 800-square-kilometre northern basalt plains mainly comprises that 18 per cent of the area made up of a network of relatively broad, shallow and poorly drained ephemeral wetlands called dambos[2]. These extensive corridors of tall, sour grasses traverse a flat and fairly arid landscape to connect with similar habitats in Zimbabwe and Mozambique, where roans once thrived. Avoidance of areas used by high-density species minimises competition and the heavy grazing and trampling that renders grass swards unsuitable for the low-density antelopes' fastidious tastes. As a consequence, they are sensitive indicators of the biological richness or degradation of those habitats and so give us a lens through which we can view environmental trends. However, their overriding niche requirement is not absence of competition, according to a study by Witwatersrand University's Johannes Chirima, Norman Owen-Smith, Barend Erasmus and Francesca Parrini, but a lowered risk of predation.

There are advantages as well as limitations to living few and far between in an inhospitable habitat – because of the paucity of prey species, predators are proportionately fewer. The low-density antelopes' legacy of early adaptation to life in a land of scanty resources has also specialised them for life in a land of low predation levels. Where other herbivores and the predators that hunt them are plentiful, these antelopes are rare or absent. In the Kruger, where lions are more numerous than in most other parts of the rare antelopes' African range, their narrow distribution is due partly to higher predation rates in areas from which they have vanished or never occurred.

Because it is the most endangered, the roan has become the poster species for the rare antelopes' plight. Although one of the most wide-ranging antelope species in sub-Saharan Africa, occurring from sea level to 2 400 metres, its strict requirements mean that the roan is nowhere common. It reaches its highest numbers in the better-watered parts of West Africa's Guinea savanna – a woodland belt stretching from Senegal east to the upper Nile basin. Senegal's 8 000-square-kilometre Niokolo-Koba (Place of the Roan Antelope) National Park protected around 1 640 roans in 2003, although that number was down from 2 180 in 2001 due to poaching, village encroachment, cattle activity and possibly ecosystem changes due to long-term rainfall declines. West Africans familiar with this big, handsome antelope admire its stately physical presence, gently backward-curving corrugated horns and long ears tipped with tufts of reddish hair. Storytellers liken its pink-greyish-brown, or roan, pelage to the subdued shades of the bush and its striking black-and-white mask, which resembles a balaclava with elongated cutouts around the eyes, to the facial scarification once adopted by Yorùbá men.

A 1999 estimate put Africa's overall roan numbers at 40 000 but, allowing for an undercounting bias in aerial surveys and for huge areas of their current range for which estimates are unavailable, such as southern Sudan, that figure has been revised to 76 000. This relatively robust continental population is classified in the latest International Union for Conservation of Nature (IUCN)[3] *Red Data Book* as at lower risk but conservation dependent. Outside protected areas they are in decline and already have been eliminated from large parts of their former range because of illegal hunting and habitat loss. Even in protected areas they are decreasing or at best stable – Kenya's last roans persist as a remnant population in Ruma National Park. Roans once roamed the vast plains of northeastern Uganda but a 2004 survey by ecologist Hugh Lamprey in savanna parks and wildlife reserves across the country could not find any. In the 1980s poachers armed with automatic rifles wiped out the formerly thriving roan population in Kidepo National Park and then followed survivors down into Pian Upe Wildlife Reserve, south of Kidepo, where their numbers had declined to just seven animals by 2002, and apparently they have since disappeared. On the positive side, in Southern and Central Africa roans are still widely distributed in Zambia, Botswana and the Caprivi, while Malawi's Nyika National Park hosts a flourishing population.

In East and southern Africa the roan has been glaringly absent from large areas in the east for as long as there have been records. Southern roans reach their highest abundance in a vast block of monotonous savanna known as miombo (a Bemba and Shona word used to describe primarily brachystegia woodlands that stretch from the Democratic Republic of the Congo to the Zambezi River and from Angola to Tanzania). These moist savannas have leached mainly infertile soils that produce poor-quality grazing with a correspondingly low herbivore-

> Outside protected areas they are in decline and already have been eliminated from large parts of their former range because of illegal hunting and habitat loss.

carrying capacity. You can drive for hours and see very few large mammals in miombo country but it does have dambo drainage systems on a far bigger scale than those in the Kruger, which suits the local roans and sables admirably. During a more arid era in prehistory, miombo would have filled much of the present Congo basin and been connected to the Guinea savannas by the Nile Valley and the western Rift, providing roans with a continuous range. The Kruger's fauna was enriched by the southward extension of such characteristic miombo species as roan and sable when, according to scientific evidence, miombo stretched much further south than at present. Or they may have come later via the mopane woodlands that now connect the miombo to the southern bushveld.

Having crossed into South Africa, roans selected as their domain lightly wooded, park-like savannas with open areas of medium to tall grasses in suitable parts of Limpopo province, Mpumalanga, North West province, the Free State and the eastern Northern Cape. In the west they ranged as far south as the confluence of the Orange and Vaal rivers. In the east they never ventured south of Swaziland, where they grazed montane pastures in the western highlands, the Lebombo Mountains and the Dumezulu and

Malindza Hills. In the 1950s, the intrepid Swaziland conservationist Ted Reilly saw small herds at Maphiveni and Sikhupe in the Malindza Hills and in 1961 recovered the remains of what he believes to be the last indigenous roan in a snare at Maphiveni. Appropriately, Reilly is spearheading the roan's reintroduction into the mini-kingdom's Mlilwane and Mkhaya game reserves.

Bushman rock paintings in southwestern Kruger indicate that roans were common in this region until relatively recently. James Stevenson-Hamilton was told in the early 20th century by village elders and old white hunters that roans had been 'very numerous' in the rolling, not too thickly wooded uplands of the eastern Transvaal middle veld and 'in the semi-open country about the foothills of the Drakensberg, while rarely encountered in the bush country proper'. By the end of the 19th century, however, the Lowveld's roans, together with elephants, hippos and rhinos, had been nearly exterminated by indiscriminate hunting. 'In the early days of the game reserve the few [roan] survivors were found living in quite thick bush, but after six or seven years they gradually abandoned

A tsessebe grazes green shoots erupting in the wake of a fire.

this for the more open country,' Stevenson-Hamilton recalled. A 1918 ground count estimated that the 4 600-square-kilometre Sabi Game Reserve, between the Crocodile and Sabie rivers, contained 300 roans, 1 500 sables and over 1 000 tsessebes, while the 9 000-square-kilometre Singwitsi Game Reserve, between the Letaba and Luvuvhu rivers, held 500 roans and 2 000 sables.

In 1923, however, a dismayed Stevenson-Hamilton recorded in his journal: 'South of the Olifants River the only country suitable to [roans and sables] was excised from the Sabi reserve, as well as that containing all of the red duiker, and nearly all the mountain reedbuck.' Further boundary adjustments in 1960/1 and 1967/8 resulted in the loss of more favoured roan and sable habitat as well the only suitable oribi habitat and some of the best grey rhebok habitat. In a 1937 report, Stevenson-Hamilton wrote of 'a westward migration in the upper reaches of the Shingwedzi River' and complained that there was 'a considerable reduction in animal numbers, especially roan and eland, attributed to these seasonal movements and the poaching to which the herbivores were then subjected'. Why a sedentary species like the roan, with its fixed home range, should undertake such a migration is open to speculation but it seems probable they were seeking better pastures. In his 1955 annual report, warden Louis Steyn noted that an improvement in the numbers of most grazers could be detected although the position 'regarding antelope such as tsessebe, roan antelope and sable antelope had deteriorated to such an extent in the Central and Southern districts during the preceding ten years or more that it would take them a long time to build up their numbers to a point where they could be considered safe. In the Northern districts the same applies to wildebeest, tsessebe and especially eland.' Steyn attributed the southern declines to bush encroachment into savanna grasslands.

The species is now listed in the Red Data Book as vulnerable to extinction in South Africa.

By the 1960s just three isolated roan herds remained south of Olifants River, in the Munywini and Batavia areas of the Central District and around the headwaters of the Biyamiti and Mtshawu rivers in the Southern District. The last of them, a herd of between 10 and 20 in the vicinity of Pretoriuskop, had disappeared by 1985. In his 1937 report, Stevenson-Hamilton could proclaim that 'north of the Letaba River, [roans] at once become numerous and continue so right up to the northern boundary of the Park'. But within a couple of decades this population, once South Africa's most abundant, long established and secure, would collapse. The species is now listed in the *Red Data Book* as vulnerable to extinction in South Africa.

Due to the complexity of maintaining a population locked up in the intricacies of its biology, roans have for a long time been closely monitored by the Kruger's wildlife managers. Different scenarios that could have led to its poor population performance were first discussed in detail as early as the 1960s when park biologist Tol Pienaar ruefully declared that they were 'the only large ungulate species of which the population growth curve has remained relatively stagnant through the years and which has not yet reacted favourably to the stringent protection afforded them'. The most likely limiting factor was thought to be habitat related, although disease, specifically anthrax, and a loss of vitality due to inbreeding were also suggested, as was predation.

One of the identified threats reappeared in 1959/60 when an outbreak of the highly infectious bacterial disease anthrax spread from the low-lying Pafuri area into regions that largely overlapped the northern portion of the roan's preferred habitat. Anthrax epizootics[4] occur every six to 20 years in the Kruger and are most prevalent during dry months when herbivores drink from stagnant waterholes infected with anthrax spores in the excreta of vultures that have fed on contaminated carcasses. Blowflies and hyaenas also spread the disease and, while most mammals are vulnerable, different species have different levels of natural immunity. The Kruger's impalas suffered hardly any mortality while in northern Tanzania's Lake Manyara National Park they were nearly wiped out, perhaps because of genetic differences between the two host populations or between different types of anthrax. The Kruger's eland were unaffected but the related kudus and bushbucks were extremely susceptible. Records show that only eight sables died of anthrax over the 11 years between the first outbreak and a second in 1970, while 83 of the closely related roans succumbed out of an estimated 250 north of the Olifants River.

Disease has long been known to regulate wildlife populations but it was now realised that epidemics could become a serious menace to endangered species that occur as small populations in fragmented habitats. Accordingly, the roans of the northeastern basalt plains came in for special attention. The entire population, except for those furthest from the main focus of infection at Mooiplaas, was immunised annually by vaccine-filled projectile syringes – later replaced by bio-bullets – fired from a helicopter. Launched in 1971, the programme was finally halted in 1992 because of concerns that the panicked roans became vulnerable to predation when they scattered in all directions at the helicopter's approach. Also, maintaining comprehensive vaccination coverage is expensive – after road maintenance it was often the largest item in the park's budget. Ultimately it was discovered that anthrax could be stopped by lacing infected waterholes with antibiotics.

Anthrax was considered, then rejected, as a factor in the roan's penultimate population collapse that began a few years after the severe 1982/3 drought. Aerial surveys began recording losses among roans and tsessebes that continued through the even more devastating drought of 1991/2. Anthrax deaths are closely monitored and none were reported during these die-offs. Illegal hunting was also quickly discounted – not only is the Kruger well patrolled, but declines were not confined to park borders where poachers are most active. It seemed reasonable therefore to assume that the deaths were due to habitat deterioration caused by prolonged low rainfall and exacerbated by competition from a zebra population that had proliferated from a Kruger-wide total of 16 000 in 1978 to 30 000 in 1983.

More than a decade earlier, in 1970, ecologist Salomon Joubert, later the Kruger's executive director from 1987 to 1994, set out to investigate the roan's social behaviour and habitat preferences at a time when scientific knowledge about them was surprisingly thin. In 1972 he went on to study the habitat preferences of tsessebes, and in 1976, the roan's population ecology. His new data challenged long-held beliefs and helped fill in large ecological holes. The 1970s was also the era of the mega Water for Game project. By 1975, 35 active boreholes – an average of just 41 square kilometres per borehole – and six dams had been built on the northern basalt plains. The programme aimed to boost herbivore numbers by opening up forage-rich areas previously inaccessible to water-dependent species and, ironically, given the events that later unfolded, to boost rare antelope numbers by safeguarding them from recurrent droughts. It also set the scene for a classic example of the Law of Unintended Consequences.

As construction of the new waterholes got under way, Salomon Joubert expressed serious concerns. 'Artificial watering points in favoured roan habitats that historically had no natural surface water could render the northern areas unacceptable to roan and, to a large extent,

Kruger's sable antelope population has declined by 75 per cent in the last 30 years.

tsessebe,' he warned. 'It has frequently been observed that herds of roan and sable withdraw to remote and waterless areas away from other wildlife. In many cases waterpoints have been provided in these waterless areas for the benefit of the roan or sable herds but instead have attracted wildebeest and zebra, resulting in overcrowded conditions.' His warning went unheeded. The ecosystem was adjusted and only then was it fully realised how finely attuned to its home on these rugged plains the roan really was.

The network of perennial dams and drinking troughs attracted sharply increased numbers of zebras and wildebeest to the northern plains during the drought and, no longer obliged to migrate in search of water, they became sedentary. Zebras are one of the roan's most important competitors; it is probably no coincidence that zebras are absent from Waza National Park in northern Cameroon where, in the 1970s, 2 000 roans achieved one of the highest roan densities in Africa. Plus, it is now known that artificial water points favour water-dependent species such as zebras above the rare antelopes during severe droughts. On the northern plains, zebras monopolised the more selective roan's preferred dry-season pastures. Degraded veld increased from six to 40 per cent between 1985 and 1989 while healthy vegetation declined from 10 to three per cent.

Poor nutritional conditions usually affect the survival rates of young animals much more than adults. Not unexpectedly, roan calf recruitment was especially low during the years of poor rainfall but rebounded when rainfall improved. It was hoped that, as was usual, overall roan recovery would be fairly rapid in the following wet cycle. Instead, deaths among adults tripled from an initial annual loss of around 10 per cent to over 30 per cent after 1986 and remained high until the population collapse. With little change in calf survival, nutritional factors were unlikely to be the main cause. Also, losses seemed more extreme than could be explained by poor grass production and a doubling of the zebra population – there had to be an additional factor affecting adult survival.

The old style of intensely managed ecosystems, with their extensive water provisioning, had disrupted the northern plains' predator–prey relationships.

Attention next turned to an increase in predators, particularly lions that had followed their staple prey, zebras and wildebeest, up north. Rangers' diaries confirmed an increase in lion sightings and two censuses on the northern plains, one in 1989 and another in 1993, found that lion numbers had doubled from 50 to 100. 'From a comparatively low-density, the area now supports a lion density of the same magnitude as the Central District during the 1970s,' observed predator specialist Gus Mills. As lions multiplied, roans, tsessebes, sables and eland began disappearing. The proximate cause of the declines was increased predation owing to a buildup of lions following the zebra and wildebeest influx, but the ultimate cause was the recent water installations. The old style of intensely managed ecosystems, with their extensive water provisioning, had disrupted the northern plains' predator–prey relationships.

The relationship between predator and prey is a delicate balance, an ongoing evolutionary struggle. Increased predation, especially to adults, may just tip the balance between a situation where a herbivore population has a small but positive rate of increase and one where a negative population growth leads inexorably to extirpation. Although roans and the other low-density antelopes fall within the lion's optimal prey weight range, their inherent rarity makes them too energy-expensive to search for. But when they lose the protection of their relative rarity they become heavily preyed on. Predator–prey relationships analysed by Tol Pienaar in the 1960s showed that both roans and sables are vulnerable to lions even when their numbers are low. He expressed their susceptibility in terms of the lion's 'preference ratings', which is a ratio between the percentage of recorded lion kills and the relative frequency and abundance of the prey species. The ratios showed that, although roans comprised only 0.16 per cent of the prey community, their relative frequency in all lion kills was 0.26 per cent, or more than one-and-a-half times as frequent as their abundance merited. Sables made up just 0.58 per cent of the prey community but comprised 1.52 per cent of lion kills, over two-and-a-half times as often as their numbers would suggest. On the northern plains, rangers' reports showed that, while the 90 roans killed by lions over a span of 22 years comprised only a little over one per cent of the lions' diet, the kills annually accounted for between four and 12 per cent of the roan population, and that was before lion numbers doubled.

Because of the possibility of losing all of the Kruger's roans, seven stragglers were captured at scattered localities throughout the park in 1994 and released as a breeding group of three males and four females into the 300-hectare N'washitshumbe enclosure. Situated roughly in the centre of the northern plains, the fenced enclosure excludes large predators and other herbivores. Released from the constraints of predation and competition, the nucleus seven animals responded by increasing to 49 by 2002, or over 25 per cent per year. This stark contrast to the fate of the free-ranging roans provides compelling evidence of the impact predation can have on a prey species naïve in the ways of big cats and perhaps nutritionally weakened by increased competition for scarce resources.

'The overriding importance of predation also helps explain paradoxes in the distribution patterns of the antelope species that are generally present in relatively low densities,' Johannes Chirima, Norman Owen-Smith, Barend Erasmus and Francesca Parrini propose in a 2010 paper that examines the sable's distributional niche in the Kruger. 'Why,' they asked themselves, 'are sable so widely distributed in rather arid mopane-dominated woodlands when they strongly seek greener grass during the dry season? Why are roan antelope, which achieve greatest abundance levels in the moist savannas of West Africa, found in KNP only in the driest region? Why are eland, with their generalist grazing-browsing habitats, so uncommon in the Kruger compared with kudu, more narrowly specialised for browsing? Why are tsessebe found in KNP mostly in the mopane-dominated north rather than in the open basaltic plains of the south that would seem more suited to their superior running speed?' The answer: the common feature of the five species seems to be their vulnerability to predation.

For example, the researchers found that the presence of wildebeest, zebras, impalas and buffaloes had a surprisingly strong influence on the presence of sable herds, over and above that of land types and annual rainfall. 'High concentrations of wildebeest and zebra are associated with high presence of lion prides because these two grazers are the prey species most strongly favoured by lions. Impala are numerically strongly represented among lion prey but make a lesser dietary contribution than wildebeest, zebra and buffalo on account of their smaller size. Nevertheless, being sedentary, impala may have a somewhat greater influence on where lion prides can establish year-round residence than the more mobile herds of wildebeest, zebra and buffalo.' The researchers concluded that the overriding niche requirement for the Kruger's sables, roans and other rare antelopes is habitat with relatively low predation pressure; that is, localities with relatively few principal prey species supporting relatively few resident lion prides. Consequently, in contrast to all other grazers, the rare antelopes avoid the more nutrient-rich regions. Conversely, the rare antelopes' drastic declines post-1986 resulted from the invasion of

Why are roan antelope, which achieve greatest abundance levels in the moist savannas of West Africa, found in KNP only in the driest region?

their long-grass home ranges by long-grass-grazing lion food in the form of zebras, following the spread of permanent surface water, and later buffaloes, as their numbers increased following the cessation of culling.

If roans are to re-occupy appropriate habitat in the northern Kruger, it is essential that their specialised needs be met. What precisely those needs are is the kind of detailed and timely information that the Kruger's decision-makers want scientists to supply. Ecological studies will have to make clear why, for example, habitat changes can be detrimental to some species and why changes in the status of one species may have far-reaching, sometimes disastrous, consequences for others. As simple, linear extrapolations of observed trends often give misleading indications of future events, even in the short-term, sophisticated computer simulation models are often preferable. In a 2003 paper by Witwatersrand University's Craig McLoughlin and Norman Owen-Smith that outlines a simulation model they developed to evaluate the viability of the Kruger's diminishing roan population, the two scientists argue that augmenting the free-ranging roan population by releasing animals from breeding enclosures would be wasteful of the gene pool while a high predation threat remains. They also quite rightly point out that experience has shown that culling lions to reduce predation pressure is futile 'as long as the prey base persists and opportunities for recolonization from surrounding regions exist'. Instead, they maintain, the challenge is how best to reduce zebras and wildebeest by judiciously opening and closing man-made waterholes while ensuring that enough water remains for the roans' personal needs during droughts.

Back in the 1970s, Salomon Joubert had predicted that 'the only feasible alternative to culling [zebras and wildebeest] would be to close down all but a few selected artificial waterpoints'. Eventually, in 1994, a minimum intervention approach was adopted that entailed the gradual closure of specific water points so as to reduce zebra and lion numbers by removing the cause of their increase. Initially 12 windmills were turned off and one critically placed dam breached in the last roan herds' core habitat. The closures plus increasing rainfall saw zebras decline from 2 500 to 1 400, although many merely moved to open water points or concentrated along drainage lines. There was also an initial drop in lion numbers, after which they stabilised at between seven and 11 lions per 100 square kilometres, according to a 2005 estimate. Alarmingly, the northern plains tsessebe population also declined after the water point closures from 100 in 1993 to less than 40 in 1998. Over the same period the basalt plains sables decreased from 60 to just three animals, although possibly because they moved west to the granites.

Africa's fastest antelope, the tsessebe, can't outrun the threat posed by competing grazers like elephants, attracted to their harsh habitat by artificial water supplies.

The roan population stabilised but despite good rains and improved grass cover their hoped-for recovery did not materialise, perhaps because they are now so few that even mild predation is a major block to population increase.

The rare antelopes are dwindling fast yet the dilemma persists. 'Lions remain and continue hunting to some extent through the range occupied by the roan herds,' McLoughlin and Owen-Smith noted. 'Closure of further waterpoints is indicated but this is difficult because water persists in large dams that cannot easily be removed. Furthermore, waterpoints are important for other herbivore species, and also for roan, as well as being tourist drawcards.' In a 2008 paper on shifting prey selection by lions, Norman Owen-Smith and Gus Mills analysed records of 49 453 animal carcasses gathered by field staff and found that the rare antelopes as a group made a very small contribution to the lions' prey base until around 1987, when their proportion rose abruptly from less than two per cent to about five per cent, with eland topping the kill count rather than the more abundant sable. The shift by lions to the resident rare antelopes seems to have been prompted by the reduced abundance of their three most favoured prey species, wildebeest, zebras and buffaloes. Until then low-density antelopes had survived by keeping out of harm's way but 'with all three principal prey species less readily available, lions turned toward alternative prey including kudu, waterbuck, warthog and giraffe, as well as the rare antelope species', Owen-Smith and Mills concluded after combing their database for fresh insights.

The rare antelopes are dwindling fast yet the dilemma persists.

One of nature conservation's most important parameters is the size below which a population ceases to be viable over the long term. While most herbivores increased after rainfall improved in 1995, that was not so for the rare antelopes, despite the closure of over half of the Kruger's boreholes, thus alleviating the conditions that led to increased predation. Instead, the declines continued. In a 2010 Witwatersrand University study that focuses on their shrinking numbers, Norman Owen-Smith, together with Johannes Chirima, Valerio Macandza and Elizabeth le Roux, investigated the role played by enduring habitat degradation and/or continuing high predation in propelling the rare antelopes on what the researchers describe as 'a ratchet trajectory towards local extinction'.

Because they are the most numerous and widespread of the Kruger's rare antelopes, much of the work has concentrated on sable antelopes. Ominously, sables have declined faster as they became less abundant. In the last 30 years their Kruger population has crashed by 75 per cent. At the same time, the disappearance of entire herds has led to a 25 per cent contraction in the sable's local distribution.

This striking-looking animal reaches the southern limit of its geographic distribution at the Kruger's southern boundary but now teeters on the brink of local extinction in places where in 1899 Frederick Courtney Selous stated 'the sable antelope is, or was until recently, plentiful in the low veldt of the Eastern Transvaal and in fact the whole of South-East Africa north of Swaziland and Delagoa Bay'. An 1892 depiction by the English artist and illustrator John Millais portrays a multitude of sables on the Nuanetsi (or N'wanetsi) plains in what is now southeast-central Kruger. In the 1920s sables in this region were so numerous that they were shot for staff rations by the land companies and by stock farmers to reduce grazing competition. In *Call of the Bushveld*, an anecdotal account of life on Sandringham game farm, near Acornhoek on the Kruger's western boundary, published in 1948 by A.C. White, the author mentions that 'not many years ago it was possible to come across herds of sable numbering up to 200, almost anywhere on the big game farms in the Eastern Transvaal ... Today few herds are to be found numbering more than three or four dozen, and not many as big as that.' A measure of the sable's rarity value these days is the R150 000 price a single animal fetches at auction.

The Wits University scientific team used aerial survey records to examine factors associated with the sable's decline such as changes in the number of herds, the size of the herds and calf/adult ratios. They found that, in the sable's case, the lack of population recovery was not related to increased zebra numbers attracting more predators. Instead, they suggest, the cause may be linked to Allee effects[5] that result in the sharp decline of reproductive success. This can arise when population density is too low for individuals to find mates, as a result of genetic inbreeding, or, in the sable's case, because of reductions in the security big herds provide against predation.

The researchers' analyses indicate that the drop in the sable population is linked to a major reduction in the number of herds, as well as a reduction in the size of the remaining herds, especially in the northern Kruger. Several of these herds were established during the high-rainfall years between 1977 and 1982, suggesting that sable losses and shrinkage in herd size were tied initially to habitat degradation in the extended droughts that followed. In 1997, only eight herds were recorded in the entire Southern District, down from a peak of over 20 prior to 1992. In the northwestern region, south of Punda

The marshes and associated grasslands in Limpopo province's Nylsvley Nature Reserve are an example of the habitat most favoured by roan antelope.

In the scientific team's two study areas, however, the sable herds' failure to increase is linked to poor calf recruitment.

Maria, the 12 to 15 herds recorded between 1982 and 1991 had been reduced to four by 1995 and only two when the study started in 2001; these had amalgamated into a single herd of about 20 animals by 2003.

Although sables are known to be highly susceptible to drought conditions, grassland monitoring has revealed that sites preferred by them recovered rapidly after the 1991/2 drought, which would seem to rule out habitat deterioration as a factor in suppressing their long-term population recovery. That leaves predator pressures, despite no evidence of increased predation on adult sables. In the scientific team's two study areas, however, the sable herds' failure to increase is linked to poor calf recruitment. That brings into contention carnivores other than lions, in particular hyaenas. The scimitar-horned sable is more aggressive in its response to threats than other antelopes, but cooperative defence may become ineffective once herds are reduced to as few as four or five adult cows. Earlier studies have demonstrated that reduced herd size greatly exacerbates the risk of extinction for small populations subject to predation. Typically, sable herds number 15 to 25 females plus young, which come together in the dry season to form groups of 30 to 75; in the past, herds of over 50 were recorded in the Kruger. Norman Owen-Smith and his team found that a lowering of the sable population growth by as little as 15 per cent – the difference between the pre-1987 and post-1986 periods – means that the population has little recovery potential in high-rainfall years to counteract shrinkage during adverse years.

Perhaps the best hope for the future of the Kruger's rare antelopes lies across the eastern border, in Limpopo National Park. This huge chunk of state-owned land in Mozambique's Gaza province has languished completely unmanaged; here the footprint of man is faint indeed. Pristine bushveld, dotted with pans and streams flowing down from the Lebombos, is crisscrossed with avenues of trees that follow the water forced

The eland is also one of Kruger's rare antelope species. Like the others, their dwindling numbers are due primarily to increased lion predation.

up along rhyolitic fault lines. Since 2004, researcher Valerio Macandza has collected comparative data on sable movements in both the Limpopo and Kruger sections of the proposed international 'peace' park. In February 2007 he joined a monitoring team that took to the skies over Limpopo Park to find out how his study herd of four naturally occurring sable cows was faring. All aboard were delighted to count three additional juveniles. A further search east and south of Giriyondo border gate revealed that sables there had increased from 17 in 2001 to over 40, and possibly more, six years later. Although much of Limpopo Park is not suitable roan habitat, the survey team found six roans reintroduced two years earlier in excellent health, with an additional two juveniles in tow. 'We believe that with the correct protection, sables and other rare antelopes will steadily increase because of the suitable habitat and relatively fewer predators,' enthused SANParks veterinarian Markus Hofmeyr, a member of the monitoring team. When the rare antelopes' Kruger habitat requirements have once again been restored, perhaps their kind can recolonise traditional grazing lands by coming west across an ecosystem free of fences.

(Top) Sable bulls aggressively assert their dominance when dealing with subordinates. (Bottom) Fights between equals sometimes end fatally.

---

1 Basalt is the commonest type of volcanic rock; usually grey to black and fine-grained, it makes up much of the Earth's surface. The basalt substrate in eastern Kruger gives rise to fertile soils whereas the granitic parent material found in the west gives rise to nutrient-poor, sandy soils.

2 Dambos (called vleis in the south) are shallow wetlands that form when rainfall is trapped by accumulated clay in shallow valley floors. They are waterlogged in the wet season and retain wet lines of drainage in the dry season. The water causes grass to grow tall and fibrous (sourveld) and most herbivores will not eat it except under drought conditions.

3 The International Union for Conservation of Nature is dedicated to finding 'pragmatic solutions to our most pressing environment and development challenges'.

4 An epizootic is a disease that appears as new cases in a given animal population, during a given period, at a rate that substantially exceeds what is expected based on recent experience.

5 Allee effects are density-dependent mechanisms in very small populations that can create critical thresholds, beyond which the chances of population recovery diminish.

5

Return of
the **rhinoceros**

**In the bush of the eastern Transvaal [present-day Mpumalanga],
forty years ago, the old bones and skulls of rhinos were often
seen, showing how numerous this animal must once have been
in the locality.**

James Stevenson-Hamilton, *Wild Life in South Africa*, 1947

erhaps more than any other living creature, rhinos evoke Africa's vanishing wilderness. Their wild temperament is a metaphor for the pristine horizons from which their species, and later ours, originally arose. In that sense, rhinos are a symbol of our untameable past, of that sweep of millennia that underlies the affairs of men and beasts.

Our understanding of rhino natural history starts with the unravelling of Earthly prehistory. Their tribe, early Eocene fossils tell us, had its beginnings some 50 to 40 million years ago when the superfamily Rhinocerotoidea diverged from other perissodactyls (odd-toed ungulates). Around 11 to eight million years before present, during the late Miocene, an ancestor of the extant black or hook-lipped rhino (*Diceros bicornis*) arrived in Africa from Eurasia. In the early Pliocene, five to four million years BP, the white or square-lipped rhino (*Ceratotherium simum*) diverged from the black rhino and spread in bountiful numbers through Africa, Eurasia and North America.

By the time the rhinos' only real predator had turned protector, the ravages of profligate hunting had pushed them close to extinction.

Because this incredible-looking relict, with those great horns protruding from its snout, hails from such distant aeons, it is little short of a miracle that it has lasted long enough for us to set eyes on it, especially since some scientists believe it has passed its evolutionary use-by date. Despite any evolutionary anachronisms rhinos may or may not have, they were clearly a highly successful, widespread and abundant model of a big herbivore for millions of years, until they encountered technological *Homo sapiens*. Their daily routine of movements within a relatively small area, returning often to favourite watering points or shade trees, made them easy targets. By the time the rhinos' only real predator had turned protector, the ravages of profligate hunting had pushed them close to extinction.

Approaching cautiously downwind, a trails guide brings visitors on a walking safari close to an unwary group of white rhinos. Poachers use the same tactics when stalking these myopic and generally placid pachyderms.

The easy-to-stalk southern white rhino was an early casualty. By 1885 it had been reduced to a remnant population of fewer than 50 in what is today the Hluhluwe-Imfolozi Park in KwaZulu-Natal. By 1991, northern white rhinos were down from 2 250 in 1960 to 30 refugees in Garamba National Park in the Democratic Republic of the Congo. They again came under relentless assault during the ongoing civil wars in the DRC and neighbouring Sudan, which lowered their numbers to the current count of just four free-living animals.

The black rhino has been brought to the edge of extinction because of human appetite for its distinctive horns.

Once abundant from northern Niger – according to 2 000-year-old rock paintings – to Cape Town, where Jan van Riebeeck's 1653 diary records them as 'common on the Cape Flats and on the slopes of Table Mountain', the black rhinoceros is represented today by an estimated 4 240 animals and classified as critically endangered. As recently as the 1960s it was thought that there were over 100 000 Africa-wide. In the 1970s an organised poaching epidemic driven by a 20-fold increase in the price of rhino horn had reduced the population to 65 000. Composed entirely of agglutinated keratin fibres, rhino horn resembles the structure of horses' hooves, turtles' beaks and cockatoos' bills, except in the rhino's case the commodity is lethal.

Rhino horn has become one of the most valuable natural substances on Earth. It is prized in Yemen for fashioning *jambiya* dagger handles, and during the 1970s up to three tonnes were imported annually into that country. A decade later that trade had declined significantly, to be replaced by the burgeoning eastern and southeastern Asian markets where rhino horn, ground into powder, is said to be a cure for a variety of non-life-threatening ailments including fever, gout and rheumatism. A recent scam on traditional medicine websites, designed to profit from families of terminally ill patients, touts powdered rhino horn as a treatment for serious illnesses such as cancer, which it manifestly is not. Clinical trials to determine whether there is a pharmacological basis for the lingering cultural belief in rhino horn's fever-reducing properties have been overwhelmingly dismissive. A study commissioned by the World Wildlife Fund (WWF) and the International Union for Conservation of Nature (IUCN) and conducted by Hoffmann-La Roche 'found no evidence that rhino horn has any medicinal effect as an antipyretic [fever-reducing agent] and would be ineffective in reducing fever'. Nor 'has it analgesic, anti-inflammatory, anti-spasmolytic or diuretic properties' and 'no bacterial effect could be found against suppuration and intestinal bacteria'. Scientists at the Chinese University of Hong Kong found that, although fever-induced rats showed some temporary cooling effect after being injected with a massive dose of rhino-horn extract, there was no effect at the dosage levels that would need to be prescribed to human patients. Though no meaningful evidence supports the notion that any constituent of rhino horn has any medical property, or none that works as well as alternative synthetic pharmaceuticals, centuries-old beliefs in the alleged magical powers of animal parts are unlikely to be discarded by Far East users simply because Westerners condemn them.

A prosperous and growing Chinese and Vietnamese middle class has fuelled an increasing demand for rhino horn that jumped from 600 to 700 kilograms a year in the late 1980s to two tonnes annually between 1992 and 1996. By 1998, registration of stocks in Chinese medicine corporations alone – not counting retail shops, private ownership and museums – recorded total holdings of almost 10 tonnes of horn. By 1992 the demand had led to a catastrophic 96 per cent drop in black rhino numbers. In 2006, in the absence of confirmed sightings or spoor of the last survivors in northern Cameroon, the IUCN's African Rhino Specialist Group tentatively declared the western subspecies extinct. Africa's rhinos, symbols of a major evolutionary heritage, had now also become symbols of Africa's conservation woes.

Even before the old Sabi Game Reserve was proclaimed in 1898, the region's last white rhino had been shot. The species had 'existed at one time all over the White River area, Pretoriuskop and no doubt in the relatively open country of the Lebombo flats', James Stevenson-Hamilton could confirm. By 1871, when trading store owner and farmer Bill Sanderson first hunted in what is now the Kruger Park, the white rhino had become little more than a legend among local Africans, although they had a definite name for it. According to Henry Thomas Glynn, son of one of the original Lowveld pioneers, a few still occurred near Lower Sabie until the late 1870s. The English hunter and naturalist Frederick Vaughan Kirby recorded: 'This year [in the early 1890s] I came upon two in that district [between present-day Skukuza and Lower Sabie], a cow and a big calf,' but after 1896 no more were seen in what would become the Kruger National Park.

Rhino horn has become one of the most valuable natural substances on Earth.

White rhinos and elephants disappeared from the region at about the same time and it seems likely that their extirpation was accelerated by the activities of the slave trader and big game hunter João Albasini. In 1845 he established a trading post at Magashula's Kraal on the Sabie River near present-day Phabeni Gate, which is believed to have been the first European settlement in the Lowveld. Albasini's well-armed local hunters made ivory and hide hunting their sole business over the course of many years, although the man himself remained for only two years before departing for the growing settlements on the Drakensberg escarpment, where he bought a farm at Ohrigstad and opened a shop.

A handful of black rhinos held on for almost another 40 years before they too died out. 'I can well remember hunting black rhinoceros … fourteen years ago [circa 1880] in the eastern portions of the Transvaal … in places where now one might walk or ride for hours without turning out so much as a reedbuck,' Vaughan Kirby lamented. He recalled that black rhinos had been quite plentiful in the dense Nwatimhiri acacia thickets on the south bank of the Sabie River, east of Skukuza; in the Gomondwane bush, south of Lower Sabie; along the Timbavati River; and in the Nyandu bush northeast of Shingwedzi.

'There have always been a few individuals located in the lower Sabi bush,' reported Stevenson-Hamilton. 'In 1902, a single one used to drink at a pool near Gomondwane. A few years later, while in camp some miles down the Sabi River from the bridge, I saw, at daylight one morning, an old bull close at hand; and at intervals single and sometimes two animals together, have been seen by the staff.' Another three black rhinos were reported along the headwaters of the Tsendze River in the Singwitsi Reserve soon after its proclamation in 1903 and solitary animals were seen in the 1920s on the Lebombos southeast of Tshokwane.

In 1923, Stevenson-Hamilton found signs of a single black rhino along the Bububu River in the Shingwedzi area. 'This was an interesting episode, being apparently the last time any traces of rhinos have been observed in that country and I suppose this particular animal wandered into Portuguese territory [Mozambique] and was killed there.' In October 1936, district ranger Harry Kirkman saw the Kruger's last recorded black rhino, an old female, on Nwatiwambu Spruit in the Nwatimhiri bush, southeast of Skukuza. 'Subsequent to 1940, no traces of the animals have been found and I am inclined to think that the species must be written off as a Kruger National Park resident,' Stevenson-Hamilton unhappily concluded. Local extinction is invariably the end result when such solitary and reclusive animals slip below a viable critical mass and become too few and widely scattered to maintain breeding contact.

It took 65 years before the white rhino's characteristic cloverleaf spoor was again seen in their old Kruger precincts. That it happened at all was due to the stringent protection afforded Hluhluwe-Imfolozi's miniscule founder white rhino population, which responded by increasing spectacularly.

It was a stunning turnaround and stands as one of the world's greatest conservation success stories. By 1960 there were so many white rhinos in the 96 000-hectare sanctuary that they began straining its ecological carrying capacity. With the development of effective capture-and-translocation techniques, surplus rhinos could be re-established in former ranges. Over the decades more than 4 000 were moved during what became known as Operation Rhino.

In October 1961 four adult white rhinos – the nucleus of a breeding herd – were released into a specially constructed enclosure on the Fayi Spruit near Pretoriuskop, traditionally one of their favourite haunts. Over the following 12 years a total of 345 were relocated to the Kruger. Most were released into the wild in the Southern District, between the Sabie and Crocodile rivers at Doispane, in the Mhlanganzwane-Panama area of the Crocodile Bridge section and between Malelane and the Mlambane River.

A helicopter and trucks try to shepherd a darted rhino away from dangerous terrain but this one collapses in a waterhole and must be hauled to safety before being loaded for translocation.

Finding themselves in unfamiliar surroundings, the first arrivals understandably took a long time to settle down. Some wandered great distances, though many returned to their release site before finally selecting more permanent residence. Gradually the immigrants began to drift south until they discovered the gently rolling hills and relatively open terminalia woodland savanna along the headwaters of the Mlambane River, about 12 kilometres north of Berg-en-Dal rest camp, an area that closely resembles their Imfolozi homeland and which they found much to their liking. Over time others joined them so that now the country around Mlambane Dam has the park's highest white rhino density. They are also plentiful between the Biyamiti and Mlambane rivers in the Pretoriuskop, Stolsnek and Malelane areas and around Lower Sabie and Crocodile Bridge.

In early 1964 it was noticed that some rhinos were crossing the Sabie River. One cow drowned in the attempt but the rest succeeded and some soon began colonising the Kruger's Central District. Here their preferred habitat is a belt of Delagoa thorn (*Acacia welwitschii*) tree savanna that runs up the middle of the Central District from the Sabie River,

It was a stunning turnaround and stands as one of the world's greatest conservation success stories.

past Tshokwane until just northwest of Satara, where it merges into bushwillow (*Combretum zeyheri*) savanna adjoining the Timbavati River. With its palatable short grazing, open low shrub layer and large number of small pans, this is highly favourable white rhino country.

In January 1964, 13 white rhino bulls and three cows were released in the northern mopane-veld region. The majority were set free along the Tsende River at Shipandani, near present-day Mopani Camp, and the remainder on the road to Mahlangeni. Most showed their disapproval of their new home by voting with their feet, travelling far and wide in search of more suitable habitat. Some covered immense distances, trekking as far north as Pafuri. A few even went beyond, into Zimbabwe, before returning to the Kruger. Several were killed by hunters when they strayed across the Lebombo Mountains into Mozambique. One crossed both the Letaba and Olifants rivers on its journey south. Several breached the western boundary fence and turned up in settled areas, but fortunately all were tracked down, immobilised and returned to the park.

all Leon Nell

One wandering bull was gored to death after a titanic battle with an elephant bull over drinking rights at Nkulumbeni-North waterhole, east of the Shingwedzi–Babalala road. In the end, four male and two female rhinos remained in the Tsende River neighbourhood. Their first calf was sighted in April 1965 and another in 1968 and their descendants can be seen there to this day.

Boosted by immigrants from the south, by 1991 there were 72 white rhinos between the Olifants and Limpopo rivers. Subsequently, white rhinos have been seen through virtually the whole Northern District where their preferred habitat is undulating mopane bush savanna with clay bottomlands that support a host of pans suitable for wallowing. Indeed, the great majority of the Kruger's reintroduced white rhinos ultimately liked the place so much that they went on to average an annual population growth rate of 8.4 per cent, effectively doubling the population every nine years. An aerial census in 2007 estimated that their numbers had swelled to 8 600, nearly as many as the total count in the rest of the world put together. These days, the Kruger's healthy, expanding population has meant that high densities in some areas have provoked territorial fights to the death. To reduce social pressure, a quota of around 100 are made available for sale or exchange each year as part of an international white rhino conservation programme.

Wallowing is an essential part of rhino hygiene. They love cooling off by blissfully lying in pans for hours on end, every so often rolling in the delicious ooze.

Research has shown that white rhinos have basic but very specific habitat requirements. Their preferred Kruger landscapes generally have an undulating topography with uplands, bottomlands and watercourses that support a moderate to dense cover of good-quality grasses. Suitable feeding grounds are a top priority for an animal that spends nearly half of each day grazing 50 to 65 kilograms of mainly short, sweet, preferably perennial grass. The open combretum woodland savannas in the southern Kruger have low to moderately tall trees and shrubs that promote a high proportion of the grasses most palatable to white rhinos. Here they typically feed on shade-tolerant species such as protein-rich guinea grass (*Panicum maximum*) that grows predominantly under tree canopies. In the high-rainfall Pretoriuskop sourveld where deep, sandy soil supports mainly tall, coarse grasses that when mature are low in nutrition, white rhinos are particularly partial to the fringe of short grasses such as sporobolus that sprout on the nutrient-rich soil of termite mounds. They are also usually one of the first animals to move onto new grass growth on burnt veld.

While doing research in the Kruger in 2008, Richard Fynn of KwaZulu-Natal University found that a white rhino's grazing unwittingly sustains and promotes biodiversity by creating short grass patches interspersed with stands of undisturbed tall grass. 'White rhinos are basically huge lawnmowers that benefit a wide variety of insects, spiders, birds and even other mammals,' he says. Some beneficiary species are short-grass specialists; others prefer long grass; some need places to hide; others prefer open spaces to keep a lookout for predators. 'It would be a good idea to relocate more white rhinos to Kruger's central basalt plains where tall grasses are currently limiting biodiversity and causing a decline in wildebeest numbers,' Fynn believes. 'White rhinos could help maintain open, short grass pastures that would make it easier for wildebeest to detect predators while at the same time providing them with their preferred grazing pastures.'

Another crucial habitat requirement centres on a rhino's water dependence. White rhinos need regular access to surface water and can drink up to 50 litres at a time, with an average consumption of 12 litres per day. In the wet season, when water is freely available, they drink daily or even twice daily, but in the dry season they may be forced to travel to more permanent waterholes with drinking frequency reduced to two- to four-day intervals. Water is also essential for wallowing, an intrinsic part of rhino hygiene. On hot days rhinos love to cool off by lying blissfully in seasonal pans and the water-filled mud holes that form in the clay-laced bottomlands of combretum woodlands, while terrapins harvest parasites overlooked by oxpeckers. Every so often they roll in the delicious ooze, coating themselves with mud that works as a sunscreen when they resume feeding

Boosted by immigrants from the south, by 1991 there were 72 white rhinos between the Olifants and Limpopo rivers.

White rhinos are basically huge lawnmowers whose grazing unwittingly promotes biodiversity by creating short grass patches interspersed with stands of tall grass, says grasslands expert Richard Fynn.

and also helps shield them from ticks and blood-sucking flies. After they rub against a favourite stump or boulder, dead ticks can be seen trapped in the dried mud.

The return of the black rhino to the Kruger began in 1971 and continued until 1990, with a total of 90 animals translocated from KwaZulu-Natal. Focus areas for the reintroductions were around Skukuza and Tshokwane, where these roughage browsers of tree foliage, shrubs and woody forbs once again live as they always did in the closed woodlands and dense thorn thickets around Skukuza-Nwaswitshaka, the Lubyelubye area near Lower Sabie and along the Sweni and N'waswitsontso rivers between Tshokwane and Satara.

Since the Kruger's black rhinos are difficult to see in their favoured dense bushland and forest habitat, it would normally be hard to know what is happening with the population. But, in order to judge how effective conservation measures are, it is essential to monitor total numbers, sexes, approximate ages, matings, births and deaths. So each year a helicopter survey photographs and records the age and sex of every black rhino encountered in a 100 000-hectare southern Kruger high-density study area. Individuals are also ear-notched to monitor population performance, dispersal and personal history. Latest reports are encouraging. Annual calf recruitment of nine per cent is higher than the parent Hluhluwe-Imfolozi breeding rate. With a population of more or less 400 – they're tough to count in thick bush – the Kruger already supports one of Africa's last genetically and demographically viable black rhino populations and the huge park has the capacity to carry at least another 2 500 of these fractious but strangely compelling beasts.

Animals the size of an adult rhino do not have much to fear from natural predators but during the early days of the Kruger's white rhino reintroductions a big bull was so badly mauled by lions at Mlakeni, northeast of Pretoriuskop, that it had to be euthanised. Attacking a mighty rhino bull so determinedly

The return of the black rhino to the Kruger began in 1971 and continued until 1990, with a total of 90 animals translocated from KwaZulu-Natal.

is very unusual but lions and packs of spotted hyaenas will sometimes pull down a calf or even a subadult. Consequently, female rhinos especially tend to be aggressive towards these two top predators. A mother will vigorously defend her young from attack and calves stay by their mother's side for as long as four or five years, until she again gives birth. Kills nonetheless occur. Rhino specialist John Goddard, while working in Kenya and Tanzania during the 1960s, estimated that in his study areas 16 per cent of black rhino calves less than two years old were lost to lions and hyaenas. In Namibia's Etosha National Park, a coalition of three male lions on separate occasions killed three subadult black rhinos. The rhinos, all three to four years old, would have just separated from their mothers and so were particularly vulnerable. In the Kruger more black rhinos have ears or pieces of tail missing than do white rhinos, suggesting that as calves they are attacked more often. But like disease, to which rhinos do not seem particularly prone, non-human predation is generally not a significant factor affecting the park's rhino population growth rate.

On a more ominous note, with rhino horn currently selling in Asia's traditional pharmaceutical markets for up to $60 000 (R483 000) per kilogram, the world's remaining rhinos are being targeted in what has become an environmental crisis of global proportions. Since 2008, poaching of African rhinos has risen 2 000 per cent. The dramatic surge is heartbreaking after so much hard work has been done to bring these heavyweight herbivores back from the edge of extinction. Given the history of rhino slaughter in the rest of Africa, one of the main hopes for their survival in the wild lay with the relatively secure southern African populations. After all, South Africa currently holds 94 per cent of Africa's white rhinos and 36 per cent of its black rhinos. But that expectation has been seriously threatened, with 95 per cent of the killings occurring in Zimbabwe and South Africa. Despite a suite of new law-enforcement measures, South Africa's losses at the time of writing in 2011 were running at up to 20 rhinos per month, placing it at the epicentre of the kill zone.

'In 2007 we only had 10 rhinos poached in Kruger,' SANParks spokeswoman Wanda Mkutshulwa told reporters. In 2008 that number spiked alarmingly to 83 countrywide, of which 76 were in the Kruger, with 28 carcasses found along the Mozambique border. The end of Mozambique's civil war in 1992 left the region awash

Rhinos need regular access to surface water. They are able to drink up to 50 litres at a time (above) and water is also crucial for wallowing (top).

with big guns and empty pockets. 'Guns were supposed to have been surrendered to the government after the war ended but some people decided to keep them and former soldiers are believed to be selling their weapons to make a quick buck,' says Captain Albert Mathonsi from the South African National Defence Force's (SANDF) joint tactical head office. The poaching escalation came amid allegations that some Mozambican government officials were aiding and protecting rhino poachers employed by Vietnamese crime syndicates operating in South Africa. Vietnamese diplomats implicated in transporting illegal rhino horn have been caught by hidden camera on SABC's *50/50* environmental news programme transacting deals in front of the Vietnamese embassy in Pretoria.

'Most poachers choose remote parts of Kruger in which to operate,' says Ken Maggs, head of SANParks' Specialized Corporate Operations, which includes the anti-poaching unit. 'They like hilly and bushy places which muffle gunfire. Rhino poaching is a sustained, ever-present threat, with drug and firearm syndicates, and even gold smugglers involved,' he warns. 'For people moving contraband, rhino horn is just another commodity.' To protect rhinos effectively is expensive and requires a lot of manpower. Rhinos are easy quarries and it is relatively straightforward to conceal and smuggle their horns, which seem such bizarre objects to be the cause of so much death.

Not all poachers choose remote hunting grounds, however. In an article published in *Africa Geographic*, photojournalist Ian Michler interviewed two brothers, the Van Deventers from Bronkhorstspruit, east of Pretoria, convicted in July 2007 of killing 19 white rhinos. The brothers told how, passing themselves off as bona fide tourists, they had used busy roads in the southern Kruger while searching for rhinos. Animals were shot within 100 metres of the road, some as close as 15 metres, and all in broad daylight. Now apparently repentant, the Van Deventers outlined the telltale signs exhibited by rhino poachers masquerading as visitors, including: vehicles parked at the side of the road for long periods; lone drivers hanging out at rest stops or reading in vehicles; and lone drivers doing U-turns along park roads. Anyone noticing suspicious behaviour is urged to report it to the nearest camp, lodge manager or ranger.

'For people moving contraband, rhino horn is just another commodity.'

As the Van Deventers found out, things do not always go the poachers' way. Poaching can be a dangerous business, even for heavily armed gangs. In 2007 a suspected poacher was killed in the Kruger during a shootout with rangers. Another five were killed near Crocodile Bridge in January 2011 when rangers returned fire in self-defence. In March 2009, rangers on patrol in the Nwanetsi concession east of Satara heard cries for help and discovered two men who had been mauled by lions. The suspected rhino poachers were armed with an unlicensed AK47 assault rifle and a pistol and, though they denied ownership, the spent cartridges at the scene indicated they had fired them to scare off the lions. In the end, the lions appeared to have escaped without injury and the would-be

This cow's long horn would be a great prize for a poacher, but even her calf would be slain for its nub now that rhino horn sells for more than gold or cocaine by weight.

poachers, Emmanuel Ngobeni and Mtlakavaka Matose of Masingeri in Mozambique, were hospitalised and ultimately charged to appear in Skukuza circuit court.

Despite the risks, the price of rhino horn has made poaching a growth industry. Although the Kruger successfully resisted the rhino massacres of the 1960s and '70s, the current wave of poaching is much better organised and the scale, sophistication and audacity is unprecedented. Well-funded and widely connected criminal networks use helicopters, night-vision scopes, silenced weapons, crossbows, poison and veterinary tranquillising drugs in multi-faceted campaigns, often conducted at night to avoid law-enforcement patrols. The conservation organisation Traffic points out that modern technology has made aspects of a poacher's life easier and the fight against poaching harder. Poachers now use cellphones to contact their pickup teams while the internet makes it possible to sell illegal horns anonymously anywhere in the world at the click of a button.

In 2009 a new South African record for rhino kills was set with 122 rhinos lost nationwide, of which 26 white rhinos and one rare black rhino were killed in the Kruger. Then came 2010, with a death rate nearly triple that of the previous year. In the country as a whole, 333 rhinos – 323 white and 10 black – were killed and dehorned, with the Kruger the hardest hit, losing 146. At the same time, 162 suspected poachers were arrested, 68 of them in the Kruger alone, compared with 29 in 2009. The number of rhinos poached in South Africa in 2011 jumped to 448, 115 more than the previous year. At a rhino summit in Pretoria in September 2010, Richard Emslie of the African Rhino Specialist Group warned that poaching was having a massive economic effect on the value of one of South Africa's primary assets. Citing potential losses of more than R1 billion, he said that 'for private game reserves, owning a rhino has become a liability. That means many are not being sold at auction and those that are, are not fetching the prices they used to.'

... modern technology has made aspects of a poacher's life easier and the fight against poaching harder.

About 20 per cent of South Africa's rhino population is owned privately and farming them has generated big business in this country. The Department of Environmental Affairs and Tourism estimated the value of South Africa's 18 880-strong white rhino population (94 per cent of Africa's total) at R4 billion. Most are sold for trophy hunting, which earned nearly R50 million in 2009. But as a result of poaching and increased legislation governing private ownership, the average price of a rhino has dropped from R275 000 in 2008 to R225 000 in 2010 as game ranchers switch to safer investments such as disease-free buffaloes and sable antelopes.

In order to halt the massacre, substantial resources need to go into law enforcement, both in Africa and Asia, where all trade in rhino horn is now illegal. SANParks has posted extra rangers to the Kruger and as of April 2011 SANDF soldiers have been deployed to patrol the whole of the park, with orders to hand over captured culprits to the police. Those arrested in and outside the Kruger have included actual poachers, couriers and kingpins in rhino-poaching circles. In September 2010 police and security agencies struck a deep blow when nine people were netted in Limpopo province, two of them well-known and respected veterinarians who owned an animal clinic involved in catching and transporting wildlife. According to police spokesman Vishnu Naidoo, they are 'the masterminds' behind a syndicate responsible for 'hundreds of rhino poaching incidents'. The involvement of vets explains how large quantities of highly scheduled veterinary immobilising drugs have found their way onto the black market.

The connection between unscrupulous trophy-hunting operators and the illegal rhino-horn trade is another concern. The lucrative rewards and easy access to guns have made the industry a natural breeding ground for rhino poaching and horn smuggling. Recently a trophy hunter based in North West province was charged with using a small aircraft to ferry poachers and spot rhinos in game parks, and then transport the horns back to his safari headquarters, which also served as a money-laundering depot. Moreover, legal hunting is being used increasingly as a smokescreen in the issuance of export permits for rhino trophies to Vietnamese nationals who pay above market price for rhino hunts despite having no previous hunting experience. In at least one instance, the Vietnamese 'client' was identified as being involved in ongoing rhino crime investigations.

Which brings us to an intriguing idea to curb the buoyant poaching of rhinos in the wild by legalising a centralised and regulated trade in rhino horn that, it is hoped, will crowd out the illegal trade. But it is a concept so controversial that it has split the wildlife community into two opposing camps. Proponents, such as wildlife professionals Jake Veasey and Cathy Dean of the European Association of Zoos and Aquaria (EAZA), which annually coordinates a year-long fund-raising and awareness campaign for threatened species including rhinos, point out that the well-intentioned ban on rhino horn contributed to massive price rises during the 1970s and '80s, increasing the incentive to poach. They argue that 'the depletion of the world's rhinos can only be realistically halted by international and national political measures that result in a decline in the price of rhino horn and an increase in the funds available for protecting wild rhinos'. The Florida, USA-based International Rhino Foundation agrees and urges that as a first step the stockpile of around 30 tonnes of rhino horn stored in various East and southern African warehouses be sold to create a legal outlet 'that would allow the Far East to continue with its medicinal traditions and at the same time pump industrial sums of money into cash-strapped African conservation bodies'.

> **The connection between unscrupulous trophy-hunting operators and the illegal rhino-horn trade is another concern.**

'This killing is absurd,' contends Michael Eustace, a South African economist on the board of the African Parks Network, a private conservation organisation that works in partnership with African governments. 'At the moment about 400 poached horns are sold into the market each year. South Africa can supply an equivalent amount of horn from natural deaths alone.' Keep supplying the market with horn at that rate for the next 10 years, he adds, and 'our rhino population will have doubled, if we can stop the poaching. We can then supply 800 horns from natural deaths from a population of 40 000, generating $64 million a year for parks and rhino conservation. At the moment 400 horns are generating $32 million a year for criminals and nothing for conservation.'

One proposal that has been around for a while but is only now gaining wider acceptance is wildlife farming, or more correctly, wildlife ranching of semi-free-ranging rhinos. 'Why kill a rhino for just one horn, when you could get several from one rhino over its lifetime?' Zimbabwean wildlife breeder Ian du Preez asked incredulously of travel photojournalist Adelle Horler in a 2010 article she wrote for *Conservation News*. A rhino's horn grows continually during its life; the amount of regrowth varies according to species, sex and age but can average as much as five centimetres a year. This allows for repeated harvesting as long as it is done with surgical care – horn is dead material but it is critical to avoid cutting into blood vessels and nerves at the base of the skull. 'People think this is a crazy solution but bring me a better one,' Du Preez challenges. 'We keep taking the same head-on approach, hunting poachers and blaming the markets that buy the rhino horns but it's not working here or in South Africa.'

According to recent media reports, China may have stolen a march on local would-be entrepreneurs by developing its own rhino-farming enterprise. The China Institute of Science and Technology in Beijing published a paper in 2008 entitled 'A Proposal for Protection of the Rhinoceros and the Sustainable Use of Rhinoceros Horn' that reveals the project is under way already. Funded by State Soft Sciences, the Sanya City Center for Artificial Propagation of the Rhinoceros has been established in Hainan province and stocked with 141 white rhinos imported from South Africa since 2000. Scientists at the Center are currently researching captive rhino breeding, rearing, nutrition and diseases.

The farming of wild animals is not a new idea in Asia. Notorious bear bile farms have been operating in East Asia for three decades, with up to 10 000 bears held in squeeze cages with steel catheters inserted into their gall bladders to drain off bile, the main ingredient of a lucrative supplement said to improve eyesight. When they outlive their usefulness they are killed, although their living conditions are so vile that death may be preferable. Another repellent example is the growing number of tiger farms in China, where more than 6 000 of the big cats are packed into tiny, crowded cages or listlessly pace treeless, fenced-in areas. If ethical rhino ranching is to have any chance of general acceptance, issues of animal welfare must be above

Squealing defiance, a white rhino refuses to give way before an angry elephant's mock charge. This time the adversaries went their separate ways but these waterhole confrontations sometimes result in rhino deaths.

reproach. And there is another equally important consideration – the benefits to wild populations that farming threatened species is supposed to bring. It worked in Australia, where legalising crocodile farms stopped the poaching of wild crocs for their skins in a way that law enforcement had not been able to. But it does not seem to be working that way in China.

Campaigners like Mark Jones, programme director of Care for the Wild, a conservation charity involved with CITES[1], cite the China example when they insist that selling parts from captive-bred creatures will not result in a halt in the illegal trade but instead will fuel demand. 'There is no evidence coming out of China that Asiatic black bear populations are increasing or even stabilising as a result of bile farms nor is their multi-billion dollar turtle farming industry helping to stem the decline of China's own wild freshwater turtles.' Farming tigers under the guise of 'sustainable use' and 'wildlife conservation' failed to save the 1 000 wild tigers illegally killed in the past decade. It is thought China has only about 20 tigers left in the wild, out of a world population of 3 200 wild tigers, down from the 100 000 that roamed the subcontinent in the early 20th century. 'On the face of it, rhino farming seems logical,' Jones concedes. 'But for many consumers there is a perception that the healing properties of animal parts from free-ranging wildlife are more potent than those from ranched or captive bred animals. Affluent people are willing to pay a premium for products from wild-caught specimens.'

> **If ethical rhino ranching is to have any chance of general acceptance, issues of animal welfare must be above reproach.**

It is also argued that, given the low starting point of rhino populations, even a legal trade could not satisfy the demand for horn, and poachers would continue killing rhinos in protected areas, except now it would be easier to launder their illicit wares through the legal market. Perhaps the biggest argument against are concerns over management and the practicalities of ensuring the trade is managed effectively in the rhinos' best interests, rather than advantaging corrupt officials in range states and countries where horn is traded. 'Before CITES is likely to approve reopening the rhino horn trade, the international conservation community will need to be convinced of the benefits, the likely control mechanisms and especially that rhino species in other range states will not be put at risk by such a move,' says Richard Emslie.

Ears pricked and attention focused on the source of strange clicking sounds, this territorial white rhino bull approaches the on-foot photographer with aggressive intent.

White rhinos are more gregarious than their less sociable black cousins.

The efforts to control the illegal rhino-horn trade have had local successes but little general influence on the demand and in particular the incentives to the organised crime syndicates. All poached rhino horns, even those that make their way to Maputo, end up in Gauteng province and here the trail goes cold. The horns simply disappear. There are still thousands of rhinos in the Kruger, sufficient to attract commercial rhino poaching, as long as the Far East medicine markets continue to flout the public opinion that helped curtail the ivory trade. As Africa's premier rhino sanctuary and a reservoir for seeding other reserves, the Kruger is the key to the southern white and southern black rhino's future. What then is their future?

As Africa's premier rhino sanctuary and a reservoir for seeding other reserves, the Kruger is the key to the southern white and southern black rhinos' future.

Right now rhinos are under siege so, although their population growth in the Kruger is encouraging, the immense pressure exerted by poaching will test our will to protect them. Their passing would be a tragedy. They are creatures from a time beyond memory but still persisting. The question is: for how much longer? How many more rhino crises can be supported? Will the pressure ever let up?

---

1 CITES: Convention on International Trade in Endangered Species. A United Nations-style organisation attended by scientific advisory groups that supervise a global framework designed to regulate the commercial sale of wild species through a set of appendices ranging from total prohibition to qualified dispensations. With the exception of rhinos in South Africa and Swaziland, all African rhinos are accorded Appendix One status, which means a total ban on trade.

6

African buffalo trails

The *Buffel* is now totally extirpated throughout the Cape Colony, where so many local names testify to its former presence ... So far, however, as the country has yet been explored, this noble beast is extremely abundant in all the eastern portions of Southern extra-tropical Africa.

W. Cornwallis Harris, *Portraits of the Game and Wild Animals of Southern Africa*, 1840

There is a lot more to African buffaloes than first meets the eye. To get a sense of what it means to be a buffalo, you need to know something about its herding behaviour. Behind the half-curious, half-timid phalanx of probing, shiny moist muzzles, lowering horns and lumbering demeanours that confronts you when you first encounter a breeding herd, is a group of families that share resources and coordinate activities in ways that resemble human society. Status among individuals is instantly recognised by subtle bovine signals such as body posture, direction of gaze, tilt of head, vocalisations and odour, all of which are broadly similar to those to which people respond but of which we are often unaware.

Herding also greatly benefits young, inexperienced buffaloes when it comes to the business of earning a living. Finding the best food at a given time in a certain habitat requires the knowledge that youngsters learn by associating with adults. To maximise the advantages derived from their elders' collective wisdom, buffaloes have developed a sophisticated communal decision-making system not unlike human voting, according to ecologist Herbert Prins, who studied their ecology and behaviour in northern Tanzania's Lake Manyara National Park.

Herding also greatly benefits young, inexperienced buffaloes when it comes to the business of earning a living.

Prins noticed that, after spending the heat of the day lying inert, quietly ruminating, individual buffaloes would stand up in the late afternoon, shuffle around for a minute or so before bedding down again. At first, he interpreted this simply as stretching their legs but then he became aware that only mature females behaved this way and always about an hour before the herd departed for their evening feeding grounds. Significantly, the cows adopted a special posture, holding their head higher than the usual resting position but lower than the alert stance, and seemed to gaze in one direction. Prins recorded the direction each buffalo looked and calculated the average direction. He found that the orientation of their bodies showed a fair degree of consensus and overlapped with compass bearings pointing the way to a choice pasture. When it came time to resume grazing, the herd arose as one and immediately moved to the feeding ground selected by a majority on the pathfinders' committee.

Their decision is critically important. Buffaloes are non-territorial, inhabiting instead clearly defined home ranges of 250 to 500 square kilometres in the Kruger that nevertheless show little overlap with neighbouring herds. Large herds move through their home range on a seasonal cyclic route, their grazing and trampling favouring rapid plant regrowth, which in turn encourages repeated foraging. Topography, soil, rainfall and the grazing and browsing of herbivores turn grasslands into a mosaic of different forms of vegetation, which determine the buffaloes' movement patterns and, true to their strong sense of cohesion, the entire herd must go along. Deciding which pastures to visit requires that the expert panel of cows arrives at a multi-factorial decision. They have to consider not only where the most suitable grass is, but also whether they have fed there recently and how long the grass will take to recover – different grasses grow at different speeds – and where to go to avoid grass patches depleted by competing herbivores. A bunch of wild cattle that operate as an information centre? Who would have thought? As it turns out, these enigmatic, quintessentially African beasts are full of surprises, which only compounds the sense of loss evoked by their steeply declining numbers across the length and breadth of sub-Saharan Africa.

In southern Africa, buffaloes occupy, or once occupied, a variety of habitats from riverine valleys to montane and lowland forests, from vleis to moist and dry savanna woodlands and grassy plains, except where rainfall, shade and water requirements are not met. In short, any place capable of supporting cattle may once have supported buffaloes until indiscriminate hunting severely depleted their numbers. Then came

A ONCE ABUNDANT SPECIES

In 18th-century Africa, buffaloes were the most abundant ungulate species south of the Zambezi River. Mighty herds up to 3 000-strong, with attendant egrets and oxpeckers, churned across winter plains in the early mornings and late afternoons on their way to water; a solid, living wall of black and tan raising swirling dust that looked like orange mist in the slanting light. It comes as no surprise then that, after settling in the Cape Colony, European colonists quickly adopted buffalo as a favourite meat. Now all that remains of those once-widely distributed coastal herds is the relict population in the Addo Elephant National Park.

The renowned big game hunter Frederick Courteney Selous tells us that right up to the beginning of the 19th century buffaloes in southern Africa's subtropical regions were still more common than any other game animal, even more than the legendary springbok herds

of old. Indeed, buffaloes are one of the most successful grazers in Africa, thriving from the forests and grasslands of the highest mountains – they've been seen at 4 000 metres on Kilimanjaro's snowline – to sea level; and in swamps, floodplains and most savannas where annual rainfall exceeding 300 millimetres gives rise to abundant, medium to tall sweet grass; ample drinking water; mud wallows; and woodlands for refuge.

the rinderpest epizootic at the end of the 19th century, which destroyed up to 95 per cent of the vestige. Afterwards, buffalo distribution was divided into pre- and post-rinderpest eras, and the present.

'The rinderpest, sweeping down from North-East Africa, ravaged the continent from Abyssinia [Ethiopia] to the Cape, and everywhere it touched, exterminated or all but exterminated the buffalo,' James Stevenson-Hamilton wrote in *Wild Life in South Africa* (1947), an early chronicle of African animal behaviour. 'For many years the species was scarce, but its recuperative powers are evidently great, for today, wherever it has received even a modicum of protection, it has increased and flourished amazingly.' Their increase was due not only to the protection afforded by the reserve, but also to the immunity the survivors had acquired to rinderpest. 'In Kruger National Park, the fifteen or twenty animals which escaped the rinderpest in the lower Sabi bush have increased to some thousands, and spread nearly all over the Park at least as far north as the Olifants River. It is probable that the herds found north of this considerable faunal barrier may be mainly immigrants or descendants of immigrants from neighbouring [Mozambique].' Today, buffaloes are distributed throughout the Kruger, without a strong preference for any particular landscape. They are, however, found in local concentrations, especially near rivers, while tending to avoid thickets near rivers, sour bushveld and mountain bushveld.

In 1964, a dry-season count revealed that the Kruger's buffaloes had surged to some 10 500 head, with over 2 000 concentrated in a 260-square-kilometre section around Crocodile Bridge. In light of this unexpectedly high number, park biologist

Behind a buffalo herd's half-curious, half-timid phalanx of moist muzzles and lowering horns is a group of families that share resources and co-ordinate activities in ways that resemble human society.

Their increase was due not only to the protection afforded by the reserve, but also to the immunity the survivors had acquired to rinderpest.

Tol Pienaar felt that because of 'additional heavy grazing pressure by other species such as wildebeest, zebra and impala, as well as the fact that the winter range in this area already showed distinct signs of over-utilisation during dry periods, culling of excess numbers would soon become necessary'. At the time, records regarding the Kruger's buffalo population dynamics were lacking in detail. To acquire the additional ecological knowledge necessary to establish safe culling procedures, veterinarians from Pretoria University's Onderstepoort research centre joined teams of local workers in the field to gather a trove of new data. Their work began during one of the park's longest droughts on record. Despite the harsh conditions, the Kruger's first aerial census in 1967 revealed that buffaloes had increased to over 15 700 and were up to 19 000 by the end of the dry phase in 1969. That year regular buffalo culls began in the Kruger, two years after elephant culling started, although the sanctioned killing of buffaloes never excited anywhere near the same public interest.

Buffaloes and elephants are counted by helicopter in the Kruger each year and for 23 years, from 1969 until 1992, around 3 000 buffaloes, or five to 10 per cent of the total, were culled annually so as to maintain the population at approximately 30 000.

The 1993 drought in Serengeti caused a 70 per cent die-off among buffaloes and 40 per cent among wildebeest.

This was done in accordance with the fervently held management principle of wildlife-carrying capacity that aimed to prevent mass deaths due to natural causes when populations increased. But this boom-and-bust phenomenon is not specific to the Kruger. All over savanna Africa most large herbivore species experience elevated mortality during prolonged droughts due to food shortages towards the end of the dry season. The 1993 drought in Serengeti caused a 70 per cent die-off among buffaloes and 40 per cent among wildebeest. Moreover, studies have shown that natural fluctuations play an important role in maintaining ecological resilience and stability and should be retained where possible.

The Kruger's nine years of drought in the 1960s were followed in 1971 by 10 years of high rainfall. The dramatically changed weather conditions precipitated startling changes in the daily affairs of a number of big game species. The first anomaly was flagged in 1972 when an intensive aerial census over the Central District recorded steep population declines for wildebeest and zebras (see Chapter 3, page 55). By 1974, with the numbers still dropping, worried researchers came to the realisation that during periods of high rainfall, lions and hyaenas take advantage of increased hunting cover and the fragmentation of big herds into smaller units to improve their hunting success of open-plains-loving animals such as zebras and wildebeest. Conversely, tall-grass-loving species such as buffaloes show the opposite trend during wet years. They directly benefit when their primary predator, the lion, concentrates almost exclusively on its most favoured prey species, the suddenly very vulnerable zebras and wildebeest. The situation for the three prey species is reversed when a drier spell returns, with lions preying more frequently and having a bigger impact on the buffalo population in drought conditions.

Butch Smuts, the ecologist overseeing the investigation, observed that culling some 3 500 buffaloes in the Central District between 1969 and 1978 – thus limiting the population to about 8 350 – had diminished their possible buffer effect in terms of lion predation; when buffaloes are abundant, lions are more likely to select them as prey. Reducing the buffalo population also reduced the grazing pressure that these somewhat indiscriminate bulk and roughage feeders bring to bear in opening up tall grasslands by trampling and pulling at long grasses, stimulating the regrowth of finer grasses for more selective species in the grazing sequence such as wildebeest. Smuts' sensible suggestion to suspend the buffalo cull, at least until a drier phase returned, was, however, vetoed.

The directive to continue culling seems strange considering that the park warden responsible for the final decision was Tol Pienaar, who just a few years earlier, as park biologist, had worked with the team of Onderstepoort veterinarians to amass

When hyaenas feast on an intact buffalo carcass it has most likely come their way as a consequence of drought or disease.

a wealth of fresh information on buffalo biology, growth and population ecology. In a scientific monograph describing his findings, Pienaar states: 'Buffalo herds range over a very large area and rarely linger in a trampled or depleted zone while there are still good stands of grass in their habitat … In this manner, the grazing habits of buffalo actually complement the requirements of species with more restricted feeding habits and others which shun old or tall grassland, such as tsessebe, wildebeest, zebra, etc., in that additional grazing range suitable to the selective requirements of these animals is opened up in the wake of buffalo herds.'

As it was clearly understood that while buffaloes exert pressure on the veld, they generally avoid overgrazing, why not cancel the cull and allow the full complement of buffaloes to fulfil their key ecological role as bulk grazers? By removing the overburden of tall grasses they would have facilitated access for zebras and wildebeest, which normally avoid such habitats. So pivotal is this role that, on private ranches that have converted from domestic livestock to wildlife, the absence of big-bulk grazers often results in swards of unpalatable rank grass. Property owners now seek to rectify this ecological imbalance by introducing buffaloes.

Between 1970 and 1980 nearly 20 000 buffaloes were cropped throughout the Kruger at a rate of between 12 and 20 per cent annually. In spite of this, following the extremely favourable rainfall years in the '70s, their numbers had climbed to 35 000 by 1981. Based on these figures, the park biologist at the time, Salomon Joubert, calculated 'that without culling, the buffalo population could have increased to well beyond 70 000. In fact, in the space of ten years, the population could have more than trebled.' That calculation seems predicated on a limitless food supply, although Joubert does concede that 'buffaloes could well be adaptable enough to fluctuate in harmony with the [region's] short term (20 year) climatic cycles.'[1]

Far from doubling or trebling, the severe El Niño-related drought of 1982/3 inflicted massive mortality on the buffalo population, which sagged to around 15 250. In times of prolonged drought, buffaloes tend to lose condition faster than other savanna ungulates. Computer simulations showed that buffaloes in the Kruger's Central District were heavily predated as their starving population declined in tandem with deteriorating environmental conditions. It was later estimated that weakened and dying buffaloes had provided lions with twice their usual food intake. Prides constantly followed buffalo herds, particularly during winter, with most kills made near watering places. Lions were recorded killing three or more buffaloes in an emaciated group and then eating only one of them.

Interestingly, buffaloes did not feature in recorded kills before 1946 and appear to have been virtually ignored as prey by lions during those early years.

As ecologists Norman Owen-Smith and Gus Mills observed in an analysis of the various factors influencing ungulate population dynamics: 'The food available to support a predator depends not simply on the prey population size but rather on the vulnerability to mortality (directly through predation or interactively with nutrition) of the individuals constituting those populations.' The authors point out that a prey population that is growing because animals are generally in good condition offers less food to predators than a similar size population that is stressed and declining. 'All dying animals constitute potential food for predators, which readily scavenge when opportunities arise. In KNP, ungulate carcasses uneaten by predators are rarely encountered, except during extreme drought years or outbreaks of anthrax.' In addition, the spread of bovine tuberculosis in the southern Kruger may have meant that sick buffaloes provided another source of easy pickings for opportunistic lions.

When the rains returned, the population again picked up. But the good seasons were followed by deadly droughts between 1991 and '95 which, combined with an outbreak of anthrax in the northern half of the park that devastated buffaloes, resulted in a

52 per cent drop in their numbers from 30 000 to 14 000. The massive crash persuaded park officials to terminate the annual buffalo cull and it was never again reinstated as a means of population control. Over the next two years, plentiful rains and improved habitat halted the decline and, apart from 2002, the park's buffaloes have steadily increased since then, jumping from 31 000 in 2005 to 33 300 a year later.

So, though buffaloes increase rapidly under good conditions, they are also highly susceptible to droughts, when deaths soar. In his 2002 master's thesis for Pretoria University, Darcy Visscher investigated the influences of culling, rainfall and density dependence on the Kruger buffaloes' population peaks and troughs. He found that, in general, buffalo numbers are kept in check through density-dependent factors – which may include food, water, space, disease, predation and competition – that affect the population because of that population's density. He concluded that, although culling had been employed to maintain the population within acceptable limits, 'those limits appeared to be within the range of densities where the buffalo population would limit its own growth'. In this instance and others, it has become apparent that there is an overwhelming natural order at work, which functions best unfettered by human interference. For example: buffalo culling was supposedly based on random selection procedures but was in practice strongly biased towards subgroups of non-breeding individuals within herds. This disruption of population structures reduced the potential for future scientific studies and may have pre-empted natural selection processes that shape buffalo characteristics.

Long-term studies in the Kruger have demonstrated the cyclic nature of ecosystems and the importance of recognising the need to conserve the system with all its facets and fluxes before management actions such as population control are implemented. Recent complementary studies have looked at the role large carnivores play in these fluctuations, with predator–prey interactions emerging as a central influence on the dynamics of many animal populations – far more so than previously suspected.

By analysing records of lion kills found by field staff over 70 years, Norman Owen-Smith and Gus Mills showed that wildebeest, zebras and buffaloes are the lion's favourite prey species in terms of the amount of meat eaten. Interestingly, buffaloes did not feature in recorded kills before 1946 and appear to have been virtually ignored as prey by lions during those early years. As a proportion of all lion kills, buffaloes amounted to only one per cent in the 1940s, going up to nine per cent a decade later. Those figures began to trend progressively upwards as buffalo numbers increased from 1960 to around

During times of prolonged drought in Kruger, starving buffaloes become progressively weaker and are heavily predated by lions.

1990 and as lions honed their buffalo-hunting techniques in times of drought when the quarry was particularly vulnerable. From 1946 to the early '70s, buffaloes in the northern half of the Kruger numerically comprised 55 to 65 per cent of lion kills, whereas prior to 1946 waterbucks appear to have been the principal prey in the north. The buffalo contribution to lion kills waned as zebras became steadily more abundant in the north following the installation of artificial waterholes during the '70s but surged in the 1982/3 and 1991/2 droughts, going back up to over 50 per cent in the latter dry period. Following a drop in the buffalo population after 1992, the proportion of zebra kills again increased.

In the southern Kruger, buffaloes only contributed five to 10 per cent of lion kills until the 1982/3 drought, when that figure shot up hugely to more than 30 per cent. The increase in buffalo kills was paralleled by a decreased contribution by impalas. Through the severe 1992 drought, buffaloes remained numerically more important in lion kills than either wildebeest or zebras but then faded following a drop in numbers, with zebras and wildebeest again increasing. The effect rainfall had on buffalo selection seems to have been similar in both halves of the park, with a significantly higher kill ratio after the 1982/3 drought than before. The buffaloes that survived the great die-off were probably the fittest, which would have deflected predation pressure towards alternative prey species. In conclusion, Owen-Smith and Mills note that 'changes in the abundance of buffalo were influenced by changing prey selection by lions but in their case vulnerability to predation cannot be disentangled from susceptibility through food deficiencies and possibly also disease'.

Buffalo births are timed to coincide with the wet season's optimal veld conditions, with most Kruger calves born between January and March.

A stampeding buffalo herd is followed overhead by its noisy flock of attendant oxpeckers.

It is evident, then, that buffalo populations are largely regulated by a dynamic relationship between periods of high and low rainfall and the manner in which lions respond to those events. Look further into the predator–prey relationship between lions and buffaloes and it becomes apparent that age and gender make certain buffaloes more susceptible to predation than others. Lions select smaller and weaker buffaloes and consequently take a heavy toll on calves, despite herd members charging en masse to the rescue in response to an endangered calf's mournful bawling. Based on population age analyses and the results of random samples taken during his 1960s study, Tol Pienaar registered high calf mortality within a Lebombo Flats herd in southeastern Kruger. Only six to nine of every 20 calves reached maturity, although their kill rate dropped to low levels after they reached two years. In contrast, a 1985 study by Russell Taylor revealed only a 16 per cent mortality rate in the first year of life for buffaloes in Zimbabwe's Matusadona National Park. The differing findings suggest another example of population density at work. That conclusion is supported by Pienaar's earlier observation that heavy juvenile mortalities occurred in large herds of over 500 animals, whereas survival was far higher in small herds of less than 100.

In their weakened state, calves lag behind or drop out of the herd altogether, becoming easy prey for lions and hyaenas.

One of the reasons buffaloes live in big herds is for defence against predators, but it is not hard to see why calf mortalities would be higher in big herds, particularly during drought, despite mothers and their offspring having an unusually long and intense relationship. Buffalo births are timed to coincide with the wet season's optimal veld conditions, with most Kruger calves born between January and March. Although the all-black, 26- to 54-kilogram newborn is on its feet within 10 minutes after birth and can follow its mother within a few hours, it needs several weeks to keep up with the herd. Pienaar found that, as the dry season advanced, the grazing in the vicinity of perennial drinking water became trampled and churned up by pounding hooves, forcing the big herd he was monitoring to range up to 18 kilometres from surface water, which they visited at least once and often twice a day. In a 1994 study, Tshwane University of Technology's Paul Funston found that, in the Sabi Sand, herds would trek up to 10 kilometres at night in search of better grazing. The long journeys at walking speeds of five to six kilometres an hour rapidly tire suckling calves and juveniles between one and two years and they lose condition in the struggle to keep up. Compounding their distress, disease and parasitic infections exert their most profound impact at such stressful times. In their weakened state, calves lag behind or drop out of the herd altogether, becoming easy prey for lions and hyaenas.

In buffalo society, all females and young live in breeding herds that may range from 50 to over 1 000 animals, of which calves less than one year old make up about 15 per cent and mature bulls just 10 per cent. Bulls associate with breeding herds on a temporary basis only, seeking mating opportunities from the end of the dry season until the beginning of the following dry season. The rest of the time they spend in smaller, male-only coalitions known as bachelor groups. A male-dominance hierarchy

Portrait of a grouchy old 'dagga' boy. Dagga is Zulu for mud and these superannuated bulls love nothing better than whiling away the day in a mud wallow.

maintained mainly by threat behaviour and seemingly playful head sparring exists within breeding herds as well as bachelor groups. This size- and strength-based male ranking reduces the later risk of serious fights over breeding rights. Dominant bulls force three- to four-year-old adolescent males out of the breeding herds but, when clashes between rivals close in dominance status occur, they are usually brief, violent – charging with chin raised, ramming and front pressing – and sometimes fatal. Defeated bulls stay within a bull herd until about 15 years old but after losing their hierarchal position they join other increasingly decrepit outcasts in post-mature groups or live as loners. These so-called 'dagga boys'[2] are notoriously irascible and can be dangerous to people on foot but, of all adult buffaloes, it is these superannuated patriarchs that bear the brunt of lion predation.

However, killing even a lone 700-kilogram buffalo bull can be a monumental task. A herd can give lions a really hard time. They even show some coordinated defence against a pride and sometimes the hunters are gored and trampled to death. In their remarkable film and book, both called *Relentless Enemies*, Dereck and Beverly Joubert document three years spent in Botswana's northern Okavango Delta capturing astonishing sequences in the eternal interaction between lions and buffaloes. They witnessed a 'fierce' lioness from the Pantry pride take on a buffalo 'that was just too much of a match for her, and she was sliced open across the stomach and condemned to a week of suffering before finally succumbing to death. One by one the rest of the pride fell to the buffalo or just disappeared.' The Jouberts' assistant cameraman filmed this attack:

Killing even a lone 700-kilogram buffalo bull can be a monumental task.

One of the Pantry pride lionesses caught a buffalo by the throat. She hung on during almost an hour of combat while the others alternately jumped on the buffalo's back and dodged the relentless attacks of a handful of supporting bulls that were determined to save their companion. One male put his head down and charged, hitting the lioness fully broadside over and over in an attack that would have killed most lions, and definitely would have at least made them release their stranglehold. But she took the hits and tensed her body against each successive blow. Eventually, without releasing her hold, she balled herself up under the victim's neck, and the attacking bull was hitting his companion as its head offered some shelter to the Pantry female. Finally she collapsed the buffalo, and as its calls faded away the rescuers left and the lioness moved off to the shade. It was the last we saw of her – a gallant battle, won but ultimately lost.

In the Kruger, the danger of falling victim to a lion is almost four times more likely for a buffalo in a bachelor group than in a mixed herd, whereas there is no statistical difference in mortality rates for adult males and females in breeding herds. Just why some ungulate species practise sexual segregation – when males and females use different habitats or occupy distinct home ranges or live in separate social groups – has for a long time puzzled and intrigued biologists. Although a number of theories have emerged, few of them have been tested in places with an intact predator community. The Kruger Park offered the perfect opportunity.

Beginning in 2000, Craig Hay from Tshwane University of Technology spent nearly six years collecting field data for his master's thesis explaining sexual segregation in African buffaloes. His painstaking research included observing the daily movements, foraging preferences, social affiliations, body condition, hormone status and mortality rates of hundreds of individually identifiable buffaloes, as well as 163 radio-collared buffaloes of both sexes living between Lower Sabie and Satara.

Hay found that the vast majority of buffalo deaths were due to lion predation. He also noted that most kills occurred in low visibility areas such as riverine habitat, similar to those used by bachelor groups. Although these low-lying areas usually have more nutritious grazing – they tend to retain moisture, which enables grasses to remain green for longer – they also provide excellent cover for stalking lions. Mixed herds, on the other hand, tended to use more open, upland areas. Along the way, Hay also collected a lot of buffalo dung, which he later analysed for nitrogen content – nitrogen directly relates to the quality of food eaten – and for the male sex hormone, testosterone. His results showed that young bulls that spend almost the entire year in breeding herds

Hay found that the vast majority of buffalo deaths were due to lion predation.

had consistently low testosterone levels. Older bulls spent most of their time in bachelor herds, only rejoining the breeding herd in the breeding season. Though the older bulls displayed a range of testosterone levels, some were exceptionally high, especially when they associated with breeding herds. Those with high testosterone are likely to be high in the social hierarchy and, driven by genetic vigour, dominant in the male rivalry contest.

By foraging mainly in productive, riverine woodlands during the dry season, bulls in bachelor groups were eating similar food to or higher-quality food than bulls in mixed herds. Because of the ready food supply, bachelors moved almost a third less distance per day than breeding herds and so gained more body condition than males in breeding herds, thus optimising their competitive edge. Females with offspring, on the other hand, choose predator-safe habitats even at the expense of food quality and energy expenditure, despite the high energy demands associated with pregnancy and suckling a calf. It seems that the benefits for bachelor buffalo bulls of eating generally better-quality food and expending less energy in order to gain condition and improve their chances in the breeding stakes outweigh the increased risk of lion predation. This form of sex segregation is known as the predation-risk hypothesis, in contrast to the forage-selection hypothesis, practised by some northern hemisphere ungulates in predator-free areas, where the sexes separate because the difference in their body size means they have different dietary needs.

Craig Hay's work, supervised by Paul Cross from Montana State University and Paul Funston, forms part of a series of interlinked projects investigating the Kruger's buffaloes, and is especially important in light of the spread of bovine tuberculosis (BTB). This highly contagious bacterial disease first entered the Kruger ecosystem between 1950 and 1960,

Being at the top of the food chain, lions are particularly susceptible to contracting bovine tuberculosis (BTB) from the many weak, old and debilitated buffaloes they eat.

transmitted by infected cattle on two farms bordering the Crocodile River. By the time it was first detected in 1990, BTB was already well established in the park's Southern District. During the '80s, it had spread like a veld fire among the buffalo herds south of the Sabie River, infecting as many as 45 per cent, and continued spreading north from herd to herd at a rate of about five kilometres a year. In the 1990s it passed to the Central District's buffaloes, where infection rates were even higher than in the south, with 10 per cent of healthy buffaloes in the Satara area infected annually. By 2005, BTB had reached the northernmost herds in the Levubu/Limpopo drainage.

Vets who had first studied the movements of collared BTB-infected buffaloes estimated it would take 40 years for the disease to reach the top of the park; instead it took just 15 years. As it spread northwards, the infection was detected in a range of new species, including lions, leopards, cheetahs, hyaenas, kudus, eland, impalas, bushbucks, baboons, warthogs, bushpigs, honey badgers and large-spotted genets. In these secondary hosts, infection often leads to severe loss of condition. Large predators, especially lions, are particularly vulnerable – being at the top of the food chain means they are at high risk of exposure to infected prey animals or carcasses. A 2003 paper by Alexandre Caron, Paul Cross and Johan du Toit reported early symptoms of BTB-related ecological disturbances. For example, buffalo herds that manifested high BTB prevalence appeared more vulnerable to drought because of a loss in condition and an increased tick load. Also, because lions selectively kill weak, old and debilitated buffaloes, their prey base accumulated a disproportionately high prevalence of BTB. A study comparing lion prides in high buffalo BTB-prevalence zones found correspondingly high infection rates in lions, a correlation that held true for lions in zones with low buffalo infection rates. Lions also infect one another through biting and airborne transmission.

According to the Kruger veterinarian Roy Bengis, the first case of BTB in the Kruger's lions was diagnosed when post mortems were conducted on two emaciated lionesses in 1995. Subsequent testing of a sample of lions from the southern Kruger has shown that approximately 80 per cent were infected by, or had been exposed to, BTB. Lions develop symptoms faster than do buffaloes, with a shorter time span between infection and the first clinical signs of the disease and eventual death. As the disease progresses, lions become extremely thin, which suggests that it may interfere with their digestive process and absorption of nutrients into the bloodstream, says Bengis. Also, many positive lions have

Indeed, veterinarians estimate that only 2.3 per cent of South Africa's buffaloes are disease free, with most of those originating from Addo.

BTB lesions in their bones and joints, compromising their mobility. A higher-than-usual number of infected lions are found during the rainy season, probably because 'lions are more stressed as their prey disperses,' Bengis suspects, which exacerbates the disease's effect. It is estimated that around 25 lions die from BTB each year.

'Even more important is the effect the disease is having on lion social behaviour,' says the Kruger's chief veterinarian, Dewald Keet. Because adult males usually dominate at kills, they eat the choicest parts, such as lungs, which are a main site for BTB lesions and bacteria. 'Lions are weakened by this wasting disease, which leads to a faster turnover of pride males, which in turn leads to more cubs being killed by the new pride males.' The eviction of entire prides from territories has also been documented, which is utterly contrary to lion behaviour elsewhere in the Kruger. The infected population is significantly younger than the non-infected, with non-infected lions, especially males, living much longer. Cub survival is higher in the non-infected population but birth rates are higher in the infected population, although it is feared that cubs may be infected in their mother's womb or through her milk. 'All of this contributes to generally lower breeding success and survival and a decrease in average lion longevity,' says Keet.

BTB is not the only disease the Kruger's buffaloes harbour. Most are infected with corridor disease (also called east coast fever) and foot-and-mouth disease and more than a quarter with brucellosis. Indeed, veterinarians estimate that only 2.3 per cent of South Africa's buffaloes are disease free, with most of those originating from Addo. A consequence of these diseases is the disruption they present to wildlife translocations, due to the national and international trade restrictions on affected species. For instance, originally because of foot-and-mouth disease, only non-cloven-hoofed animals such as elephants, rhinos, hippos and zebras may be moved out of the park. A programme to breed disease-free buffaloes has been established near Skukuza, where wild-caught cows are held in sterilised bomas so that disease-free calves can be reared and weaned under quarantine conditions, and then relocated to other conservation areas in South Africa. This strategy aims to ensure that a gene pool of the Kruger buffaloes is safeguarded well away from the BTB zone as a kind of insurance against any catastrophic future calamity.

These various diseases often have only minor or no ill effect on the buffaloes themselves. BTB may take years to kill its host, spreading slowly, usually without showing external symptoms such as emaciation until the terminal stage, and consequently has proven difficult to detect in living animals. So it persists in buffalo populations, which then act as disease reservoirs. Although BTB poses no direct threat to humans, the potential for spillover infection to cattle from buffaloes that stray beyond the Kruger's boundaries is very real. From there the disease could spread to people who drink unpasteurised milk from infected cows, an almost certainly fatal outcome for anyone who is HIV-positive.

BTB also afflicts wildlife in northern Tanzania's Serengeti and Tarangire grasslands and woodlands and the Masai Mara in southern Kenya but, according to long-time Serengeti lion researcher Craig Packer, who is also professor of zoology at the University of Minnesota, it is not as important an issue there. 'While we still have BTB in Tanzania, it isn't a problem that we worry much about. Surveys have demonstrated exposure of Serengeti lions to BTB since at least 1984 but it seems that it is a worse problem in Kruger than elsewhere. It is still not clear that the disease is as devastating as people originally claimed,' he says. But experts in the Kruger do worry. The big question: why does BTB seem to be a problem in the Kruger but not elsewhere in Africa?

As with human tuberculosis, no vaccine yet exists to treat BTB, making it currently impossible to eradicate in a free-ranging ecosystem. At one point in the late 1990s, park management was so worried that they considered shooting thousands of buffaloes in the most heavily infected herds. The late Bruce Bryden, the Kruger's senior ranger at the time, said it could be done but would involve a huge and expensive logistical operation to dispose of so many carcasses. Ultimately, it was decided that the dire ecological consequences of such a far-reaching cull

both Malcolm Macfarlane

Buffaloes are selectively darted from a helicopter (top), then transferred to a quarantine boma at Skukuza where disease-free calves are reared (bottom).

would be worse than the disease itself. Because the BTB pathogen is considered an alien species in the Kruger, authorities are obliged to remove it but they also have an obligation to protect the host species.

Vaccination remains the ultimate control measure for BTB but, until that day comes, resources have been focused on monitoring the spread of the disease. Buffaloes are gregarious animals with a herd structure that Herbert Prins likened to a fission-fusion society, in that herds split up and come together again at intervals, depending on the season and the best available local grazing, as part of their foraging strategy as bulk grazers and ruminants. Drought conditions may favour the spread of BTB by prompting herds to explore new areas and mix with previously unassociated herds. Research by Princeton University's Anna Jolles found that, in KwaZulu-Natal's Hluhluwe-Imfolozi Park, buffalo bulls spent only three to four months with breeding herds but their peripatetic ways led to higher infection rates than in cows. It is a perfect system for a disease like BTB to spread its pathogens among a great many buffaloes through the air, when they breathe, cough or sneeze droplets into each other's faces.

Summing up the present state-of-play in the ongoing BTB crisis, scientists from South African and American universities investigating the epidemic in the Kruger report that it 'epitomizes many of the difficulties that arise in the management of wildlife disease. Early action would have improved the likelihood of disease control or eradication but limited data existed on the long term impacts of the pathogen, making it difficult to argue for aggressive management. Almost 20 years later, it is still unclear how BTB-induced reductions in lion densities could have cascading effects upon the ecosystem.' Complete eradication of the disease is unlikely given the size of the Kruger's buffalo population and the many alternative spillover hosts that can maintain the infection independent of buffaloes. The best hope may lie in the steep decline in buffalo numbers that occurs during or just after severe drought, which would 'improve the chances of holding BTB prevalence down through aggressive test-and-slaughter and/or vaccination campaigns as the population recovers'.

> Almost 20 years later, it is still unclear how BTB-induced reductions in lion densities could have cascading effects upon the ecosystem.

---

1 Much of southern Africa experiences a 20-year rainfall oscillation consisting of approximately 10 years of above-average and 10 years of below-average rainfall.

2 A popular name among the people of the bushveld, 'dagga boys' are old buffalo bulls that love nothing better than spending long hours wallowing. Dagga means mud in Zulu and refers to the thick coating of mud the bulls acquire. The same mud is used to build huts in African villages of wattle (acacia) and dagga (daub or mud).

7 A **giraffe's** eye view

The great giraffe conveyed an idea of old-world life; they seemed what they were – things utterly apart, a different creation. Other animals herded with them, but they were not of them; they had nothing in common, save the reposeful contentment occasioned by their surroundings.

Frederick Vaughan Kirby,
In Haunts of Wild Game, 1896

The 18th-century English writer Samuel Johnson's description of the giraffe as 'an Abyssinian animal, taller than the elephant but not so thick' needs elaboration. This stately, extraordinary-looking creature is Africa's gentle giant, or not so gentle if you happen to be a hunting lion. It is the tallest mammal on Earth; bulls stand over three metres at the shoulder but their two-metre-long neck means the height at the top of their horns can be five-and-a-half metres. The giraffe is also the world's biggest ruminant – southern adult males can weigh up to 1.4 tonnes. Appropriate to a species that relies on vision for social reasons as well as an early warning system, a giraffe's soulful brown eyes are the largest of any land mammal. There are other curiosities: so as to pump blood through its elongated system, the giraffe has the highest blood pressure of any animal, which has required it to evolve the thickest hide of all living mammals – 16 millimetres, seven millimetres thicker than the hides of elephants and hippos. The giraffe's thick skin acts like a built-in compression stocking by pressing against the blood vessels to prevent blood pooling under extreme pressure.

... so as to pump blood through its elongated system, the giraffe has the highest blood pressure of any animal, which has required it to evolve the thickest hide of all living mammals ...

Startlingly outsize yet graceful and serene, the giraffe is one of those distinctive beings that for centuries have stirred the imagination. Karen Blixen likened it to a gigantic, long-stemmed flower. The word giraffe may come from the Arabic *zarafa*, 'one who walks swiftly' or *xirapha*, meaning 'graceful one'. The Roman poet Horace fancied the giraffe's bizarre appearance resembled that of a camel with leopard markings, which together with its Arabic name gave the giraffe the scientific title *Giraffa camelopardalis*.

Surveys taken in the Kruger reveal, perhaps not surprisingly, that this fabulous beast is the species most photographed by visitors to the Kruger. Not only is it an appealing subject, with its strikingly handsome coloration contrasting dramatically against the summer landscape's vivid green, but it is also easy to find if you are in the right place. Giraffes occur throughout the southern half of the Kruger, particularly in knobthorn-marula bushveld on the eastern basalts. They are also well represented in mountain bushveld but avoid the northern sandveld and to some extent mopane woodlands. Though their numbers are slowly increasing in the northern half of the park, the relative scarcity of suitable browse, in particular

A giraffe's sticky, 45-centimetre-long prehensile tongue comes in handy when removing ants or other insects that scramble up its nose while its browsing. It is thought that the tongue's purplish-black colour may help protect it against sunburn.

acacias, has always stifled their population growth there. The Central District has the Kruger's highest giraffe density of about seven per 10 square kilometres, although that is likely an underestimate; in Serengeti they attain a regional density of 12 per 10 square kilometres and in Timbavati Reserve the population has stabilised at 26 per 10 square kilometres.

Giraffes are also hard to miss. Their lofty bearing gives giraffe-spotters a high visibility target to look for. A plus for photographers is the giraffe's nonchalant acceptance of our presence. After the Kruger was opened to visitors in 1928, giraffes quickly became accustomed to vehicles and ever since have taken very little notice of them. If one happens to be in the middle of the road, it usually waits until the vehicle is about 20 metres away before ambling off with its curious gait – first the two immense legs on one side swinging forward and then the two on the other side, its tail tightly curled over its rump – before obligingly pulling up to stand gazing unconcernedly from the roadside.

Today there are close to 6 000 giraffes in the Kruger but their situation was critical in 1902 when James Stevenson-Hamilton was appointed warden of the Sabi Game Reserve. No more than 15 survived south of the Olifants River, while to the north there were even fewer. Other than that remnant, all that remained of the once-plentiful species were 'giraffe shin-bones everywhere in the veld, showing how numerous the animals must once have been', Stevenson-Hamilton remembered. The rinderpest pandemic that devastated cloven-hoofed animals in the Lowveld around 1900 must have played a major role in the giraffe's great die-off, as it was one of those most severely affected by the virus. But its precipitous decline started earlier, the result of unsustainable hunting.

After the Kruger was opened to visitors in 1928, giraffes quickly became accustomed to vehicles and ever since have taken very little notice of them.

'Until protected by legislation, giraffes suffered terribly from the attacks of hunters both European and native; for the tails were worth, among the low country Bantu, the equivalent of £1 each, and the hides were valuable to white men for making sjamboks, the lashes for the long wagon whips, and other purposes,' Stevenson-Hamilton recalled. 'It is related that in the old days one man used to kill giraffes in the country now constituting the Kruger National Park in order to sell the bones as manure, and a friend, who hunted here in the late [1870s] told me he often passed wagons loaded up with giraffe hides and bones.'

In his autobiography, Harry Wolhuter, Sabi Reserve's first game ranger, tells of joining a hunting trip to the Lowveld in 1892, when he was 15 years old. 'The next morning we set out, and I was a happy lad! We did a little shooting on the way, and finally we arrived in the area now known as the Satara section of the Kruger National Park, which was then, as now, the best giraffe country.' Young Harry was instructed to herd a troop of giraffes towards the hunter. 'I immediately galloped after them, and as the country was fairly open succeeded twice in bringing them near enough for him to shoot, but on turning them the third time I could not locate him.' Harry chased after the giraffes until they entered a boggy watercourse, where one of the cows became

GIRAFFE EVOLUTION

The giraffe is marvellously adapted to the Kruger's bushveld savanna environment but it was a long and tortuous journey getting there. Along the way the mighty mega-herbivore underwent an evolutionary transformation to reach its present form that was crucial to that still-contentious question: how did the giraffe get its long neck? To find answers we must go back in time to the giraffe's mysterious origins. DNA studies and fossil remains tell us that the giraffe – which is a true ruminant, with a complex four-chambered stomach like other even-toed ungulates such as cattle, antelopes and deer – is descended from an ancestral deer that was developing in a new direction. Though the lineage from the first ruminant to the modern giraffe is far from obvious, it can be traced back to the early Eocene some 50 million years ago. The giraffids, a family of which the giraffe and okapi are the only two living members, appear to have evolved from a three-metre-tall deer-like mammal that roamed Europe and Asia. Separation from deer occurred around 25 million years ago with the advent of the modern giraffe's progenitor, which still resembled a deer with large, weirdly shaped antler-like ossicones (skin-covered horns) but with longer legs than usual, although it still looked nothing like a giraffe.

Between 15 and 10 million years ago, the first recognisable giraffine, *Canthumeryx syrtensis*, gave rise to okapis and giraffes via four intermediate species: Giraffokeryx, a slender, fallow deer-sized animal that had a clearly elongated neck and reduced horns; Palaeotragus, of which the okapi is the extant 'living fossil'; Samotherium and Bohlinia. Fossilised remains recovered from Greece, dated eight million years old, show that Bohlinia – which had an anatomy almost identical to that of the modern giraffe – is its closest ancestor. Stimulated by climate change, descendants of Bohlinia entered China and north India where they evolved into typical giraffe species, and then died out four million years ago. Also following their preferred habitat, early giraffes entered Africa seven million years ago and, apparently unaffected by changes to the climate that were pushing their Asian counterparts towards extinction, evolved into three relatively small and two large species. They did not stay the course and disappeared, but not before giving rise to the present-day giraffe, which appears for the first time in East African fossil deposits that date back a million years.

mired. As he was without a rifle, he was at first unsure how to proceed, 'and then quite suddenly it struck me that I might as well try and cut her throat with my pocket knife … When I had come close enough I took out my pocketknife and slashed away at the poor beast's neck as high as I could reach: and since the animal was of course held fast in the mud it could neither move nor defend itself in any way. I continued to saw away at its neck, with blood splashing all over me, until from sheer loss of blood the huge beast toppled over; and then, the excitement being over, I was conscious of a sense of regret, and it seemed to me that I had perpetrated a dreadfully cruel and bloodthirsty thing – almost a crime!'

As Stevenson-Hamilton remarked: 'In old South African days it was customary to ride the herds down on horseback, a deadly and wasteful, if exciting method of hunting, which more than any other was responsible for the species having been almost exterminated in [much of southern Africa]. Apart from the commercial side of the question, it is difficult to understand what possible satisfaction could be obtained from the killing of a giraffe. It is so gentle and harmless a beast, that the thrill of excitement – outside pure blood lust – is absent; so big, that it requires no skill to plant a bullet in its body; and it provides no trophy worth preserving except possibly the tail. Moreover, it is so exceptionally harmless as regards all man's works that there is not even that excuse for its destruction.'

Their unique evolutionary design has required profound adaptations to the giraffe's circulatory system.

In the wake of hunting massacres and deadly rinderpest came absolute protection. It soon paid handsome dividends. By 1912, giraffes were increasingly seen along the Olifants and Timbavati rivers and by then had recolonised the present western boundary between the Olifants and Nwaswitsontso rivers. Ground counts in 1918 estimated there were 200 giraffes in Sabi Reserve and a further 60 along the eastern boundary north of the Shingwedzi River. The country between the Sabie and Olifants rivers had always had the highest giraffe density and the population radiated from there. The Pretoriuskop long grass veld was re-entered in 1933 and by this time the Olifants had been crossed from the south and in 1953 the Letaba River was also forded.

In their analysis of the origin, evolution and phylogeny of giraffes, Graham Mitchell, a zoology professor at the University of Wyoming, and John Skinner, professor of zoology and mammalogy at the University of Pretoria, make a compelling case that the giraffe's divergence from its forest-dwelling ancestors 'has depended on and been stimulated by the emergence of a woodland scrub' as Africa became drier and rainforests shrank, opening up

A neck of such unusual length requires specialised equipment to pump blood over two metres uphill to the brain.

This old giraffe bull cranes his head and neck at full vertical stretch and extends his tongue to reach the leaves and seed pods on the underside of a mature tree's canopy. Females usually feed with their necks curled over about 130 degrees, selecting leaves at body and knee height, thus reducing competition between the sexes.

the way for the spreading savanna. 'This biome is rich in leguminous browse that provides the nutrients their skeletons require and camouflage … It is a biome to which giraffes are adapted and to which they seem irretrievably bound' and 'there is a strong suggestion of co-evolution between it and giraffes'. But, the authors warn, 'it is a biome that is shrinking and with it so has the range of giraffes'.

Their unique evolutionary design has required profound adaptations to the giraffe's circulatory system. A neck of such unusual length requires specialised equipment to pump blood over two metres uphill to the brain. It was once thought that to do so the giraffe had a very big heart but research has shown that the body cavity lacks sufficient room for that option. Instead, it has a relatively small heart, with the power coming from a very strong beat – up to 170 times a minute, double that of humans – while pumping the highest-known blood pressure of any mammal, again double that of humans. This is possible because of the left ventricle's incredibly thick walls and small radius – at its thickest, the left ventricle's wall is four centimetres thick. The right ventricle is only about one centimetre thick, but then it needs to pump blood only a short distance to the lungs, whereas the left ventricle has to pump blood all the way up to the head against the hydrostatic pressure of the blood already in the long vertical artery.

Seeing a giraffe lower its long neck to drink, early observers wondered why the blood rushing down to the head did not cause it to black out or bring on a fatal haemorrhage. To withstand a surge of blood when its head is raised, lowered or swung rapidly, the giraffe evolved control valves in its jugular veins and an unusually elastic network of blood vessels at the base of its head known as the *rete mirabile caroticum* – wonder net of the carotids – that acts as a pressure-regulation buffer and helps keep blood pressure constant in the brain. Equally marvellous is the fact that blood does not pool in the legs nor does a cut on the leg bleed profusely, even though arteries near the feet are under great pressure because of the weight of fluid pressing down on them. In other animals, such pressure would force the blood out through the capillary walls. In giraffes, however, these blood vessels are thick walled and less elastic, with a very tight sheath of thick skin around the lower leg, which maintains high extra-vascular pressure. So effective is this coordinated system of blood-pressure controls that NASA scientists studied it extensively when developing the anti-gravity suits worn by astronauts. Giraffes also have a very rapid respiration rate for such a big animal. They breathe 20 times a minute – compared with our 12 and an elephant's 10 – as the trachea tube connecting the back of the throat to the lungs via the long neck contains partially inhaled and exhaled air that must be cleared.

The ecologist Harvey Croze defined the giraffe as 'a product of evolution that has solved its problems by elongation'.

Nursery groups of two or more giraffe calves and their mothers will gather together to form what is known as a 'calving pool'. Social cohesion in these nursery groups is maintained by the bonds formed between calves of the same age.

The ecologist Harvey Croze defined the giraffe as 'a product of evolution that has solved its problems by elongation'. He was referring, of course, to its long neck and legs, which are widely regarded as a classic example of evolutionary biology based on foraging competition. Because the giraffe's incredible height lifts it above the common herd, this hypothesis proposes, it is able to avoid competition with most other animals by browsing high up in the canopy. It is further aided in this upward yearning by a modified atlas joint connecting the skull to the spine that allows it to tip its head back vertically; this, together with a long, muscular, prehensile tongue, gives it even greater reach. Its height also bestows advantages on researchers investigating feeding ecology[1] because it is easy to observe what a giraffe is eating, unlike ungulates that feed close to the ground.

Eating is the single most important activity in a giraffe's generally peaceful day; most of the night is spent ruminating while sitting or lying down. The chief research scientist at the Serengeti Research Institute in the 1970s, Robin Pellew, analysed and compared giraffe food consumption and energy budgets to their calving frequencies. He noted that adult female giraffes browse year-round for a relatively constant 53 per cent of each day. During the dry season and prior to breeding they seek high-energy food containing increased levels of phosphorus. In this way they obtain the necessary nutritional and energy requirements to calve at all times of the year, without the usual seasonal constraints imposed on grazing ruminants. That said, a study in the Timbavati Reserve, west of the Kruger, found that 60 per cent of giraffe conceptions occur during the late wet-season months of December to March, when leaf production is at its greatest.

Giraffes are tree pruning specialists and as such are almost exclusively selective browsers.

Because of their efficient foraging strategy, Pellew dubbed female giraffes 'energy maximisers'. Bulls, on the other hand, wander in search of oestrus cows approximately once every two weeks and so have evolved a 'time minimiser' strategy. They spend less time foraging – around 50 percent of their day in the dry season and 40 percent in the wet season when food is more plentiful – but more time walking – 22 per cent of their day, or six kilometres, as against 13 per cent for females. Unusually, giraffes chew cud while walking, which maximises their feeding opportunities.

Giraffes are tree pruning specialists and as such are almost exclusively selective browsers. Adults may consume around 60 kilograms of plant material daily. In the Kruger they prefer deciduous plants during the wet growing season but, as the dry season advances and deciduous trees lose their leaves, they rely increasingly on less palatable evergreen and semi-evergreen plants growing along drainage lines. At the end of the dry season they turn to unpalatable evergreens growing in riverine thickets and forests flanking the bigger rivers, devoting more time to foraging as the quantity and quality of the food declines. This seasonal selection of woodland types allows them to maintain a high-quality diet throughout the year, except sometimes towards the end of the dry season.

In the central Kruger, giraffes feed on 42 different species of trees and shrubs, although acacia leaves provide them with their most important food source. They are especially partial to tender, new growth on branch tips, which is eaten thorns and all, before thorns have a chance to harden. Succulent, unhardened acacia shoots contain higher levels of protein, fat and minerals than most other plants, so, although giraffes have similar rates of food intake to other ungulates, their food is better quality. Like pruned hedges, acacias respond to browsing with increased shoot production, which thickens their surface area, providing giraffes with a greater leaf table to feed from. Flushing shoots also comprise up to 74 per cent water and permit giraffes to go for long periods in the wet season without drinking. When shoots harden, giraffes strip leaves from the branches by running the shoot tips over their lower incisors and bite off shoot ends. In the dry winter months, up to 15 per cent of their diet comprises hard woody roughage such as twigs, compared with five

This giraffe is stripping leaves from a tree's prickly limbs by dragging the branch between its lobed canine teeth with a backward pull of its head. Its lips, tongue and inside of the mouth are covered in papillae – taste buds that sit on raised protrusions – that help protect against thorns.

per cent in the wet season. Herbs, including vines, climbers and taller forbs – but no grass – make up between 0.2 and seven per cent of their year-round diet in different areas. Giraffes also seek out flowers when available and the hard, baseball-sized fruit of the Transvaal gardenia and monkey apple and the sausage tree's huge woody pods.

Unlike elephants, giraffes are 'neat' eaters. A casual observer watching a giraffe fastidiously nibbling on first one tree and then the next could be excused for assuming that the big animal is having little impact on the plants it browses. But look closely and you will notice that repeated foraging has left an obvious visual impression on the giraffe's preferred food trees. Browse lines on the underside of a woodland canopy are trimmed off sharply below six metres or pruned into a dumbbell shape. In fact, giraffes, their extinct relatives and other browsers are thought to have shaped the biology of favourite food trees, including the evolution of defensive thorns and chemical deterrents. A 2001 study in northeastern KwaZulu-Natal's Ithala Game Reserve by William Bond and Debbie Loffell found that giraffe feeding had a significant effect on the structure and composition of plant communities – so much so that, within 25 years of their introduction, giraffes had browsed some sensitive acacia species to local extinction and heavily affected others, except in areas too steep for giraffes to access. Research has shown that selective browsing by giraffes can suppress the environmental dominance of some plant species, providing opportunities for other species to increase, while even low levels of leaf loss make certain plants less successful competitors or hold them at a height range that makes them vulnerable to veld fires.

Clearly images of delicateness where giraffe foraging is concerned can be misleading. Interestingly, the umbrella thorns (*Acacia tortilis*) in Ithala showed no or very little mortality, undoubtedly because they are common in parts of Southern and East Africa with large giraffe populations and have of necessity developed appropriate defences. Trees subjected to high browsing intensity have significantly longer thorns, smaller leaves and higher total cyanide (prussic acid) concentrations than trees with low browsing intensity. The umbrella thorn is the only acacia to have both straight and curved thorns, but all African acacias have evolved thorns of some kind. Some are recurved, claw-like and flesh grabbing, others hide-piercing, five-centimetre-long, needle-like spikes. On the Highveld, however, where giraffes rarely ventured, the sweet thorn (*Acacia karroo*) and common hookthorn (*A. caffra*) lose their thorns with maturity.

The Kruger's savannas are divided into two main ecological types – broad-leaved savanna comprises 75 per cent (of which 50 per cent is mopane) and 25 per cent is fine-leaved acacia bushveld. Giraffes concentrate in the latter although it seems amazing that any browser would attempt to penetrate the trees' bristling, wicked-looking defences. Giraffes, however, are completely undeterred. Their flexible upper lip is made for gathering the acacias' tiny leaflets and the narrow, 45-centimetre-long tongue pulls food with unerring dexterity into the mouth, which is lengthened and narrowed for the purpose. Giraffes inadvertently bite off some thorns but a horny skin covering the palate and thick, latex-like saliva protects inside the mouth, while sturdy molars crush the thorns. Any thorns that get embedded in the tongue's mucous covering are gradually shed as it is replaced by new cells. Experiments have shown that, though thorns do not prevent giraffes from browsing, they slow the feeding rate by restricting bite size and bite rates – consumption rates are three times higher on trees that have had their thorns removed.

In a 1990 paper, Johan du Toit, a large-mammal ecologist now at Utah State University but at the time at the University of Witwatersrand, asked: are giraffes that feed on acacia flowers predators or pollinators? His research focused on the knobthorn (*Acacia nigrescens*), a staple tree browsed by giraffes in the central Kruger. After late dry-season leaf-fall in August and September, this five- to 18-metre-tall tree produces a profusion of creamy-white, unscented bottle-brush flowers that are highly sought after by giraffes. Which begged the question: did giraffes also provide a pollination service while feeding? Some mammals such as fruit bats and thick-tailed galagos (bush babies) have long been recognised as pollinators of certain trees like baobabs, picking pollen up and carrying it in their fur. Big, non-flying mammals, however, did not seem to fit the bill. But, Du Toit noted, giraffes collect visible amounts of pollen on their heads and necks while eating flowers so it seemed quite feasible that they might distribute pollen to other flowering knobthorns within their 80- to 120-square-kilometre home range.

> Experiments have shown that, though thorns do not prevent giraffes from browsing, they slow the feeding rate by restricting bite size and bite rates ...

In 2003, Johan du Toit was back in the central Kruger, this time together with Patricia Fleming from Murdoch University in Australia and Sally Hofmeyr and Sue Nicolson from Pretoria University, to re-examine the relationship between giraffes and knobthorns. The researchers compared the nutritional content of knobthorn flowers with alternative browse, the amount of flowers eaten and the subsequent fruit set in the presence and absence of giraffes. The study revealed that the flowers contained 50 per cent more water, almost twice as much protein and about 33 per cent less acid detergent fibre – the fibrous, least digestible portion of roughage – than alternative browse. Despite the fact that they contain almost three times as much condensed tannin as leaves, giraffes ate around 85 per cent of the flowers within reach, which significantly reduced fruit set at heights accessible to giraffes. Most fruit set on the tops of trees, beyond the reach of giraffes, suggesting pollination by the many insect visitors like wasps, flies and bees. The researchers ultimately concluded that giraffes were effectively predators of knobthorn flowers.

One particularly odd item on the giraffe's menu is the occasional bone, a dietary craving known as osteophagia. A 2008 paper in the *Onderstepoort Journal of Veterinary Research* by Ian Bredin and John Skinner from Pretoria University's Faculty of Veterinary Science and Graham Mitchell from the University of Wyoming asked: 'Can osteophagia provide giraffes with phosphorus and calcium?' The researchers observed that in the Kruger the eating of bones occurs about 10 times more frequently from April, when acacias start losing their leaves, to October, when early rains have leached calcium from the soil, and the fast growth and high water content of leaves lowers their calcium concentration. 'A giraffe's calcium requirement is formidably large,' the authors note, because its '...tallness brings its own price: the costly maintenance of an elongated and stronger skeleton'. By analysing giraffe and buffalo bones collected at various sites throughout the Kruger, the researchers discovered that the amounts of calcium and phosphorus required by a giraffe to support this growth are two to three times the amounts required by a buffalo. 'For the first year of life, about 7 grams daily is available in milk (and like most mothers, the giraffe cow will deplete her skeleton to provide for her calf's) but thereafter the calcium must come from preferred vegetation and perhaps from the intermittent eating of bones. Interestingly, giraffes prefer legumes, especially acacia leaves, which contain three times as much calcium as grass does.'

Tracking what goes down a giraffe's long throat in the form of food and supplements brings us back by a circuitous route to that intriguing question: did the giraffe's long neck evolve as a means of opening up a largely unexploited food niche? Many people think so and with some justification. A 1990 study by Johan du Toit in the central Kruger's Tshokwane region found that niche separation is not confined to grazers. Using a real-time computerised data-capture system, he recorded the length of time giraffes, kudus, impalas and steenbok browse at various heights. Giraffes foraged almost 90 per cent of the time above the feeding height ranges of the other three. Kudus allocated

Lara Tranter

Giraffes are sometimes seen picking up the bones of dead animals and chewing them – probably to maintain their enormous skeleton. During those months in the Kruger when naturally occurring calcium is in short supply, giraffes combat the onset of the giraffine version of osteoporosis by resorting to this unusual dietary supplement.

33 per cent of their feeding time to a height range of 1.2 to 1.7 metres, which was little used by giraffes and impalas, and beyond the reach of steenbok. Although there was clear stratification in average feeding heights among the four species throughout the seasonal cycle, Du Toit observed considerable overlap in the feeding-height ranges of kudus, impalas and steenbok, whereas giraffes were separated from the other species. He noted that giraffe bulls fed at a higher level than cows, often with head and neck extended vertically to gain access to nutritious new shoots in the upper canopy.

The hypothesis that the giraffe's long neck evolved as a consequence of competition seemed so plausible that until the beginning of this century no study had been designed to test it explicitly. That situation was addressed by Elissa Cameron, director of the Mammal Research Institute at Pretoria University, and Johan du Toit. Between November 2001 and July 2003 they conducted field studies in Sabi Sand's Lion Sands Game Reserve within the Greater Kruger ecosystem, to provide the first real experimental evidence supporting this textbook example of natural selection. To do so they investigated whether foraging competition with shorter herbivores could explain why giraffes feed mostly on leaves in the upper canopy, despite being able to feed at lower levels as well. An earlier study by Andrew Woolnough and Johan du Toit had established that giraffes obtain more leaves per bite when feeding on knobthorns around 2.5 metres above the height used by kudu-sized browsers. It was unclear, however, whether this resulted from competition – highly selective smaller browsers depleting leaves at lower levels – or because trees respond to this attack by putting more effort into growing their upper canopy.

One particularly odd item on the giraffe's menu is the occasional bone, a dietary craving known as osteophagia.

In the most recent experiment, Cameron and Du Toit created nine exclosure plots by building 2.2-metre-high fences around individual knobthorns that were taller than four metres and had branches throughout their height range. The fences excluded all small browsers and partially excluded larger browsers except giraffes, who could freely forage at all heights except the lowest. After a complete growing season the researchers found little difference in the number of leaves per shoot on the fenced trees but significant differences on the unfenced control trees, revealing that competing smaller browsers had selectively foraged for higher-quality leaves, leaving fewer nutrients per bite for a large bulk forager like the giraffe. 'We conclude that giraffes preferentially browse at high levels in the canopy to avoid competition with smaller browsers,' the authors reported.

But not all animal behaviourists agree that the giraffe's neck evolved to outreach competitors. One of the more fanciful counter-theories was hatched by the British zoologist, author and committed anti-espionage exponent, Chapman Pincher, in his 1949 book *Evolution*. He suggested that the 'most extraordinary feature of the giraffe is not the length of the neck but the length of the forelegs', which had permitted giraffes to outrun potential predators except for lions. The neck had then been obliged to follow the legs so that the giraffe could reach ground level to drink. That explanation misses the obvious: under direct threat a giraffe does generally beat a hasty retreat (though a mother

Zebras and other prey species are noticeably more relaxed when giraffes are in attendance at a waterhole. From their great height, giraffes can scan their surroundings for a distance of at least a kilometre, helped by their large, bulging eyes that give them good all-round colour vision. Their senses of hearing and smell are also sharp.

shepherding an infant will usually stand her ground) but, long legs notwithstanding, its top speed is about 56 kilometres per hour, not much faster than a lion and no match for a cheetah at 70 kilometres per hour. Also it tires quickly, so it could not outrun a pack of hyaenas or wild dogs. It is not speed but size that makes an adult giraffe virtually immune to all predators other than lions.

In the Kruger the lion's largest prey animal is a bull giraffe, which weighs approximately 10 times as much as the predator. And giraffes are a lot tougher than they look. If brought to bay, they defend themselves with powerful kicks with their hind feet or chop kicks with the forefeet, or they strike with the whole stiff foreleg. Kicking in all four directions, they are capable of killing a lion. A safari operator in Tanzania, Russell Douglas, spotted a blood-spattered although seemingly uninjured giraffe bull. He backtracked the blood spoor and came upon what looked like a blood-stained rag that on closer examination turned out to be the remains of a lion trampled into oblivion. On another occasion, safarists watched a mother with calf almost sever a lion's head with a kick from her dinner plate-sized front hoof. When hunting giraffes, lions that fare best have developed highly cooperative hunting techniques or operate in big prides, with pride males playing an active role. Then they can fell even mature, healthy bulls. Indeed, males are more vulnerable because they are quite often alone and so lack the benefits of group vigilance. Of 108 giraffes killed by lions in the Kruger between 1966 and '68, 56 per cent were males and 31 per cent females (the remaining 13 per cent could not be sexed). In lion-rich areas the giraffe population may well be skewed towards a majority of females.

Another hypothesis conjectured that long necks evolved so that giraffes could keep a high-rise eye on predators. Matched with sharp eyesight, their height does give them an early warning advantage against lions during the day, so much so that antelopes and other prey species are noticeably more relaxed at waterholes when these mobile watchtowers are present. However, a fascinating study of vigilance behaviour in giraffes by Elissa Cameron and Johan du Toit found that 'predation risk does not appear to be a significant modifier of [giraffe] vigilance behaviour, although a constant level of anti-predator vigilance is probably maintained'. The researchers observed that although vigilance in prey species is thought to have a predominantly anti-predator function, with the frequency and duration of scans per individual decreasing with increasing group size, where giraffes are concerned group size has little effect on scanning behaviour in either bulls or cows, nor does the presence of calves. Instead, 'bulls scanned the most when they were in groups with larger bulls and least when they were with smaller bulls' and less time was spent scanning when a bull was alone. 'Cows were significantly more vigilant when an adult bull was close, or was the nearest neighbour.' The researchers concluded that, surprisingly, social influences are the most important in giraffe vigilance behaviour.

It used to be widely believed that giraffes suffered relatively low predation rates but it is now known that lions kill a lot more giraffes than was formerly assumed. Infants are particularly vulnerable. In the weeks after birth, giraffe mothers try to hide their young in dense cover and it is while lying out[2] that their coat markings provide ideal camouflage. Nevertheless, conservation biologist and past SANParks director Anthony Hall-Martin found a 48 per cent mortality rate among the Kruger's calves in the 1970s, while a 2006 report by Norman Owen-Smith gives calf mortality as between 33 and 55 per cent in the first year, with most losses occurring in the first month after birth. Although a youngster's chances of survival improve dramatically in its second year, as with most large mammals, high giraffe infant mortality is compounded by a slow birth interval averaging 20 months – together they effectively stabilise the Kruger's giraffe population growth.

It is not speed but size that makes an adult giraffe virtually immune to all predators other than lions.

In his extensive analysis of 46 181 carcasses identified by rangers throughout the whole of the Kruger from 1933 to '46 and 1954 to '66, park biologist Tol Pienaar recorded 675 giraffes killed by lions, or fewer than two per cent of all kills, which coincides with the two per cent representation by giraffes in the park's fauna. In a follow-up analysis from February 1966 to January 1968, Pienaar listed 108 giraffes killed

Hyaenas scavenge the remains of a giraffe killed by lions. Even a pack of hyaenas presents no threat to a healthy adult giraffe, but during its first few days a newborn is vulnerable to hyaena predation despite the valiant efforts of its mother to protect it.

by lions, or five per cent of the total. In the Kruger's Central District, where giraffes achieve their highest density, giraffe meat represents a much more substantial portion of the local lions' diet. Here, giraffes make up 11 per cent of recorded lion kills but because of their bulk they comprise 43 per cent of the lions' food intake, according to a stomach contents analysis of 257 lions killed in the Central District between 1974 and '78. Over this same period, giraffe contributed 32 per cent of the lions' diet in the southern half of the Kruger.

Despite a relatively high kill rate, giraffes in the Kruger nonetheless qualify as an alternative prey species for lions. Their selection is influenced by the changing abundance and vulnerability of the lions' three principal prey species, wildebeest, zebras and buffaloes. A shift in prey selection toward giraffes was evident in the mid-1970s when buffalo vulnerability was low because of the excellent grazing following high rainfall – when veld conditions deteriorate so do buffaloes, making them easier to pull down – and the relative scarcity of wildebeest and zebras. However, this had little or no effect on the giraffes' population trend. A study by Jason Turner in neighbouring Timbavati Reserve found that most giraffe kills occur during the late dry season, suggesting that, as in the case of buffaloes, malnutrition renders them more vulnerable. In adjoining Klaserie Reserve, as much as half the giraffe population died in September 1981 following a spell of exceptionally cold weather, with the consequent frosting of evergreen foliage in the bottomlands resulting in the loss of a critical dry-season food resource. Turner also noted that in these private game reserves giraffes were the most vulnerable prey animal to predation by lion prides, despite being 'one of the least abundant prey animals in the study area from 1979 to 2003'. This occurred as lions shifted prey selection away from the preferred but declining zebra and wildebeest populations toward more numerous impalas and larger giraffes and buffaloes. 'It's possible lions selected giraffes because they provide a high energy return for the energy expended per hunt,' Turner surmised.

Lions are marvellously adaptable, able not only to develop special techniques that allow them to tackle such formidable prey as adult giraffes successfully, but also to take advantage of special conditions that put prey at a disadvantage. In the Kruger it is widely reported that lions have realised that giraffes struggle on paved roads: they run more slowly, get less traction and are liable to slip, and so are easier to pull down. And once a giraffe is downed by lions it stays down. Occasionally other hunters will try catching a giraffe, with varying success. In his analysis of carcass data, Pienaar records that two giraffe calves were killed by cheetahs and two adults by crocodiles. Sometimes, though, a crocodile's best efforts to snag a giraffe can go wildly wrong, as recorded in a remarkable amateur photograph published in a popular magazine back in the 1970s. An adult giraffe stooped to drink from the Sabie River and a crocodile lunged. The photographer tripped the shutter just as the giraffe reared up with the croc clamped to its face – a moment later it let go and dropped nearly five metres back into the water.

It seems improbable that the giraffe's long neck developed either as a by-product or direct consequence of an evolutionary anti-predator strategy. An alternative to the feeding hypothesis was proposed in 1996 by Rob Simmons, an ecologist and giraffe expert from the Percy FitzPatrick Institute at the University of Cape Town, and Lue Scheepers from Namibia's Etosha Ecological Institute. Their novel theory proposes that giraffes' necks have been shaped by sexual selection, a specific form of natural selection responsible for the evolution of traits that promote success in competition for mates. In support of this idea they cite males fighting 'for dominance and access to females in a unique way: by clubbing opponents with well-armoured heads on long necks … Larger-necked males are dominant and gain the greatest access to oestrus females. Males' necks and skulls are not only larger and more armoured than those of females (which do not fight), but they also continue growing with age.' The head of a giraffe bull does get heavier throughout its life, as it develops protective bony deposits and can weigh 30 kilograms by the age of 20. However, Graham Mitchell argues that, if sexual selection was responsible for the giraffe's long neck, males would have evolved longer necks than females. 'Neck length is not unique to one sex and so does not meet the requirements of sexual selection.'

Perhaps the question cannot be answered because there is no single answer. Selective pressures are complex and interdependent, with forces other than natural selection at work, such as genetic drift and pre-adaptation. Maybe differing hypotheses are interconnected: longer necks extended access to food and later males seeking to establish dominance and no longer able to fight head-on resorted to 'necking' and 'head clubbing'. Why giraffes took the tall-necked path and other African mammals did not may simply be a product of the quirkiness and contingent nature of evolutionary history, which often entails a degree of chaos. The dominant factors – the broad brushstrokes – can be defined, however. They may not deliver a clear-cut explanation but nature is notoriously uncaring of our human need for simple truths.

Sean Weber

Giraffe capture is a specialised operation and requires a skilled team to get the job done. Once the giraffe has been darted, the ground crew secures it before it falls down. Ropes are twisted around its legs and it is brought down to a sitting position and then blindfolded prior to being loaded and relocated in a modified furniture removal trailer.

1 Trophic or feeding ecology is the study of the structure of feeding relationships among organisms in an ecosystem.
2 Lying out, either singly or in a group, involves an infant giraffe lying or standing in one place without an adult within half a kilometre. Unless seriously disturbed the calf remains in the same area and is visited by its mother between two and four times throughout the day to nurse.

8

Lions
and their prey

I found that fleeting hesitation between the end of the stalk and the final explosive rush a moment of almost unbearable tension, a drama in which it was impossible not to participate emotionally, knowing that the death of a being hung in the balance.

George B. Schaller, *The Serengeti Lion*, 1972

E cology may be complex but it is never short on images to stimulate our appreciation of nature's cast of players. That is particularly true where the Kruger's apex terrestrial predator, the African lion, is concerned. Ensconced at the top of the food chain, the large toothy end of the wildlife spectrum is hard to ignore. Lions are the most visible, most gregarious and noisiest of the cats. The patriarchs are dramatic to behold, with a cloud of mane as fragrant as dried grass – the only cat, domestic or wild, that displays such ornamentation. Add their high-voltage amber stare, deep chest and shoulders striated with muscle and sinew flowing under a golden skin as they drift through the bush, disappearing, reappearing, disappearing again and it is plain to see why few other animals rivet the imagination as vividly as the lion. It is the emblem of power and savagery. And the Kruger Park is famous lion country. Nightly roars – first a throaty cough, then a rising, resonant '*Wauugh-aara RRRAR*', followed by a series of grunts in diminuendo – transform the darkness beyond the rest camps' perimeter fence into a place of stealth and danger. But, even for the park's top predator, life in the bushveld is far from certain. A hunter's life is hard, dogged by the constant threat of deprivation and death.

The ecological relationship lions have with their prey is fascinating and intricate: they have evolved together over millennia in an arms race, with neither gaining an ultimate strategic advantage. The late Miocene, around 10 million years ago, when Africa's present-day cat lineages began to emerge – the panoply of lions, leopards, cheetahs and assorted smaller felines – was their evolutionary Golden Age. As forests gave way to savannas, allowing herbivores room to gather in bigger herds, big cats played predatory catch-up, honing their behaviour and bodies to facilitate the capture of prey. In so doing, Africa's pre-eminent big cat, the lion, came to symbolise the world in its primitive state: for every lion that lives free there must be herds of wild herbivores to support it and enough wild country to maintain a territory.

Lions are the most visible, most gregarious and noisiest of the cats.

To safeguard effectively the wildlife communities we wish to conserve, it is crucial to understand the relative importance of predation in determining a game park's community structure. It is a subject that has attracted a great deal of attention among South Africa's conservation-minded citizens over the last century or so. Where the charismatic lion is concerned, public opinion has swung the full spectrum from abhorrence to adoration. It took experience and a willingness to change his mind to transform James Stevenson-Hamilton's perception of the big cat's status. On reconnaissance patrols through Sabi Game Reserve, he concluded that there were too many lions and other predators, which, he noted, had been little affected by the profligate hunting and rinderpest pandemic that had ravaged the herbivore populations.

Initially he supported calls for carnivore control to protect prey species. During his early years as an avid sport hunter and later when culling carnivores was the order of the day in Sabi, Stevenson-Hamilton personally shot, by his own reckoning, over 150 lions. He made the conversion from hunter to protector soon after arriving at Sabi, and it was here that his powers of intelligent observation led to the firm conviction that nature functions as an entity and has its own regulatory system, which is best served by a hands-off relationship with humans.

'Left to themselves carnivora never increase out of due proportion to the game on which they prey, as is sometimes ignorantly stated,' he wrote in the 1940s. 'I have always felt that Nature is able to manage her affairs better than Man can do it for her, and, where possible, have worked on that conception. It may have been a mistake to try to keep down the carnivorous animals in the days of the Sabi Game Reserve, but it was a policy forced upon us by circumstances.'

LIONS AS WILDLIFE MANAGERS

In the days of the Sabi Game Reserve, when predatory animals were destroyed as a matter of routine, it was discovered that lions could barely be kept static in numbers. So easy was it for them to catch their prey, that a lioness was accustomed to produce cubs at about twice the normal rate; in place of the usual two or three, she brought forth as many as four or five in a litter; while of these, instead of one or two only, probably all, or nearly all, were able to survive to maturity. When, after the inauguration of Kruger National Park, it was decided to permit Nature, so far as possible, to take her course, the same accelerated rate of increase tended to persist, until entire prides of twenty or more, mainly cubs and half-grown animals, were by no means unusual. Presently, as the game began to lose the unnatural advantage which it had hitherto enjoyed, it was noticed that the younger lions were often in poor, even emaciated condition, that cubs were dying, and that the number of lions of all ages, especially young animals, slain by their companions, was greatly increasing. The reason, of course, was obvious. A large party of lions would kill, for example, a wildebeest. The old members would devour the whole of it at one sitting, while the younger would either have

to stand aside still hungry, or pay the supreme penalty for trying to help themselves unasked. A ranger once found no less than five young lions, their mature teeth not yet fully developed, slain by their companions round the remains of a kill. It seems, therefore, that Nature is trying again to adjust her balance, temporarily upset by human effort.

James Stevenson-Hamilton

Thirty years later, George Schaller, the doyen of East African lion researchers, broadly concurred with Stevenson-Hamilton's assessment. 'Predators are the best wildlife managers,' he concluded in his classic study of predator–prey relations. 'The predators weed out the sick and old, they keep herds healthy and alert ... They help maintain an equilibrium in the prey populations within limits imposed by the environment ... To this task they bring a discernment that cannot be matched by man.'

By influencing population dynamics, behaviour and evolutionary processes, large carnivores affect their prey and even one another in a number of different ways in space and time. Although predation may not necessarily be the dominant force influencing prey numbers, it is an integral component of these relationships. By not addressing, or realising, the complexity of that reality, Sabi Game Reserve and, for a time, the Kruger adopted a policy that mandated the destruction, although not the eradication, of a daunting list of carnivores and others. The targeted species included lions, leopards, cheetahs, wild dogs, hyaenas, jackals, caracals, servals, civets, genets, polecats, African wild cats, honey badgers, otters, poisonous snakes, pythons, eagle owls, hawks, eagles and even baboons, porcupines and bushpigs. Over 18 000 animals were shot, trapped or poisoned as opportunity presented until 1933; thereafter only large mammalian carnivores and crocodiles were killed.

Records show that between 1902 and 1969 the official number of lions killed inside the park was 3 031, although this figure does not include those poisoned or wounded and never found, so it is safe to assume that a minimum total of around 4 000 lions were killed in the park over the 67 years. It is estimated that a further 1 000 to 2 000, or 15 to 30 a year, were killed outside the park's boundaries.

In 1926 the Parks Board decided that no more lions were to be shot 'for the time being'.

But a new way of thinking about carnivores, particularly big cats, came about once tourists started arriving in the Kruger. Almost immediately lions shot to the top of the must-see list. A sign of the changing times is illustrated by two meetings regarding lion culling that took place 50 years apart. In 1926 the Parks Board decided that no more lions were to be shot 'for the time being'. In light of later events, it is ironic that board members agreed that the general public should not be informed of the decision because of the anticipated uproar when it was learnt that 'vermin' was being mollycoddled. Another lion-culling programme in the 1970s was also kept quiet by park authorities, but this time to shield themselves from the fickle public's outrage that 'magnificent' lions were doomed. On this occasion the secret got out and ignited a firestorm of fury.

Decades of officially sanctioned slaughter seem to have had little effect on the overall lion population, however. In 1956 a comprehensive survey found that the Central District's lion population had climbed to around 425. By 1963 it was estimated there were over 1 000 lions in the park, with approximately 375 in the Northern District, 500 in the Central District and 200 south of the Sabie River. Twenty years after the 1956 survey, Senior Research Officer Butch Smuts counted an additional 12 prides in the Central District that had colonised areas around recently installed boreholes and dams. He calculated that the Central District's lion population had almost trebled in 50 years, from 250 in 1925 to over 700 – living in 60 prides, with a density of 13 lions per 100 square kilometres – by 1975. This was due, he correctly believed, to an increase in sedentary prey congregating around a greatly increased number of artificial waterholes. That situation presented lions with unprecedented hunting opportunities. Their predatory success was linked to a steep decline in the Central District's wildebeest and zebra herds during a succession of particularly wet years in the 1970s (see Chapter 3, page 58). Good management requires that, once a threatened population is identified, the second stage is to assess the circumstances accurately and devise an appropriate plan to aid recovery. This process led to mounting pressure from some officials to cull large numbers of lions and hyaenas to relieve pressure on the wildebeest and zebras.

An experimental cull was authorised to remove lions and hyaenas from one small area in the Central District and hyaenas only from another.

Butch Smuts had been staggered to discover that in the Central District the number of lions to prey was one to 110. That was the lowest number of prey relative to lions he had heard of in any large African reserve. To stem the alarming drop in zebra and wildebeest numbers he considered it critical to learn whether predators were severely impacting foals and calves, as was suspected. An experimental cull was authorised to remove lions and hyaenas from one small area in the Central District and hyaenas only from another. All scientific material yielded by the operation was to be collected and documented. At one stage up to 20 people were weighing, measuring, skinning and eviscerating culled animals in the field. Skulls were cleaned for age estimates, reproductive material and tissue samples preserved, internal and external parasites collected, while a team of veterinarians conducted post-mortem examinations.

At the same time, wildebeest and zebra counts were under way in four study areas.

After the cull, the continuing counts indicated that there was a significant increase in the zebra foal survival rate in the area where both lions and hyaenas had been removed. Where hyaenas only had been culled and in the two non-culling control areas, foal survival remained low. Lions, it was apparent, were focusing on baby zebras under a year old. By contrast, wildebeest calves in all four areas showed similar survival rates. That meant lions were not selectively hunting young wildebeest, but taking from all segments of the population. So, though lions kill similar numbers of wildebeest and zebras in the Kruger, the impact on wildebeest is more profound despite their higher birth rate, because losing adults that contribute to reproductive output has a greater effect on a population than the loss of young, which can be replaced quickly.

Further data were provided by analysis of the stomach contents of the 252 culled lions. In spite of the good hunting conditions, 48 per cent of the stomachs were empty. The remainder contained 10 different prey species. Impalas topped the table at 30 per cent but, though strongly represented numerically among lion prey, impalas make a lesser dietary contribution on account of their smaller size. Being sedentary, however, impalas may have a somewhat greater influence on where lion prides can establish year-round residence than the more mobile wildebeest, zebras and buffaloes. Next came wildebeest at 24 per cent, followed by giraffes (15 per cent), zebras (11 per cent), warthogs (eight per cent), waterbucks (five per cent), and kudus and buffaloes (two per cent each). A goat that must have strayed in from outside the park, porcupines and an unidentified animal contributed the remaining three per cent. Statistical analysis based on each animal's size revealed that giraffe meat made up the greatest bulk of the lions' diet (43 per cent), followed by wildebeest (23 per cent) and zebra (15%). Zebra and wildebeest remains found in hyaenas appeared to have been scavenged from lion kills, except for calves and foals, which presumably were killed by the hyaenas themselves.

Lionesses may give birth to up to four cubs but litters of two or three are more common. Cubs start eating meat at about six weeks old but continue suckling until they are six to seven months old.

In 1974/5 the lion cull was expanded to the Stolsnek and Sithungwane areas in the Southern District to allow newly released mountain reedbucks and oribis to establish, while in the Mnondozi area a predator cull was initiated to ease pressure on the Central District's last herds of tsessebes. It was decided that the major tsessebe range would be kept completely free of lions by periodic culling operations and hyaenas would be reduced by 50 per cent during the first cull only. Concern was also expressed about the declining sable antelope population in the Central District's western Manzimahle region. Here the plan was to cull one entire pride and half of another. The survivors were marked and only they were allowed to remain in the area, the idea being to reduce the lion density to an artificially fixed level. Again, the hyaena population was reduced by 50 per cent. In all, lion and hyaena culling operations were carried out over 40 per cent of the Central District's 5 560-square-kilometre total area, or 11 per cent of the entire park, and accounted for the deaths of 335 lions, or about 112 per year between December 1974 and early 1978. That is far fewer than the number of cubs born annually in the Central District, which means it would have been necessary to cull a much higher number to reduce the lion population significantly. Between 1974 and 1977, 297 spotted hyaenas were also culled. Unsurprisingly but certainly unfortunately, the hyaena deaths went unmourned by the general public.

This was the first lion cull in the Kruger since the 1950s, when 450 were shot, and it would be the last. In the end, the objectives of the cull were not realised; the removal of hundreds of lions and hyaenas failed to halt the decline in wildebeest and zebra numbers. That was achieved by a return to a drier climatic phase, whereupon the lions gradually shifted their prey selection to buffaloes in particular, plus waterbucks and kudus. The exercise rammed home the message that controlling large carnivores in the hope of promoting healthy predator–prey relationships is futile as long as the prey base persists and opportunities for recolonisation from surrounding regions exist. It also reinforced Stevenson-Hamilton's contention that well-meaning intervention, even in such a relatively simple ecological equation as lion-eats-zebra, often causes more problems than leaving things alone to sort themselves out.

Butch Smuts was also astonished by the speed of reoccupation of territories in which lions had been reduced. Of the three culled areas in the Central District, the first, comprising 380 square kilometres, recovered to 90 per cent of its pre-control levels within 17 months as a result of immigration and the survivors' higher birth rate. Natural increase and lions dispersing from unaffected areas resulted in a 97 per cent reoccupancy within just 15 months in the second area of 600 square kilometres, while the third area of 95 square kilometres took eight months to recover to 79 per cent of prior occupancy. Their amazingly speedy bounce-back led Smuts to conclude that culling lions was like taking a bucket of water from a pool: the space was quickly filled.

Lion density is related to the amount of prey available to eat, which depends on the amount of vegetation, which in turn depends on the soil and rainfall, but working out more precisely how many lions there are in the Kruger has never been an easy task.

These two pride males were patrolling their territory when they suddenly spotted a reedbuck nearby and immediately rushed it. The antelope instinctively hid behind a clump of grass but it was a fatal miscalculation – by the time it realised its mistake it was already too late.

Counting them from the air does not work, as typically lions are lying-up in shade and cover by mid-morning. Most previous estimates were based on Butch Smuts' 1970s count in the Central District. Extrapolating from his figures and other data, a frequently quoted estimate for the park as a whole had been about 2 000. That turned out to be an over-estimate according to the first park-wide lion census, completed in 2006, which estimated that there are 1 600 lions in the Kruger, give or take 225 animals.

Led by Paul Funston from Tshwane University of Technology and Sam Ferreira from the Conservation Ecology Research Unit in Pretoria, the survey was carried out during the winter months of 2005 and 2006. The operation demonstrated what huge commitment it takes to study lions. It is much less exciting than most people might expect – for every highlight there are hours of boredom. 'Lions are supremely adept at doing nothing,' Craig Packer and Anne Pusey discovered while researching the Serengeti's lions. 'To the list of inert noble gases, including krypton, argon and neon, we would add lion.' To obtain the Kruger count's time-consuming results, two Tshwane students, Andrei Snyman and Hennie de Beer, spent many cold nights sitting inside a steel cage on the back of a bakkie waiting for lions to turn up at loudspeakers broadcasting a buffalo calf's distress calls.

During the census 422 lions visited 229 calling stations scattered throughout the park and a further 273 lions were spotted as the researchers went about their work. No attempt was made to count all the lions in the park; instead a sampling method was used to arrive at a final population estimate. Information was also obtained on age-

Their amazingly speedy bounce-back led Smuts to conclude that culling lions was like taking a bucket of water from a pool: the space was quickly filled.

specific survival and reproduction in order to evaluate population growth rates. To do so, the researchers used a digital camera and laser range finder to record each lion's shoulder height, enabling them to estimate its age. Lions were also scored for body condition on a scale of one to five, with five indicating it looked healthy with lots of muscle tone and mass, four if it was slightly off peak condition, three if it was thin with major bones starting to show through, two if it had not eaten in weeks, and one if it was close to death.

'Over 98 per cent of the lions observed during the survey were either in good or very good physical condition,' Paul Funston noted. The latter finding was particularly pertinent as several emaciated lions had been euthanised over the previous several years after contracting bovine tuberculosis (BTB). 'At this stage we detect no effects of BTB in the Kruger lions in terms of population size and structure [sex and age ratios]. Both are almost identical to surveys done in the central district in the early '70s before BTB is believed to have been present.' However, the Kruger veterinarian Roy Bengis cautions, 'Any impact on lions will possibly only be apparent when the prevalence of BTB in buffaloes and other prey species reaches the same levels as in the south.'

According to the survey, there are 12 to 15 lions per 100 square kilometres in the Southern District's eastern basalts and seven to eight lions per 100 square kilometres in the northeastern basalts. Lion densities in the Kruger's western granite-based landscapes were slightly under the five to six lions per 100 square kilometres in the north and 10 to 12 lions per 100 square kilometres in the south, as anticipated by Funston and Ferreira. 'Lions had never before been surveyed north of the Olifants River or south of the Sabie, so we had to extrapolate from other areas which would have contributed to the slight over-guess,' Funston explained. On average, the Kruger has 12.7 lions per 100 square kilometres while Serengeti has a close 12 lions per 100 square kilometres.

The difference in the Kruger's lion densities is largely determined by prey availability and habitat suitability, as is the size of a resident pride's home range. In the central and southeastern basalt regions, home ranges are around 100 square kilometres, whereas in the drier northern basalt mopaneveld they are about 250 square kilometres. Prides occupy a hunting territory of a size that can sustain them during times of scarcity and, though territories may overlap, each pride maintains a core area where most activities are undertaken, with little interaction with other lions. A lot of territorial behaviour occurs along drainage lines in the Kruger, probably because rivers are often natural borders between home ranges and they offer male lions better hunting opportunities. In both the Kruger and Serengeti the average pride comprises 13 members; the average composition of 14 Kruger prides totalling 181 lions was 1.7 adult males, 4.5 adult females, 3.8 subadults and 2.8 cubs. Adult females are usually related – mothers and daughters, sisters and aunts. They are the core of the pride and stay within the natal range unless there is a scarcity of food, when two-year old females are forced to leave. All males are forced to leave the natal pride at two to three years of age. The number of lionesses in six neighbouring Kruger prides remained constant for two-and-a-half years, even though the actual membership of the prides changed. Each pride seems to support a maximum number of females – if that falls below the capacity for the home range, subadult immigrants may be allowed to join.

All males are forced to leave the natal pride at two to three years of age.

Although the survey's findings indicated that the Kruger's lion population has changed little over the past few decades, ecosystems are inherently dynamic and it is only through long-term studies that the full spectrum of ecological adaptations and population cycles can be appreciated. Much of the mortality in ungulate populations is attributable to predation, and possibly most populations are limited in this way, especially those that are both resident and occur at low densities in large, closed, actively managed parks like the Kruger. The Kruger's complex multi-species predator–prey systems are further complicated by the often extreme fluctuations in environmental conditions. This strongly influences the selective way in which lions choose their prey, which in turn has a marked influence on prey populations. Using records of animal deaths over 35 years, Norman Owen-Smith investigated the vulnerability of 12 lion-prey species in relation to the Kruger's changing seasons. His data revealed that buffaloes, kudus and giraffes were more likely to fall prey during the late dry season, while wildebeest and zebras were more vulnerable in the wet season. Impalas, waterbucks, warthogs and rarer antelopes became more prominent in kills during transitional periods between seasons.

In times of drought, herbivore distress allows lions to thrive. In the wake of the extreme 1991/2 drought, lion densities in the northern Kruger rose from one per 30 square kilometres in 1989 to one per nine square kilometres in 1993, as lions benefited from a glut of animals weakened or killed by malnutrition. In a 2006 monograph that documented the many factors influencing the population dynamics of 11 ungulate species in the Kruger over 20 years, large-herbivore expert Norman Owen-Smith and large-carnivore expert Gus Mills found that carcasses of animals vulnerable to predation because of below-average wet season rainfall from 1981 until 1994 effectively doubled the estimated food intake of lions between 1981 and '83, with a further rise after 1987. 'This was due largely to substantial natural mortality among buffalo during the 1982/3 drought and later under the dry conditions of the early 1990s, coupled with the steady increase in zebra and wildebeest abundance [in the northern half of the park]. These three species accounted for about two-thirds of the food base for lions.'

In times of drought, herbivore distress allows lions to thrive.

As hunters, lions are supreme opportunists with a catholic diet that runs the gamut from birds such as ostriches, bustards, guinea fowls and francolins to reptiles like terrapins, tortoises, pythons and crocodiles, and they will happily partake of the eggs of all of the above. Different prides may have different traditions and preferences of what prey species they favour – one pride in the Kruger made 14 of the 15 porcupine kills observed by Gus Mills. The pride's oldest and presumably wisest lioness led the way, darting in to immobilise the porcupine with a bite or slap on the snout as it attempted to fend off the other lions with a barrier of ominously erected and rattling quills. Killing porcupines is a specialist skill and there are many rangers' tales of emaciated lions with quills lodged in their paws or jaws. Contrary to popular theory, Mills believes that these lions were not disabled by the quills but were already in poor condition due to old age, injury or illness and, driven by hunger but lacking the requisite technique, had attacked the prickly rodent in desperation.

Closely related lionesses form the stable core of the pride, while males are exchanged every few years. Females synchronise reproductive cycles so litters are born at roughly the same time. This allows for co-operative cub raising.

But lions are too big to survive on small prey alone – the energy expended in catching them is not compensated for by the energy gained in eating them, plus a bigger carcass is able to feed more lions, an important consideration for a social cat. Instead, they concentrate on hoofed animals. Wherever lions occur, their diet is dominated by locally abundant ungulates approximately half to twice their weight. Carnivores usually prey on animals smaller than themselves but predators such as lions that hunt in organised groups can take much larger prey. Indeed, prey twice their own weight contributes significantly to the diet of the Kruger's lions, despite a low proportional kill rate, according to Norman Owen-Smith and Gus Mills, who used records of found carcasses and cause of death assembled over 46 years to arrive at an assessment of the size relationships between large carnivores and their ungulate prey. They found 'that ungulates larger than 250 kilograms contribute in aggregate more towards supporting the lion population than species within the favoured size range of 100–250 kilograms.' They also reported that 'the largest carnivore overwhelmingly dominates the large predator guild in Kruger', commandeering 65 per cent of the biomass of prey killed by virtue of its 'predator biomass, as well as by aggressively excluding and frequently killing other carnivores'.

Wherever lions occur, their diet is dominated by locally abundant ungulates approximately half to twice their weight.

In Kruger, warthogs comprise 13 per cent of lion diets but are nonetheless considered non-preferential prey as they are usually only hunted when larger, preferred species have migrated out of a lion pride's territory.

In the Kruger, six species – wildebeest, zebras, buffaloes, impalas, waterbucks and kudus – account for more than 90 per cent of lion kills although, when converted to dietary intake on a weight basis, impalas and similar-sized species constitute only 14 per cent of the food consumed by lions, with the remainder spread fairly evenly across larger prey categories, including giraffes. A study by Paul Funston and Gus Mills, which investigated the influence of lion predation on the population dynamics of common large ungulates in the Kruger, found that lions preyed proportionally most heavily on the resident buffaloes and wildebeest, less so on the semi-migratory zebras and had the least impact on the high-density impala population. 'The selection was largely in accordance with the abundance of the larger species,' the researchers reported, 'but not for impala, which were relatively under-represented.' The researchers also found that male lions preyed more heavily on buffaloes than did lionesses, with females preying mainly on wildebeest, zebras and impalas.

It is popularly believed that lionesses are invariably the active hunters and pride males merely lazy chauvinists that co-opt their kills. In the Serengeti's rolling grasslands it is true that lionesses do the majority of the hunting, while males that tag along usually hang back until a kill is made, but in the Kruger's bushveld male lions are frequent and successful hunters. Based on 679 hunts seen in the Kruger by Paul Funston, Gus Mills, Harry Biggs and Philip Richardson while investigating male lion hunting, it became apparent they kill most of their food rather than scavenging it from lionesses. Indeed, males succeeded in 30 per cent of the observed kills compared with 27 per cent for females, although this difference is negligible when the appropriate statistical tests are applied. The researchers discovered that resident males in the Kruger's savanna woodlands spend less time with pride females than is the case with lions living in more open habitat, tending to hunt in male coalitions. This may be because the Kruger's extra cover gives lionesses with cubs a better chance of hiding them from potentially infanticidal male lion intruders, so pride males invest less time and energy guarding their offspring.

Prey selection, kill frequency and the food consumption rate of male lions also differ from that of females. Buffaloes are the main prey species of all-male groups, particularly non-territorial males. Males also kill impalas – which they often encounter by chance rather than selection as they pass through thicker bush while patrolling territorial boundaries – and warthogs. Lionesses concentrate on wildebeest and zebras in more open country. Hunting success was found to be least for medium-sized prey such as wildebeest, kudus and zebras (20 per cent) but climbed to more than 50 per cent for buffaloes. The conspicuously maned male lions had better hunting success in moderate to dense woody vegetation and in medium to long grass than they did in open and short-grass areas, while female hunting success was significantly affected by grass height but not by shrub cover.

These stalk-and-ambush hunters are built for speed, not for distance. Their legs are fuelled by glycogen, a chemical that releases a concentrated burst of energy but it is short lived. Although they can reach speeds of 45 to 60 kilometres per hour in a rush, they have no stamina and quickly abandon a chase, panting heavily after 100 to 200 metres. So, to catch prey, lions have to be smart tacticians. Nearly 90 per cent of lion kills in the Kruger are made at night when their well-adapted eyes provide them with night vision that is approximately six times better than ours. And for the most part they rely on stalking, using physical features such as vegetation and gullies and rises to approach with cat stealth, chest low, every move sure and purposeful, slipping through the undergrowth with barely a rustle, eyes fixed on the quarry, until within 20 to 30 metres.

However that is not always their hunting scenario. Catching impalas and other medium-sized prey is significantly more successful when lions charge immediately on detecting them, relying on surprise to snatch a sick or an old animal, or spook one into stumbling or running in the wrong direction or into an obstacle. Buffalo herds are often followed without any attempt to stalk. African buffaloes are one of the strongest, most aggressive animals in the world and they do not give up easily. Weighing up to 870 kilograms and formidably equipped to defend themselves, they are a daunting adversary and many hunts are foiled by the collective defence mounted by the herd. So the lions' objective is to break up the solid phalanx of horns guarding the young

by panicking the herd into a stampede and then isolating a victim in the confusion. Even then they are not assured of a meal. A herd member's distress bellow will very likely rally the herd, which then hurries back to try to rescue it.

Buffalo and giraffe hunting is where the big males come into their own – it is their burly bodies and extra muscle that allow lions to subdue oversized prey. When hunting the world's tallest animal, lions first trail their quarry behind a shield of darkness, preferably on cloudy or moonless nights when the giraffe can hardly see them approaching. Next the lions encircle the giraffe to within a metre of its hooves. Now the giraffe's only option is to fight. Its back kick is its most lethal, like a fast swinging sledgehammer, but experienced lions have learnt how to weave in and out of the legs to avoid the hoof punch. Working in rotation, some lions move in while others retreat. They get tired but would be exhausted if they did not take turns. Suddenly one springs on the giraffe's back and attempts to bite into the neck vertebrae, while other lions, attacking from behind, try to cripple it. The battle may continue for a while yet but ultimately the giraffe topples whereupon it is strangled or suffocated like most other prey.

One of the most intriguing items to feature on the lion's menu is the biggest herbivore of them all: the elephant. Until recently most people imagined that the elephant's size made it all but invulnerable to predation; this was until Dereck and Beverly Joubert's remarkable TV documentary *Ultimate Enemies* and companion coffee-table book *Hunting with the Moon* (1997) revealed how in Nxwazumba Valley, northeast of Savuti in Botswana's Chobe National Park, a pride centred on a waterhole used by big breeding herds of elephants developed techniques for hunting the largest animals in their range. Once the lions had honed their skills, the Jouberts began seeing more and more elephant hunts.

In 2009 John Power and Shem Companion from the Endangered Wildlife Trust's Carnivore Conservation Group confirmed that Savuti's lions have hunted elephants increasingly frequently over the

In a night capture operation that entailed luring lions to a fresh carcass by playing a recording of a distressed buffalo calf bawling, these researchers darted and collared several lions as part of ecologist Norman Owen-Smith's investigation into how predation risk affects wildebeest habitat selection and abundance.

last 20 years, when their conventional prey migrates away during the late dry season in August to November. They recorded a pride of 30 lions killing one elephant every three nights, with seven out of eight hunts targeting four- to 11-year-olds. A similar situation exists in Zimbabwe's Hwange National Park, where buffaloes, elephants, giraffes, wildebeest and zebras made up 83 per cent of all observed lion kills and 94 per cent of the biomass of kills, according to principal researcher Andrew Loveridge from Oxford University. Elephant calves made up 23 per cent of those kills. Although calves are usually well protected, Loveridge suggests that elephants crowding around limited water sources during the dry season may deplete their food, forcing them to travel long distances between water and forage. At times like these calves can become separated from mothers. Although lions killing elephants has not yet been recorded in the Kruger, just as local lions learnt to hunt buffaloes when they became weakened by drought, so they might learn to hunt elephants as the mighty pachyderms' population continues to grow and they become more stressed and thus vulnerable to big prides' hunting cooperatively. If so, lion predation could become another factor helping to stabilise the Kruger's elephant population naturally and thus do away with the need to cull.

On Etosha's flat, open, semi-arid plains, some lions specialise in catching one of Africa's fastest antelopes, the springbok.

Lions hunting cooperatively bring a greater probability of success but there is a recurring question among scientists as to whether pre-planned cooperation is occurring or if lions are simply making use of opportunities brought about by the presence of other lions. Flip Stander, a field research officer in Namibia's Etosha National Park, has no doubts. On Etosha's flat, open, semi-arid plains, some lions specialise in catching one of Africa's fastest antelopes, the springbok. A single lion would have no chance, so circumstances have forced local lions to develop the art of teamwork to a remarkable degree. Stander draws an analogy between their tactics and a rugby team's strategy, in which the wings circle the prey while the centres wait in place. Each lioness has her own position in the hunting formation. Once the trap is set, the stalking wings charge the springboks and the centres grab them as they flee. Hunts are more likely to be successful when each lioness is in the correct position than when they are not.

A fine example of leonine resourcefulness and inventive ability to make the most of a specific hunting opportunity was demonstrated in the Kruger beginning in the 1940s. As they became accustomed to frequent human contact, lions living along the south bank of the Sabie River east of Skukuza learnt to take full advantage of the slow-moving tourist vehicles to stalk the great herds of impalas that collect each mid-morning during the dry winter months to drink at the river. The lions padded nonchalantly down the middle of the Lower Sabie Road accompanied by cars in front of, behind and on either side of them, which the sagacious big cats artfully used as stalking horses to get close to the always-alert antelopes. The Kruger's impalas are supremely indifferent to the presence of cars, which they associate with noisy visitors but do not consider dangerous, and so were relatively easy to catch for a hunter that suddenly rushed from

Eyes locked on her quarry, a lioness stalks stealthily closer, using all the cover available before a final burst of speed at the end.

behind a rank of vehicles. I saw those lions in action on my first visit to the Kruger as a seven-year-old in the early 1950s. The excitement of the close-up chase left an indelible impression on me, fuelling a boyhood passion to understand more about the lives of wild animals that remains with me to this day. Sadly, shortly after I had been enthralled by those entertaining and enterprising lions and the innovative hunting method they had passed from generation to generation, they were lost when they became part of the 450 lions culled over a five-year period.

Recognising the predatory watchfulness in the terrible intensity of a lion's stare surely accounts for much of the fascination and horror we reserve for those creatures that are capable of eating us. Man-eating tends to be regarded as unnatural but if man-eating lions are not shot at once, the general principle of availability operates for us no less than for any other prey – we become just another flavour of meat. The Kruger has a history of man-eating that almost certainly goes back a long way before that evening in August 1903 when a young ranger named Harry Wolhuter was knocked from his horse by a male lion. Dragged by the shoulder and painfully aware of the lion's loud purrs in anticipation of its meal, Wolhuter nevertheless managed to draw his sheath knife, concentrate his mind, then stab his nemesis with two quick backhand strokes behind the left shoulder and directly into its heart. That feat saved Wolhuter's life but in the Kruger's more recent annals the human victims have not been so fortunate.

Lions, like other predators, instinctively take the easy prey. Just such an opportunity was presented by the thousands of desperate Mozambican refugees fleeing war, famines, plagues, floods and droughts in their own country for the relative safety of South Africa. The Kruger comprises virtually the entire border between the two countries, and its wilderness provided cover for illegal immigrants coming on foot. By 1993, the number of refugees, many of them passing directly through the Kruger, reached an estimated 1.7 million a year. As Zimbabwe's economy imploded, massed numbers of refugees from that benighted country added to those arriving via the northern Kruger. Columns of sick, starving, weak people, some of them dying on their feet, stumbled blindly forward, without caution. Unprotected pedestrians crossing their territory at night understandably triggered new behaviour in the lions they encountered.

The vulnerable refugees were subjected to a leonine reign of terror. Rangers on patrol began finding scraps of bloody clothing in the middle of nowhere, a single shoe, an abandoned suitcase full of possessions, footprints that suddenly just ended. And, occasionally, the remains of consumed corpses. Most of the killings occurred in the north of the park, which has the lightest tourist traffic but had some of the heaviest refugee traffic. Many refugees used the Cahora Bassa power lines to navigate their way westwards across remote and otherwise largely featureless bush country. Some lions, specialising in human prey, began staking out the power lines. One such pride operated in the vicinity of Klopperfontein waterhole, northeast of Punda Maria. They first announced themselves to park officials when they tried to attack field staff on patrol. Shortly afterwards a woman sitting among other staff personnel on a Friday afternoon shopping trip was nearly taken by one of the lionesses from the back of an open truck.

The number of people killed by lions in the Kruger is officially unknown.

Just about everyone working in the Kruger knew what was happening on the refugee trail but not much was said about it. The official policy regarding man-eaters states that if a lion clearly has become a man-eater then it must be shot but if it is not absolutely clear then it must be given the benefit of the doubt. Some say quietly that while most prides in the north may not be full-time man-eaters, many have eaten humans when the opportunity presented. In the case of the Klopperfontein pride, their behaviour marked them as beyond redemption. Park management determined that they had to be destroyed. Writing in *African Lion News* in 2003, Douw Grobler, a SANParks veterinarian at the time, described the lions' reaction to him when he stepped out of his vehicle 30 metres from a zebra carcass he had lured the lions to. 'Normal lions would scatter immediately but these lions saw it as an opportunity to supplement their zebra meat and approached me immediately. My hair stood on end seeing the stare especially from the male and we proceeded to euthanize them. It was a gross sight dealing with the necropsies afterwards as they were filled with human remains, clothing with ID books and purses still intact.'

The number of people killed by lions in the Kruger is officially unknown. No central records were kept and the actual number of deaths must be much higher than the bodies found. Previous to the Kruger experience, the most egregious recorded case of man-eating occurred in the Njombe district of Tanzania between 1932 and '47 when approximately 2 000 people were killed. The Kruger's toll almost certainly exceeds that number. In April 2005 the South African government announced a new policy: Mozambicans and Zimbabweans could enter the country and were not required to have a visa for visits of 30 days or less. It is hoped that now the killings will stop.

9

The secret life of **leopards**

Gentle hunter, his tail plays on the
ground while he crushes the skull
Beautiful death, who puts on a
spotted robe when he goes
to his victim
Playful killer, whose loving
embrace splits the
antelope's heart

Yorùbá oriki (praise poem)

This haunting West African panegyric exquisitely evokes the essence of the leopard – beautiful and terrifying, a perfectly evolved beast of prey, splendid in its savagery. Secretive and silent, it is a creature of the dark and even in darkness it travels alone. A long, muscular body, thick limbs and heavy paws give the leopard an aura of great strength. It combines this potency characteristic of big cats with the versatility and grace of the smaller cats – like many small cat species, it is an agile climber. But even when snoozing in a favourite tree – legs dangling, lethal weapons sheathed, pale green eyes closed against the sun's glare, with only the tip of the tail curling and twitching with a restless spirit of its own – this consummate master of concealment embodies the heart and soul of a hunter.

The riverine thickets, gallery forests and dense reed beds flanking the Kruger's perennial rivers are prime leopard real estate. The year-round bounty of food, water and shelter along the banks of the Sabie River supports more leopards per square kilometre than perhaps anywhere else in Africa. Not that visitors can expect to see many of these elusive predators. Leopards are renowned for organising their lives so as to avoid encounters with people. Unlike lions, they are furtive and solitary, appearing and vanishing like a hallucination. They are cloaked in elegant camouflage that is ideally adapted to the dappled light of forest and bushveld, their cryptic pelt a superb device designed to make leopards invisible to quarry and enemies alike. Patterned with black rosettes that come in an infinite variety of forms, the mottled pelage is a manifestation of that process of genetic winnowing through the millennia known as natural selection. It also sets individual leopards apart – no two sets of markings are alike.

Just how adept a leopard is at avoiding the human gaze was demonstrated to me early one evening as I drove along the Lower Sabie Road on my way back to Skukuza. A couple of hundred metres ahead a leopard suddenly stepped onto the tarmac. It froze the instant it saw me, hesitated and then, crouching low, dodged behind a roadside shrub. I noted where it had disappeared, put the gears into neutral, turned off the engine and quietly glided up to it. Somehow, miraculously, the meagre cover the leopard was hiding behind had caused it to vanish. Any animal with disruptive colouring is difficult to see, particularly if it remains motionless against a suitable background, but this was astonishing. I waited and a minute or so later the cat realised her cover was blown and nonchalantly stood up. After eyeing me for a long moment she proceeded across the road directly in front of my vehicle. I realised that she hadn't been hiding from me out

Leopards are renowned for organising their lives so as to avoid encounters with people. Unlike lions, they are furtive and solitary, appearing and vanishing like a hallucination.

of fear but rather out of habit – she simply didn't want to be seen. That old piece of bush folklore about far more leopards seeing people than are seen got it absolutely right.

Persecuted animals become more secretive and often change their activity patterns to avoid humans; leopards become extremely nocturnal and stay in heavy bush by day. Their wariness is a hangover from generations of armed conflict between our two species. When the chance presented, leopards killed and ate people's sheep, goats, calves, foals, fowls, cats and dogs and occasionally the people themselves. Because they keep such a low profile, leopards are able to live in close proximity to their old enemy. They still kill sheep in the mountains within 100 kilometres of Cape Town and there is a small subpopulation thriving in the Magaliesberg, near Pretoria. A study done in the 1970s discovered that no fewer than 25 leopards roamed within a five-kilometre radius of Skukuza village, with its 1 000 or so permanent staff members. On more than one occasion residents have surprised a leopard in their garden.

Tragically, some meetings have ended fatally. The remains of a Skukuza-based game scout, Salomão Mongwe, were found by a police dog unit in nearby bush, shreds of bite-punctured, blood-smeared clothing evidence of a leopard attack. In 1992, Thomas Rihlamfu, a gate guard at Shingwedzi, was killed and partly eaten by a leopard that entered his room through an open window. The culprit was shot by the regional ranger, Louis Olivier, no more than 10 metres from the gate. While escorting a group of tourists, Charles Swart, a night-drive guide stationed at Berg-en-Dal rest camp, stopped at Matsulwane Bridge for a smoke break just as he and other guides did whenever they came this way. It was very probably the predictability of their routine that set up the leopard's ambush. Silently it stalked up behind him in the darkness, sprang onto his back and killed him instantly with a crushing bite to the neck. The only sound the tourists heard was the clatter of his rifle as it dropped to the road. It was not long afterwards that a Skukuza resident, Kotie de Beer, was killed by a leopard with the same neck-vertebrae-crushing bite while on an afternoon stroll through the village. Again the victim was alone and the path she took was popular with walkers.

> **In 1992, Thomas Rihlamfu, a gate guard at Shingwedzi, was killed and partly eaten by a leopard that entered his room through an open window.**

In turn, leopards have been hunted relentlessly. In the Sabi Game Reserve, starting in 1903, leopards were part of a carnivore-control programme initiated to protect prey populations, but they did not make it easy for those bent on their destruction. 'Had we to depend upon fair shooting alone to keep down the increase of so stealthy and elusive a member of the cat tribe as the leopard, failure would certainly have attended our efforts,' James Stevenson-Hamilton conceded. Instead, leopards were targeted using

packs of dogs to bring them to bay. They were also caught in baited iron-jawed traps attached by a chain to a fallen branch to slow the enraged animal's inevitable charge when it was followed up by rangers. Between 1903 and 1927, the on-again-off-again anti-predator campaign resulted in the deaths of at least 660 leopards.

This leopard's long tail helps her balance on the branch and sharp claws give her traction. Leopards are the best tree climbers in the big cat family. Cubs start learning tree-climbing skills as early as three or four months to avoid enemies like lions, hyaenas and wild dogs.

Given that the Kruger's total leopard population is estimated at about 700, 660 may sound like too many dead leopards. In reality, predator reduction policies probably had little impact on the long-term leopard population. Rather than causing an overall drop in density, this form of control creates 'holes' in carnivore distribution, leaving the culled individuals' territories vacant. Since these spaces in the home range mosaic usually offer good hunting prospects with few competitors, they are soon reoccupied. The loss of a resident female is usually compensated for by a young female living on the border of the same range, while a missing male's territory is claimed by a young male emigrating from an adjacent area. Research in the Kruger has shown that leopards, particularly subadults, regularly go on exploratory forays of up to 24 kilometres outside their normal home ranges, presumably looking for better areas. In the natural course of events, when all territories are occupied, there simply is nowhere for newly independent subadults to move to. Without a home they live a harried, marginalised existence, always on the run; hunger and stress soon take their toll. Studies have shown mortalities of over 40 per cent for the Kruger's subadult leopards, with starvation the leading cause of death.

By not being dependent on big game, the leopard has far more entrées on its menu than does the larger-prey-specific lion.

It was largely ecological rather than man-made influences that ultimately determined the Kruger's leopard density. Even before the end of the predator-control era it had become apparent that the leopard population self-regulated by means of a stable number of breeding adults and an adequate food supply. Whether measures to limit their numbers were severe or relaxed, the park's leopard population curve fluctuated primarily due to favourable or poor hunting conditions – nothing affected the fate of the Kruger's leopards more than the population swings of their principal prey, the impala.

While leopards show distinct preferences in their prey selection, they also have the most diverse diet of all African cats. In the Kruger they are known to prey on at least 32 species and 24 in Serengeti, while over the whole of sub-Saharan Africa their hunting tally exceeds 100 species, from winged termites and frogs to the calves of giraffe and eland. Just how flexible a leopard's diet can be was demonstrated by Nairobi University graduate Patrick Hamilton's 1974 analysis of leopard scats. Faecal analysis is a valuable method in ascertaining leopard diets, as it registers small creatures like birds and mice that are usually swatted with the paw and swallowed on the spot, something that is seldom seen and leaves no trace. Collected in Kenya's Tsavo West National Park, Hamilton's results showed that 35 per cent of the scats contained rodents, 27 per cent birds, 27 per cent small antelopes, 12 per cent large antelopes, 10 per cent hyraxes and hares, and 18 per cent arthropods, including grasshoppers, centipedes and scorpions. Among the granite koppies of Zimbabwe's Matobo National Park, scat analysis revealed that hyraxes, hares and klipspringers make up more than 50 per cent of leopard kills. Pioneering work in the 1970s and '80s on the range and diet of leopards in various Western Cape mountain habitats by Cape Nature Conservation field researcher Peter Norton turned up similar results. Here leopards average half the size of their Kruger cousins because, Norton suggests, their prey is much smaller. These leopards are also mainly diurnal to coordinate with their diurnal hyrax and small antelope prey.

By not being dependent on big game, the leopard has far more entrées on its menu than does the larger-prey-specific lion. In difficult times a leopard may depend heavily on locally abundant small prey and this is reflected in the richness of its diet, which extends to spiders, snakes, lizards and fishes – one leopard, stranded on an island by Kariba Dam's rising waters, subsisted by fishing for tilapia even though impala and duiker were present in low numbers. Its diet also includes shrews and gerbils – 3 900 metres up Kilimanjaro, leopard diets consist mainly of rodents. They will eat hares, spring hares, hyraxes, warthogs, bushpigs, chimpanzees, gorillas, jackals, lion cubs, cheetahs, civets, genets and pangolins, and occasionally resort to cannibalism. Birds – from turtle doves to ostriches – are preyed on, with guinea fowls and francolins regularly recorded. Some leopards select truly unusual prey. An astonishing sequence of images by wildlife photographer Hal Brindley show a big male dragging a grown crocodile, tumbling and thrashing, from Silolweni Dam, south of Tshokwane, before suffocating the mighty reptile and hauling it into thick bush to eat. Later I was told by a ranger that particular Kruger leopards are thought to specialise in hunting crocodiles.

Though a hungry leopard will take virtually whatever food is on offer, it is not a non-selective predator as has been suggested in the past. Preferred prey varies between different individuals and regions but it tends to be locally abundant medium-sized ungulates in the 10- to 40-kilogram range, with an optimum weight of around 23 kilograms. Although capable of killing larger prey, they seldom do so. It seems they focus on prey in a specific size class rather than a specific species. When a species killed falls within the large-class size, it invariably involves calf or juvenile ungulates. For example, all eland and wildebeest kills reported in a Zimbabwe study were calves, as were all gemsbok, hartebeest and wildebeest kills recorded in the southern Kalahari. Prey preferences are based partly on what a leopard learns from its mother and partly after hard-won experience has taught it to hunt those animals that provide the most benefit for the least effort or danger.

Juveniles and smaller prey species are clearly under-represented, as often they are eaten without leaving a trace.

Until the second half of the last century the leopard remained an enigma to science, but since then there has been a magnificent leap in the understanding of the spotted cat's ecology. An important advance occurred in the 1960s with a breakdown of the Kruger's large mammal predator–prey relationships by park biologist Tol Pienaar. In an exhaustive piece of interpretation, Pienaar analysed carcass returns of 46 181 kills by 13 different predator species submitted by field staff from 1933 to 1946 and 1954 to 1966. His overview provides a complex and fascinating tale of what goes on in the wild.

In terms of actual numbers of prey killed, Pienaar's statistics revealed that the Kruger's leopards ranked second only to lions in their impact on the prey community. The 5 487 leopard kills recorded represented one in six of all the animals killed during the full survey period. During that time, as the leopard population increased, their share rose from one in 10 to almost one in four.

Admittedly, there are methodological problems in determining the relative numbers of different species taken by any predator, especially when kill data are gathered by analysing the remains of kills, as data are biased in favour of large species and adults. Juveniles and smaller prey species are clearly under-represented, as often they are eaten without leaving a trace. Subsequent analyses, with built-in corrections to compensate for this bias, plus studies based on direct observations, showed that a higher proportion of small antelopes are killed in the Kruger and adjoining Sabi Sand Private Game Reserve than was at first realised. But despite errors that crept in due to unadjusted figures, Pienaar's examination of the Kruger's leopard–prey relationship presents penetrating insights into an aspect of the spotted cat's ecology that until then had received only cursory attention.

'There are today [1969] more leopards in [the Kruger] than at any stage since its proclamation,' Pienaar observed. Since leopard numbers correlate with prey abundance, Pienaar was able to report that 'the leopard population has increased over recent years parallel to their most important prey species – impala'. Due to changes in the fire regime during the survey period, the Kruger had undergone a rapid expansion of its bush cover, providing the type of habitat in which impalas thrive. They had responded by increasing exponentially until they made up well over half the prey mammals in the park. Thickening vegetation also meant more stalking cover for leopards, an important factor for a big cat that relies on getting exceedingly close to its quarry before pouncing. A 1970s study showed that, of 50 kills recorded in the Kruger, 46 per cent were found in dense riverine vegetation, 44 per cent in medium to dense thornbush thickets and only 10 per cent in open habitats. The stage was set for a leopard population boom, which has subsequently stabilised.

Annually, leopards accounted for 34 per cent of all predator-killed impalas, Pienaar discovered. That is more impalas than were killed by any other predator, including lions. Impalas comprised 77 per cent of the leopards' overall diet, although that varied from 92 per cent in Skukuza's acacia woodlands – where impala densities are very high – to only 53 per cent in the Punda Maria sandveld, where there are fewer impalas. So attuned are they to their favourite prey that most leopard births in the Kruger coincide with the early wet-season arrival of impala fawns in November and December. Over 80 per cent of leopard cubs are born at this time, when stalking cover is at its thickest, baby antelopes abound and the hunting is good. Cubs arriving outside the peak birth period have a significantly higher mortality rate.

Despite impalas making up the bulk of the leopard's diet, when looking at the preference rating for each prey species – arrived at by dividing the kill frequency per species by the relative abundance of that species – Pienaar discovered that, although

A baby leopard – its fur still a dull, smoky grey with its spots not yet clearly delineated – is groomed by its mother. During the first eight months of life, cubs remain hidden in the den when the mother is away hunting and only venture out to play when she returns.

the bushbuck comprised only four per cent of leopard kills, it came out on top because of its relative scarcity. It was followed by waterbuck and reedbuck, with impala only ranking fourth. Pienaar believed that impalas were a buffer species, reducing leopard predation on other, less numerous ungulates such as bushbucks. He also found that the leopard is the Kruger's most important predator of the common duiker, bushbuck, steenbok, Sharpe's grysbok, reedbuck, nyala, klipspringer and primates.

Contrary to popular belief, baboons are not high on the leopard's menu, although they are the only predators in the Kruger actively to hunt primates. Pienaar's analysis of predator-killed carcasses shows that only one in 100 leopard kills is a baboon. Pienaar also attributes over 77 per cent of baboon kills in the Kruger to leopards, which may at first seem counterintuitive but simply reflects the very small impact predation from any source has on the baboon population. When leopards do stalk baboons, it is invariably at night when the cats' huge pupils and the light-reflecting cells within their eyes give them a distinct advantage. Rather than defend themselves as they do during the day, the baboons retreat to the outer branches of the highest trees in an attempt to escape. In daylight hours, on the other hand, leopards are all too aware of the adult male baboons' formidable canine teeth and the troop's highly effective defence system, to attack anything other than stragglers. 'Occasionally however, a leopard is driven to rashness by hunger and attempts to snatch one out of a troop in broad daylight,' Pienaar recounts. 'In such cases a number of big male baboons will usually come to the aid of the shrieking victim and in the ensuing free-for-all the leopard is often severely wounded or torn to pieces by the enraged primates.' Young leopards sometimes pursue vervet monkeys through the branches from tree to tree with remarkable success, but adults are too heavy and must learn to ignore the abuse hurled by the monkeys from the safety of the treetops. The Kruger's leopards probably hunt primates only when larger prey animals are scarce. So, though leopards are the main enemy of baboons and vervets, that does not make them the leopard's main prey.

Almost 40 years after the publication of Tol Pienaar's vital statistics, ecologists Norman Owen-Smith and Gus Mills extended the database to cover the period between 1954 and 2000. The authors' summary of assorted carcasses killed by various predators in the Kruger over the whole period show that 12 336 out of 49 453 total kills were the work of leopards. That is 25 per cent of all kills or slightly less than half the kills made by lions. Broken down according to prey species, the Kruger study using carcass records found that impalas made up 76 per cent of leopard kills, while bushbucks and reedbucks together accounted for eight per cent, the same as steenbok and duikers combined. In MalaMala, where safari guides have kept detailed records of wildlife sightings since 1988, Frans Radloff and Johan du Toit from Pretoria University found that impalas made up just 48 per cent of 1 452 observed leopard kills, while steenbok and duikers combined went up to 24 per cent and bushbucks to 9.5 per cent. When looked at in relation to the number of prey killed relative to their availability, Owen-Smith and Mills found that leopards actively select smaller antelope species inhabiting denser woody vegetation, notably bushbucks and duikers, with impalas next.

The Kruger's leopards probably hunt primates only when larger prey animals are scarce.

A huskier build – Kruger males weigh in at an average 60 kilograms as opposed to a female's 35 kilograms – together with a massive skull that provides ample room for the attachment of powerful jaw muscles means male leopards typically take heavier prey than do females. This marked sexual dimorphism[1] might be an adaptation for different food habits between the sexes. In their MalaMala study, Radloff and Du Toit found that the median prey type for a male leopard was an adult female bushbuck (average weight 34 kilograms), while for a leopardess it was an adult duiker (25 kilograms). In the Kruger, adult males are estimated to kill an average five kilograms per day and consume 3.5 kilograms, while adult females kill and consume an average four kilograms and 2.8 kilograms per day respectively.

Included in the leopard's menu, but by no means the rarest item, is carrion. Leopards are inveterate scavengers and will readily eat meat other than their own kills, no matter how rotten. Their attraction to a cache of smelly meat means that they can be caught relatively easily in baited cages, which proved a boon to wildlife biologist Ted Bailey. Starting in 1973, he trapped 30 leopards 112 times as part of an intensive three-year leopard research project in the southern Kruger that to date remains the most comprehensive profile of the park's notoriously unobtrusive big cat. Adapting methods he had used to study bobcats in his native Idaho, Bailey mounted radio transmitters on collars and fastened them around the necks of 24 of the trapped leopards. He then released them and using an antenna picked up signals that tracked their direction and approximate distance. It was one of the first field studies in Africa to use radio-telemetry and it enabled Bailey to follow closely his collared leopards' movements and activities. Combined with direct and indirect observations plus capture-mark-recapture techniques, radio tracking provided him with a detailed account of leopard population dynamics, age and sex ratios, reproduction, mortality, territory size and characteristics, daily and seasonal movements, the leopard's role as predator and its relationships with other large predators.

The setting for the study comprised two contrasting sites: his 17-square-kilometre Sabie River study site lay between two perennial rivers and supported high concentrations of wildlife during the dry season; the second, nearby site, was an 81-square-kilometre block bisected by the ephemeral Nwaswitshaka River, which, because of its seasonal lack of water, supported a prey biomass 15 per cent lower than the Sabie River site. To investigate the leopard's role as predator, Bailey collected a considerable amount of interpretative information, as visual observations were for the most part not possible. To do so he adopted a dual approach. The amount of small prey in his study leopards' diet was arrived at by scat analysis. He located larger kills by stalking radio-collared leopards on foot. In the beginning the latter method proved heart-stopping work. Even with a constant radio signal indicating the precise location, it was often impossible to see the cat. But he soon discovered that leopards immediately fled – invariably before he saw them – when approached within 80 metres on foot.

To avoid losing their meals to larger carnivores, Bailey's leopards cached 84 per cent of their large kills in trees, sometimes as high as 11 metres; favourite storage trees in his study areas were tamboti and jackalberry. Hauling a heavy deadweight up a vertical tree trunk requires enormous strength, and kilogram-for-kilogram the leopard is almost certainly the most powerful of all cats. Lowveld pioneer Bill Sanderson once saw a disembowelled giraffe calf, which could not have weighed much less than 125 kilograms, lying across a four-metre-high branch – no mean feat considering that Bailey's two heaviest collared male leopards topped the scales at 70 kilograms while the largest female weighed just 43 kilograms. Trees also provide leopards with a critical escape route from enemies, which probably accounts for leopards' higher densities compared with cheetahs in the Kruger's multi-predator community.

Bailey found that 57 per cent of trees with cached leopard kills were visited by other predators such as hyaenas, wild dogs, lions and even other leopards. Lions can climb trees and sometimes rob a leopard in this way, but the worst kleptoparasites[2] in the bushveld are hyaenas. They will monitor a leopard's movements and frequently shadow a hunting leopard in the hope of scavenging an easy meal. For all its terrible ferocity, a leopard is well aware that hyaenas are more powerful and that a fight to save its prize would risk its life. The high incidence of hyaenas at leopard kills suggests that these aggressive thieves may have significantly influenced the leopard's prey-caching strategy and its preference for tall tree habitats.

While filming leopards in MalaMala, wildlife cinematographer Dale Hancock witnessed almost as a weekly event hyaenas stealing impala kills before the

A leopard stores larger kills – like this adult impala – in a tree, where it can feed in relative safety. Both lions and hyaenas will take away a leopard's kill if they get the chance.

leopard could tree them. 'These supreme opportunists were very quick to pick up on the fact that if they hung around for long enough, the leopard would catch something … On some evenings, knowing full well that these two [hyaenas] were trailing her, Tjellers [the leopardess] would sometimes catch an impala and hand it over to them without any argument. By the way she reacted, one could tell she was not surprised by their sudden appearance to claim her meal, only seconds after the impalas' alarm calls had filled the air. Knowing they were now preoccupied, Tjellers would leave the scene immediately to move off in search of another meal for herself.' Sometimes the tables are turned, however: one of Ted Bailey's collared male leopards killed and ate at least two hyaenas attracted to his kills. He also found the treed remains of a juvenile hyaena. Yet despite the occasional retaliation, it is probable that the leopard's solitary and concealed behaviour developed as a way of overcoming the costs of competition with bigger, more gregarious predators.

More males were killed in the dry season than the wet and 63 per cent of male impalas killed by leopards were less than two years old.

Bailey's radio-tracking information suggested that healthy male leopards kill one large prey – of which 87 per cent were impalas – about once a week, a total of 45 impala-sized antelopes a year. Impalas selected were mainly subordinate males and older females. More males were killed in the dry season than the wet and 63 per cent of male impalas killed by leopards were less than two years old. Bailey believes that male impalas become vulnerable to leopard predation during the dry season rut when subordinate males are evicted by territorial rams from their territories on the Sabie River's open brackish flats and forced into dense grewia thickets, which provide leopards with excellent stalking cover. Of all female impalas killed, 81 per cent were adults, although adult females made up only 61 per cent of the population. Bailey notes that older females become vulnerable during lambing when they retire to dense, leopard-friendly bush to give birth in seclusion and afterwards hide their newborn.

Leopards are also particularly successful at ambushing prey. Bailey once followed warthog tracks in a muddy road to where one of his radio-collared male leopards had been waiting in 70-centimetre-high grass. Signs at the kill indicated the warthog had walked within three metres of the hidden cat before he attacked. Bailey found that 28 per cent of leopard kills were near game trails where the hunter had waited for prey on their way to a waterhole. Despite their seeming hunting prowess, however, he reports that leopards are not particularly successful at capturing prey. If only his visual observations are considered, just two (16 per cent) of 13 stalks were successful. Other studies suggest a slightly improved 20 per cent of attempts succeed. Yet leopards seem indifferent to failure and are just as quick to abandon a hunt as initiate one. With so little energy expended on the short missed charge – leopards will chase fawns but rarely adults – they simply resume the search for new opportunities.

The Kruger's leopards are largely, but not exclusively, nocturnal hunters. Bailey found that the highest rates of daytime activity were recorded when leopards stalked impalas feeding in thorn thickets during the wet season. Generally, however, they are most active between sunset and sunrise and kill more prey at this time. Nightfall also provided Bailey with his most rewarding observations. Leopards displayed more confidence at night, allowing his vehicle to approach closer than during the day and they quickly became conditioned to his spotlight. 'Seeing a leopard at night is more rewarding and exciting, in my opinion, than in daytime. During the day, leopards are usually resting or inactive. During the night they are usually on the move or stalking prey. Adding to the excitement is the suddenness with which leopards appear out of the darkness. At night they are truly observed in their own element.' Ever the statistically minded scientist, Bailey calculated that although less than 25 per cent of the distances he drove on tourist roads were after dark, 36 per cent of all leopard sightings occurred then, with an average of 530 kilometres between each daytime observation compared with 310 kilometres for each one at night.

'Slowly travelling at night along roads or tracks used by leopards as travel routes is an exciting experience,' Bailey enthused. Indeed, roads are such popular travel routes for leopards that they use culverts and bridges as territorial signposts and anoint them with urine, anal sac secretions and faeces. Leopard scent could be detected for up to a month, he noted, and the average interval between new scrapes was 26 days. The importance of these rigorously scent-marked sites in demarcating territorial boundaries and advertising the condition of females in oestrus was apparent by the frequency with which they were visited by neighbouring leopards.

A LEOPARD WATCHER'S FIELD NOTES

A page from Ted Bailey's field notes gives an insight into the life of a leopard watcher on what was undoubtedly a particularly eventful evening.

Lower Sabie Road, 6:00 p.m. to 6:55 p.m. A leopard sits on the edge of the road looking into the darkness ... Suddenly at 6:15 the leopard jumps up, looks behind and crosses the road. Slowly it stalks into the vegetation and within two minutes the night is filled with piercing squeals and rattling sounds. Driving to where the leopard disappeared, I focus my spotlight on the leopard wrestling a ratel [honey badger] in its mouth and front paws. The back of the ratel's scalp has been bitten off. There are deep bleeding wounds on the leopard's chest and front legs [inflicted by the ratel's long, sharp foreclaws]. In the struggle the leopard releases the ratel, which runs away squealing loudly and running erratically in circles. The leopard does not pursue the ratel but spends the next ten minutes licking its wounds. While cleaning itself, the leopard becomes alert again and stalks into the darkness in the opposite direction taken to the ratel. Several minutes later I see the leopard standing over a freshly killed civet.

Bailey's data confirmed that leopards are solitary animals except during mating or when a female is accompanied by juveniles. 'All monitored leopards, regardless of age, sex or degree of home range overlap, were usually at least one kilometre from their nearest radio-collared neighbour during the day.' Scent-marking and their characteristic wood-sawing vocalisations – which sounds like a piece of wood being sawn with short, sharp double strokes – were important means to bring animals together for mating or to space out rivals so as to reduce the chances of aggressive encounters. Sawing can carry for two to three kilometres under favourable conditions and, though leopards do not vocalise frequently, it is the call most often heard, usually in the early evening, just after sunset, and more often during the dry season. Female calls differ from males'; females have more strokes per call, more calls per calling session and longer intervals between calls, as well as longer total calling periods. Bailey was able to identify individual leopards he was tracking by their calls and it seems probable that leopards also recognise the calls of neighbouring animals.

Caught in the spotlight, a Kruger leopard at night is truly seen in its element. Primarily nocturnal, it usually rests during the day in a tree or thick bush. At night a leopard is more confident and more active and it is then that it does most of its hunting.

During his study, Bailey found that territories of male leopards overlapped, sometimes completely, the territories of as many as six resident females. Meetings between individuals occurred most frequently between males and females intent on courtship. Oestrus in females averages seven days and mating usually takes place over two to three days, mostly in the late dry season, which coincides with the maximum concentration of impalas. If the female does not mate, oestrus recurs every 20 to 50 days.

In Bailey's Sabie River study site, male territories averaged 28 square kilometres and those of females 18 square kilometres. Female ranges were centred on prey-rich riverine ecozones, while those of males included lower-quality habitat. There was little overlap between male territories. Although Bailey never observed fighting among his study leopards, wounds and old scars on males indicated that fights had occurred. He reported that adult leopards in his study area were sometimes killed by other predators, less often by prey – two per

Illuminated by the camera's flash, the eerie green glow in this leopard's eyes comes from a layer of mirror-like cells at the back of the retina, called the tapetum lucidum, *that collects and reflects light back to re-stimulate the retina's rods. This special night vision adaptation allows a leopard to see extremely well in even the dimmest light, a vital ability for a nocturnal hunter.*

cent of his collared leopards were killed and eaten by crocodiles in the Sabie River – and rarely by other leopards. In Tsavo, Patrick Hamilton recorded a number of fights between territorial males resulting from accidental encounters and, in one case, deliberate interception. However, Hamilton pointed out that contact is clearly avoided within overlapping areas and fights develop only after normal avoidance behaviour has failed. So while the size of the Kruger's leopard population is controlled by the availability of food, the number of breeding adults is regulated by social behaviour.

In the Kruger, 65 per cent of the leopard population are breeding adults, although their mating success rate appears to be low. In Bailey's study sites only two (15 per cent) of 13 suspected matings resulted in the birth of cubs, which is similar to the low 20 per cent conception rate for the Kruger's lions. If a leopardess fails to conceive or loses a litter, she is capable of mating again within 50 days. Those that do conceive have a gestation period of 90 to 105 days and produce an average litter of two or three cubs, with a sex ratio of 1:1. In the Kruger, the interval between successive litters is 16 to 17 months. Inaccessible caves in granite koppies are preferred birth dens but thick vegetation at the bottom of deep gullies and abandoned burrows in the sides of scrub-covered termite mounds are also used. Births peak in the wet season in November and December, providing mothers with more cover to conceal their cubs as well as a plenitude of impala lambs. Cubs are born blind and unable to walk for the first couple of weeks. With their babies so helpless, a single mother faces a dilemma: she needs to protect them from other predators but must also leave them to find food. She tries to reduce the threat from other predators by moving the cubs to a new lair every few days, but sooner or

Cubs that survive suckle for their first 12 weeks, although they start on solids when eight weeks old and are fully weaned at four months.

later she must depart on a hunt, and the outcome is often fatal. Leopard cubs suffer high mortality rates; Bailey estimated that only 50 per cent of all cubs in his study areas lived to become adults, with predation by lions and hyaenas the main cause, although mange also took a toll.

Cubs that survive suckle for their first 12 weeks, although they start on solids when eight weeks old and are fully weaned at four months. In his Cambridge University study on the ecology of asociality[3] in Namibian leopards, Flip Stander noted that, despite their solitary nature, female leopards spend a large proportion of their life with dependent cubs. While monitoring three radio-collared females for seven-and-a-half years in the semi-arid Kaudom Game Reserve and adjoining Bushmanland communal area in northeastern Namibia, he discovered that for 50 per cent of that time they had dependent cubs. However, they did not actually spend long periods in the cubs' company – the mothers were alone for nearly 70 per cent of the time and always hunted alone. 'Surprisingly, larger cubs did not follow females on foraging or wandering trips and were left alone for periods lasting between one and seven days. Females spent more time with suckling cubs than with attending cubs.'

Usually upon capturing prey, Stander's collared females with cubs old enough to follow would eat a little, then return and lead the juvenile to the carcass. At such times a leopard's tail provides a striking visual signal; usually carried limply, the tail of a mother leading young is looped up, exposing the white underside. After the kill was consumed, the juvenile would remain there while its mother set off on another foraging expedition. However, mothers led young only to 75 per cent of recorded kills; the rest, even those over 10 kilograms, were eaten alone. Cubs are fully weaned at four months and from the age of eight months start making their own kills such as squirrels, mongooses, baby scrub hares and impala lambs. Juvenile leopards leave their mother at 13 to 18 months old, shortly before the birth of her next litter.

'Contrary to the belief of most tourists, leopards were observed more often from tarmac roads than firebreak or dirt roads.'

Ecological constraints such as rainfall and prey density determine leopard density, so, in order to estimate the Kruger's total leopard population, Ted Bailey drove throughout the park recording species and numbers of prey along the major roads. The relationship between leopards and prey was then extrapolated to similar areas throughout the park. He arrived at an estimate of 670 leopards for the 1975 dry season, with 28 per cent south of the Sabie River, 49 per cent in the Central District and 23 per cent in the Northern District. Revealingly, he estimated that 50 per cent of the Kruger's leopards inhabited perennial riverine zones, even though this habitat makes up only 16 per cent of the park's total area. In decreasing order, the Sabie, Crocodile, Olifants, Letaba and Luvuvhu rivers appeared to support the highest impala populations and therefore the highest leopard populations.

Bailey assumed that leopard densities were also higher around seasonal rivers, dams and waterholes because prey was more abundant and resident there throughout the year. He calculated the park's overall leopard density at 3.5 leopards per 100 square kilometres, but that varied widely from place to place. In the marginal short grass plains of the Central District and the low-prey density areas in the Northern District, where the biomass of leopard prey is only five to 25 per cent of the prey biomass in the riverine thickets, each leopard may require 23 to 167 square kilometres. In contrast, the high impala density corridor along the Sabie River averaged 9 500 impalas and 30 leopards per 100 square kilometres.

With so much time spent looking for leopards, Bailey naturally has a few tips to pass on to visitors keen to see one for themselves. 'Contrary to the belief of most tourists,' he advises, 'leopards were observed more often from tarmac roads than firebreak or dirt roads.' Most of his observations occurred along two well-travelled roads: the paved roads from Skukuza to Lower Sabie and from Skukuza to Tshokwane, which required driving an average of 188 and 260 kilometres respectively between sightings. 'Leopards along seldom-used firebreak roads were much shyer than those living along well-used tourist roads,' he reports. Population density of leopards, visibility and distribution of prey appeared more important than volume of tourist traffic in observing leopards. 'Few leopards were seen along the Naphe, Kruger, Diospan and Nwaswitshaka Waterhole roads because prey and leopard density were low. Most were seen along riverine areas because it is excellent leopard habitat and because leopards there were conditioned to passing traffic. Along the Lower Sabie Road leopards were often visible in overgrazed areas near the Sabie River.'

The first leopard that one meets in this way, in its wild state and up-close, is a wildlife experience that transcends all others.

The good news for leopard enthusiasts is that, over many persecution-free generations, some of the Kruger's once very timid leopards are shedding their shyness and becoming more tolerant of visitors' vehicles. As happened earlier in the adjoining private game reserves, this is probably due to the advent of guided evening drives that encounter leopards in their own element, at night, and have conditioned some of them to tolerate vehicles. The leopards living along the Lower Sabie Road are particularly well habituated, as is a pretty young female that is often seen lounging in one of the giant sycamore figs that flank Phabeni Spruit where the bridge of the same name crosses the paved road between Satara and Orpen Gate. She will remain patiently in place all day, ignoring the hubbub of cars coming and going until the sun is low on the horizon. Then she starts looking around for something to eat. If there are any impalas or bushbucks in the vicinity, she stealthily descends the tree and, using the parked vehicles for cover, makes her approach. I watched her almost catch an impala ram – if the buck had delayed its escape a second longer he would have left it too late.

But anyone who has spent long hours and days looking for leopards will tell you that searching for them is an uncertain proposition at best. The soundest advice is to drive slowly through prime leopard habitat – riverine woodlands are always a good bet – and hope to chance on one around daybreak or sunset while it is still active. The first leopard that one meets in this way, in its wild state and up-close, is a wildlife experience that transcends all others. As it pads away you are left feeling that you have seen something special, that you are as close to the wild world as it is possible to get while still in a vehicle.

---

1 Sexual dimorphism refers to the distinct difference in size or appearance between the sexes of an animal.

2 A kleptoparasite is an animal that steals food or prey from another animal, especially one with which it habitually lives in close proximity.

3 Asocial means not social, given to avoiding association with others: leopards are asocial and secretive.

10

Bushveld
cheetahs

Hunting conditions for the fleet-footed cheetah are not particularly good over most of the Kruger, except on the marula-knobthorn savannas in the east. This, coupled with the fact that the area supports a high density of competing and predatory lions and hyaenas, explains why Kruger's cheetah population numbers a modest 200. Although this population is in no immediate danger, the park's rangers need to be vigilant and monitor conditions closely.

Gus Mills, *The Complete Book of Southern African Mammals*, 1997

A cheetah has many enemies. While there are tens of thousands of herbivores in the Kruger Park, there is a correspondingly large number of predators living off them, and the relentless competition between predators has created a fine edge to the business of survival. For any cheetah, making a kill is only half the battle – defending it can be even harder. One summer sunrise in Etosha National Park I watched a lone spotted hyaena, alerted by springbok alarm whistles, come loping across a wide open plain near Namutoni towards a mother cheetah and her four nearly full-grown cubs grouped around a freshly slain springbok ewe. The hungry cats hissed and snarled and mock charged the approaching thief, which paid not the slightest heed. Without breaking stride, the hyaena headed straight for the carcass, picked it up seemingly effortlessly and trotted away, while the five furious cats could only look on. A cheetah's delicate build is no match for the hyaena's bulk and powerful jaws. Cheetahs are low in the large predator hierarchy and must avoid conflict with stronger competitors at all costs, as they cannot afford the slightest injury that might interfere with hunting.

Natural selection has refined the cheetah's predatory habits, making it the fastest animal on four legs and one of the most successful hunters in Africa.

Natural selection has refined the cheetah's predatory habits, making it the fastest animal on four legs and one of the most successful hunters in Africa. But its greatest asset comes with genetic sacrifices. It has been said that the cheetah is almost over-specialised – so streamlined for great bursts of speed that it is poorly equipped to fight larger predators. Its small, rounded, aerodynamic head and foreshortened face with big eyes set well forward – the better to focus on prey – allow for increased airflow, but translate into a small mouth with weak jaws and shortened canine teeth too small to use as daggers and certainly no match for a lion, leopard or hyaena's powerful bite. The cheetah's lightweight skeleton keeps it quick and agile, but small bones mean less surface area for muscle attachment and consequently less strength. About 60 per cent of the cheetah's muscle mass is packed onto its backbone where it is used to power a perfectly engineered spine that expands and contracts with enough force to add three quarters of a metre to its stride, allowing it to lunge nearly eight metres in a single bound and to change direction instantaneously when in pursuit of prey. The cheetah's evolutionary arsenal of high-speed skills includes cleat-like, semi-retractile claws. Except for the dewclaw on the cheetah's wrists, the more conventional heavily hooked, very sharp claws of the 'traditional' big cats have given way to specialised claws that act like the spikes on a sprinter's track shoes, giving the cheetah constant traction and the sharpest turning radius of all of Africa's big cats. But they hardly qualify as dangerous weapons.

With so many ruthless competitors around, cheetahs, of necessity, chase fast, kill fast and eat fast – anything else and they risk losing out. Unlike leopards, they are unable to cache their kills in trees; instead they adopt avoidance strategies such as reducing visual and audio cues by killing silently by asphyxiation after a short chase and dragging kills into cover so as not to attract vultures to the carcass. They also hunt mostly during the day when their major competitors are lying up. Most predatory mammals are disinclined to be up and about when the sun is at its brightest and hottest, but cheetahs have an adaptation to handle the harshest sunlight. Dark 'tear' lines running from the corner of their eyes to the corner of their mouth act to dampen the glare like the black grease some athletes smear beneath their eyes when playing in the middle of the day. They are the only cat species that has them.

Once a cheetah has made its kill, it gorges its food as if expecting to be interrupted at any moment. Most large predators eat the soft belly first and the rest at leisure but the cheetah starts with the protein-rich muscle masses on the hindquarters. Using its rear knife-like carnassial teeth, it then shears off meat from the back, limbs and base of the neck. Time permitting, it will eat the heart, liver and kidneys but usually leaves the face, skin, lungs and the rest of the neck untouched and rarely returns to the remains of the kill. Minimising contacts with lions is vital as it is not merely a meal a cheetah risks losing in a hostile encounter – there is a very real danger it could lose its life.

The deliberate killing of weaker carnivores by other species in the same guild has been recognised for some time, but it is only since the early 1990s that it has been fully appreciated what a profound ecological effect this is having. Intensive research has revealed that interspecific competition is the chief cause of natural mortality in both cheetahs and wild dogs and limits their densities to well below their ecological carrying capacity. As recently as the 1970s, the highly respected field zoologist George Schaller could only wonder that 'the cheetah population in the [Serengeti] is surprisingly low

considering the available prey and success the cats have in catching it'. Although sub-Saharan Africa's cheetah population may have been small even at the best of times, a disturbing 1970s report for the IUCN/WWF by environmental scientist Norman Myers indicated that with numbers down to 14 000 Africa-wide –12 000 at the time of writing and listed as vulnerable – they could be genuinely threatened.

A formidable coalition of four cheetah brothers crowds around a freshly caught warthog piglet. These male groups may last a lifetime. If there is a lone male cub in a litter, two or three such cubs may form a group, or a lone male may join an existing group.

Back then, theories as to the cause of the decline abounded. Heavy poaching in East Africa was held to be at least partly responsible – over 1 500 cheetah pelts entered the United States each year in the 1960s to service the spotted-cat fur trade. It was also mooted that outside of protected areas the nervous, shy cheetah was being crowded out of open grassland ranges by mankind and his cattle. Disease was mentioned; Schaller noted that four young cheetahs that had died in Nairobi National Park were infected with feline enteritis, a fatal viral disease. Park biologist Tol Pienaar recorded in the '60s that 'malnourished or vitamin-deficient' cubs were not infrequently found in normal litters in the Kruger. Kruger cheetahs are also prone to a type of mange caused by mites. Associated with stress, this is a rare disease in cats but sometimes develops in newly independent subadult cheetahs struggling to make a living.

Minimising contacts with lions is vital as it is not merely a meal a cheetah risks losing in a hostile encounter – there is a very real danger it could lose its life.

In Kenya and Tanzania, where vehicles are permitted to drive off some game park roads, tourist harassment also came in for a share of the blame. Convoys of mini-buses were accused of spoiling hunting opportunities for cheetahs as they pursued gazelles across the open plains. This inconsiderate behaviour, it was argued, caused cheetahs to die out or move out of suitable national parks and reserves. The controversy was still raging in the 1990s when I spent a prolonged period in Kenya's Masai Mara. The evidence seemed damning: there were twice as many cheetahs in the surrounding Maasai grazing lands as in the park itself, conclusive proof, some folks reasoned, that cheetahs were fleeing the tourist hordes in the Mara for the relative peace and quiet next door. In fact, it was just another example of putting two and two together and coming up with five. The reason for the disparity was the cyclical build-up of lions and hyaenas in the Maasai grazing lands to the point where the herdsmen began worrying that their livestock was in potential danger. They solved the problem by lacing carcasses with deadly cattle dip or battery acid. The baits killed many lions and hyaenas but were ignored by the last wild dogs – which were wiped out by rabies instead – and cheetahs. In the absence of their main enemies, Maasailand's cheetah population flourished.

A similar situation existed in Etosha when I was there in the 1970s, and probably still does. Cheetah densities on the cattle ranches surrounding Etosha were estimated to be eight times higher than in the park itself. Again, any lions or hyaenas that got through the boundary fence and into cattle country were summarily trapped and shot, whereas cheetahs were more or less tolerated. The main difference between Kenya and Namibia was that, though it had not been scientifically tested, the rangers and researchers in Etosha had accurately surmised the real reason for the higher cheetah numbers outside than inside the park. Given that lions are not only the cheetah's main competitor but also its main predator, it seems that, paradoxically, cheetahs may fare better in areas that are not protected, as long as they are tolerated by pastoralists.

In 1983 a new danger was identified when 18 cheetahs in Oregon Zoo in the USA died of a viral infection. Subsequent research on captive and wild cheetahs revealed that cheetahs from all over the world are nearly identical in their genetic composition – so much so that skin grafts from one cheetah to another produce no immune reaction. In human and most wild animal populations, in contrast, all individuals except identical twins are genetically unique. The finding caused geneticists to rethink the cheetah's evolutionary history. About 20 000 years ago the cheetah's range spanned the globe, but it seems the population suffered a near-extinction catastrophe roughly 10 000 years ago and today all cheetahs appear to be descended from a relative handful of survivors. What are the genetic implications? Some biologists believe that cheetahs may be unusually vulnerable to any small change in their environment and particularly susceptible to an epidemic. Others suggest that having survived the population bottleneck and recovered, free-living cheetahs show no ill-effects from generations of close inbreeding.

A far more important factor affecting cheetahs than their reduced genetic variability is likely to be lion and to a lesser extent hyaena predation, says Cambridge University-trained veterinarian Karen Laurenson. Starting in 1987, she spent three years with the Serengeti Cheetah Research Project studying cheetah behaviour and ecology for her PhD, during which time she found that, across nine different protected areas in Africa, cheetah biomass is negatively correlated to lion biomass. Since the mid-1970s, the cheetahs of Serengeti's southeastern plains have been part of an ongoing long-term study. Each is recognisable by the distinctive spot patterns on its flanks, face and chest, or banding on the tail, and individuals are tracked throughout their lifetime. Together with colleagues Tim Caro and Markus Borner, Laurenson set out to study female cheetah reproduction and offspring mortality on Serengeti's central plains where 500 to 900 cheetahs share the 3 000 square kilometres of open woodlands and grassy plains with 2 500 lions, up to 1 000 leopards and 5 000 hyaenas.

They killed them to eliminate competition on their patch, regardless of whether prey was plentiful or not.

The researchers chose 20 of the roughly 200 females inhabiting the central plains for detailed study. The selected animals were immobilised, carefully examined and radio-collared. Each month they were relocated by a Cessna 182 using fixed antennae mounted to each wing strut and a receiver that scanned the collared cheetahs' frequency bands. The intensive research revealed that females and non-resident males have huge overlapping home ranges averaging over 800 square kilometres that allow them to follow the migration of their main prey, Thomson's gazelles. Territorial males, on the other hand, have a very different land-tenure system. They scent-mark and defend small territories of less than 50 square kilometres in the best habitat, which contain a high year-round supply of prey and sufficient cover for stalking and shelter from their enemies – in other words, areas that might be expected to attract females.

Previous work had shown that adult female cheetahs live alone or with their dependent cubs, which after independence remain together as a sibling group for six or seven months until females leave to lead a solitary life. Males become either solitary[1] or band together in coalitions of between two and four, usually comprised of brothers. Although they can breed throughout the year, Serengeti cheetahs are more likely to conceive in the wet season, probably because of increased food availability in the form of newborn gazelles. Gestation varies between 90 and 95 days and, if

In a classic pose, this cheetah shows why the species has been described as a cat with a greyhound chassis. Light-boned, swaybacked, with long, thin legs and a short neck, a cheetah is built for speed. Although top speed is an incredible 110 kph, average speed during a chase is about 60 kph.

cubs die at an early age, a subsequent litter can be produced within months. The researchers found that more than 70 per cent of cheetah litters contain three or four cubs. However, they also discovered that cheetahs experience extremely high levels of cub mortality, with only five per cent of the cubs in the 36 litters they kept under observation reaching independence at 18 months old. Predation accounted for 73 per cent of the deaths. Lions were observed actively seeking out cheetah lairs. If a lion caught sight of a mother sitting up in a thicket or, in one instance, a sedge-choked marsh where cubs were hidden, it would rush the cheetah family and kill the defenceless cubs with a bite through the head or spine. They did not kill them because they like the taste of cheetah; as often as not they did not even eat them. They killed them to eliminate competition on their patch, regardless of whether prey was plentiful or not.

Cubs were still subject to high mortality after leaving the lair. From the time the 10 surviving litters (28 per cent) emerged from the lair until they were approximately three months old, three were lost entirely and all suffered some reduction in number, resulting in a further 53 per cent mortality rate. Another 41 per cent of those died in their fourth month, although by 14 to 16 weeks they were usually swift enough to outdistance predators. In a follow-up study published in 2007, Nathalie Pettorelli and Sarah Durant from the Zoological Society of London noted that larger litters survive less well than smaller ones, perhaps because litter size correlates with detectability by predators. They also found that some mothers are better at raising cubs than others. More mothers than expected performed really well and more than expected performed extremely badly. For example, one female reared nine cubs in two breeding events, while three were unable to rear a single cub in five years. Not surprisingly, young females performed less well than more experienced mothers.

Even after independence 50 per cent of males are lost, mainly due to competition with other males over access to territories. Yet, despite such heavy losses, cheetahs can replace themselves during a lifetime of about seven years because on average two of their cubs will eventually reach reproductive age. Karen Laurenson and her colleagues concluded that, while high cub predation depresses the cheetah population, it is a process of natural biodiversity that also keeps it stable. Maintaining this ecological balance may be nature's way of levelling the predatory playing field. Some life-history traits, such as early sexual maturity and large litters, suggest that cheetahs have evolved to compensate for high cub mortality. Like wild dogs, it is likely that their numbers fluctuate around ecological conditions, with their density rising when competition is weak and dropping when it is high. When lion density decreased in Serengeti in the 1970s, cheetah numbers increased, and when lion density rose in the 1980s, cheetah reproductive success dropped.

Cubs spend about 18 months with their mothers learning how to survive and it may take them another year or two to become good hunters.

But, in the absence of lions, cheetah survival soars. In 1981, eight adult cheetahs were relocated to the 13 400-hectare Suikerbosrand Nature Reserve, an hour's drive south of Johannesburg. Within two years their population had risen to 24. Their impact on blesbok and springbok numbers was so severe that it was decided to remove them altogether. 'The absence of other large predators was thought to have contributed significantly to the cheetahs' rapid increase,' predator expert Gus Mills wrote in a paper on large carnivore management. In 2007, after an absence of over 100 years, four cheetahs were released into Mountain Zebra National Park in the Eastern Cape. They adapted so well that by the end of 2010 they had multiplied to over 30; excess animals are now being relocated to other parks and zoos. Significantly, the dominant predators prior to their arrival were the less aggressive brown hyaena and caracal.

When seven cheetahs were introduced into Pilanesberg National Park in South Africa's North West province in 1981/2, soon after the park's inauguration, their only competitors were a few resident leopards and brown hyaenas and, with plentiful prey, there were limited constraints on their growing population. Before long park authorities were complaining that too many cheetahs were killing too many calves of rare and valuable antelope species such as waterbucks and tsessebes, and the cheetahs were removed except for a coalition of three males. In 1993 lions were reintroduced and in 1995 it was decided to expand the park's cheetah population with the staggered release of 17 cheetahs from Namibia. Some 'were almost certainly killed by the park's other predators', according to field ecologist Gus van Dyk – a male lion was seen running down a subadult cub. Others disappeared without trace. Today there are only two cheetahs left in Pilanesberg, while lion density is high.

Cheetahs were never abundant in the Kruger, according to James Stevenson-Hamilton. Nevertheless they were included in the systematic predator control measures that operated until the 1960s. From 1904 to 1927 a minimum of 269 cheetahs were shot, although 'it is difficult to understand the logic' Tol Pienaar later complained. 'Cheetahs are not important predators in this area and of all the carcasses recorded during the period 1933–1966, cheetah kills contributed merely 5.82 per cent ... They are also the least abundant of the major predators and the latest estimate of numbers (1964) indicated that there were no more than 263 of these sleek and graceful carnivores in the whole Park. Of these, 90 inhabited the southern district, 110 were found in the central district, while the whole of the vast northern region harboured only 63.' That averaged a minimum of one cheetah per 39 square kilometres in the Southern District or one cheetah per 72 square kilometres for the whole park.

Based on accumulated data from predator kills, Pienaar concluded 'there has been a definite decline in the number of cheetah'. He attributed the decline to predator control operations and 'in part to a progressive deterioration in the suitable hunting range for cheetahs, through bush encroachment'. The latter development, he felt, was a matter 'demanding urgent attention and the Nature Conservation Section has already embarked on a long-term project of reclamation of such overgrown savanna areas', particularly on the eastern Lebombo plains. Whatever the intentions, the legacy of the ill-fated reclamation project is today nowhere to be found.

In 1968, concerns regarding the Kruger's dwindling population prompted the transfer of 16 cheetahs from Namibia, the first of three batches intended to boost local numbers. While in quarantine at Tshokwane, most of the young animals contracted the tick-transmitted bacterial infection rickettsiosis. Two died but after intensive treatment four adults were released at Kumana, between Tshokwane and Satara, and the rest at Tshokwane itself. Judging by photographs of the introduced cheetahs – they still retained the short ruff of fur on the nape of the neck that remains until adulthood – they were too young to be hunting successfully on their own. A cheetah's deadly finesse does not come easily. Cubs spend about 18 months with their mothers learning how to survive and it may take them another year or two to become good hunters.

Although the cheetahs released at Tshokwane seemed to settle, they soon followed the example of those at Kumana, which split up and dispersed – a male was seen at MalaMala a few weeks later. A second group of eight was set free near Crocodile Bridge and another 10 along the Sabie River and at Tshokwane. Several returned to their holding pens in an emaciated condition and had to be artificially fed or were recaptured; the rest simply disappeared. It is now known that male coalitions defending their territory make newcomers very unwelcome. Trespassers are forced into less suitable habitat where they are unable to survive. Moreover, wildlife professionals have learnt that, when stocking newly established game parks, it is essential to release cheetahs well ahead of lions and hyaenas, to give them a chance to acclimatise.

A project to determine cheetah population demographics, distribution and habitat preferences based on photographs sent in by visitors to the Kruger – a system that earlier had worked spectacularly well when used to monitor wild dogs – concluded that the park's cheetah population had declined from Pienaar's 1960s estimate of 263 to around 170 in 1991 – or a minimum of one adult per 190 square kilometres – 'with the decrease occurring along a south–north gradient'. A 2005 census, supervised by SANParks and the Endangered Wildlife Trust (EWT), tallied a minimum of 103 cheetahs in the Kruger as well as the private nature reserves on the western boundary and Limpopo National Park to the east. However, that may have been a blip, as their 2009 survey received photos of 172 cheetahs in total, many of them seen only once. The majority, 92, were photographed in the 4 057-square-kilometre Southern District between the Crocodile and Sabie rivers. Only 69 cheetahs were seen in the 6 192-square-kilometre Central District (which included the private reserves on the western boundary) although impalas, their favourite prey, are abundant; the open plains provide ideal opportunities for hunting but also support a higher lion density than in the south, which has less ideal habitat. The 2009 census also found that in all three districts adult cheetahs outnumbered young animals and the ratio of females without cubs to mothers with cubs was higher than in other regions. In the 11 102-square-kilometre Northern District, only 11 cheetahs were identified, although the census coordinators stress that this is a minimum count and, as with earlier figures, may be a big underestimate of actual numbers. Nonetheless, it is perhaps no coincidence that the downward trend in cheetah numbers, particularly cubs, north of the Sabie River parallels an increase in lion densities in both regions since Pienaar's estimates.

Cheetah cubs in Kruger's more wooded landscapes are harder to detect than they are in Serengeti's open grasslands, so cub predation is reduced.

Interestingly, of the 172 cheetahs photographed, 54 were adult males and only 31 adult females (67 were cubs and 20 could not be sexed). A predominance of males in the adult sex ratio was noted also by Tol Pienaar. He records that, of 51 cheetahs destroyed at random during control operations between 1954 and 1960, 70 per cent were males and 30 per cent females. He also refers to 471 live cheetahs subsequently sexed, where 60 per cent were males and 40 per cent females. 'If the predominantly male adult sex ratio is real,' he cautions, 'then this may be a further factor inhibiting population growth.' In contrast, George Schaller calculated that in Serengeti in the 1970s, adult female cheetahs outnumbered males two to one. Litters born in captivity and others sexed in the wild suggest an equal sex ratio at birth.

The cheetah's specific niche in the Kruger's ecosystem is similar to that in Serengeti's in some respects but very different in others. As in Serengeti, the Kruger's cheetahs feed mainly on the most abundant medium-sized antelope in the area. In Serengeti that is the migratory Thomson's gazelle, which contributed over 90 per cent of prey animals recorded by George Schaller, with two thirds of the gazelles captured less than a year old. In the Kruger, on the other hand, the sedentary and evenly distributed impala comprised 77 per cent of all reported kills in a survey by Norman Owen-Smith and Gus Mills. It is the difference in the habits of their favourite prey species that accounts in part for the two cheetah populations' differing social organisation. Unlike the Serengeti females' huge home ranges, female home ranges and male territories in the Kruger are about 185 square kilometres each. Males scrupulously avoid crossing into other males' territory but females' home ranges overlap the domains of male coalitions, ensuring a steady supply of potential mates.

Most cheetah studies have focused on Serengeti's open grasslands because of the relative ease with which cheetahs can be observed there and the suitability of the environment for their hunting methods. Cheetahs also occupy a wide range of bush, scrub and woodland habitats but little was known about their ecology and behaviour in this thicker terrain. Then, starting in 1987, biologists Gus Mills, Lynne Broomhall and Johan du Toit used continuous field observations over four years to assess the feeding ecology of seven radio-collared cheetahs that ranged across the southeastern Kruger's basalt plains. In their scientific monograph, the researchers posed the question: is the cheetah a successful hunter only on open grassland plains? Their answer, together with other recent cheetah studies in woodland habitats, provides new awareness about the way these unusual felines earn a living in a quite different type of environment from Serengeti's open grasslands.

Mills and his co-researchers noted that cheetahs require good visibility and a straight trajectory of attack, without obstructions, when reaching speeds of 100 kilometres per hour during hunts. It is therefore reasonable to assume that they need open habitat to hunt successfully and the literature on cheetah ecology has supported that assumption. While acknowledging that woodland savanna might inhibit cheetahs from reaching top speed, they wondered if it might also confer benefits such as better cover, which would help them stalk closer to their quarry before the chase. In addition, concealing kills from scavengers and newborn cubs from predators might be easier in bushveld.

What they found was that the thick bush in the Kruger's western granitic belt does restrict the cheetah's main hunting advantage. Hunts in this type of terrain are often quick lunges or short chases with only limited success. On the eastern basalt plains, both male and female cheetahs prefer the more open savannas and centre their core area or entire range there, though they use all habitats according to their availability. Females use denser woodlands more often than males, probably because their main prey, impalas, favour this habitat and it provides better cover for cubs. But, though impala densities are higher in acacia thickets and the adjoining Lebombo Hills, the researchers found that

'If the predominantly male adult sex ratio is real, then this may be a further factor inhibiting population growth.'

their study cheetahs killed significantly more impalas in open savanna. Broad drainage lines provided particularly good hunting grounds, as cheetahs could stalk prey through the thick bush on the margins of the watercourse and then chase at high speed across the drainage line's more open spaces. In this type of terrain the average chase distance for a successful hunt was 190 metres, less than half the distance of a Serengeti chase.

Kelly Marnewick

Kelly Marnewick

Johan Marais

Unlike Serengeti's open grasslands where carnivores can see for kilometres, the Kruger's more wooded landscapes mean that fewer cheetah kills are appropriated by hyaenas and lions. In Serengeti they are robbed of around 13 per cent of their prey, compared with 12 per cent in the Kruger and 10 per cent in MalaMala. Mother cheetahs and cubs are also harder to detect in the Kruger's thicker bush, so cub mortality is reduced. The critical period in the Kruger is when subadults become independent and seek their own piece of suitable living space. How difficult that is can be seen by the contrast in cheetah densities in the Kruger as a whole – just one cheetah per 100 square kilometres – compared with prime cheetah habitat in the Kruger's southeastern marula/knobthorn tree savanna, which supports more than twice that number, the same as on the Serengeti plains. 'The cheetah is more adaptable to habitat variability than is often thought,' the Kruger study concluded, 'and is not only a successful hunter on open plains.'

Earlier, Tol Pienaar observed that 'the manner in which cheetahs have been found to adapt themselves to a more overgrown habitat in the Kruger Park may be deduced from the number of bushbuck which are killed'. Still, his data showed that impalas made up 70 per cent of their overall kills and up to 75 percent in the high impala-density Southern District, compared with 58 per cent in the lower density north. Despite the predominance of impalas in the cheetah-kill tally, Pienaar ranked them fifth on the prey preference scale, after reedbucks, waterbucks, kudus and tsessebes. In fact, he found that cheetahs accounted for over 20 per cent of all reedbucks killed, more than by any other predator. He also noted that 'apart from impala, of which all age classes are killed (particularly females and young during the breeding season) cheetahs are fond of killing the newly-born young of larger prey such as wildebeest, waterbuck, kudu, zebra, tsessebe and sable antelope'.

Gus Mills and his colleagues found that three species comprised 70 per cent of the 68 observed kills made by their study cheetahs, which consisted of a three-male coalition, a two-male coalition, a single male and four females with and without cubs. Impalas totalled

A comatose cheetah (top) is blissfully unaware that it's about to become airborne for the first time in its life. Kelly Marnewick (middle), the Endangered Wildlife Trust's Carnivore Conservation Programme Manager, records a tranquillised cheetah's vital statistics. Fully recovered from its sedated state (bottom), a newly radio-collared cheetah seems unfazed by the experience.

46 per cent of all kills – of which 78 per cent were male impalas[2] and 22 per cent females – while common duikers and steenbok each contributed 12 per cent. In neighbouring MalaMala's mixed combretum/terminalia woodland, impalas comprised 70 per cent of male cheetah kills, while female cheetahs selected 65 per cent impalas, followed by steenbok (12 per cent) and duikers (11 per cent).

A mother cheetah and her three cubs use a termite mound's elevation to scan their surrounds for potential prey. Keen eyesight allows cheetahs to spot prey as far as 5 kilometres away.

The Kruger researchers noted that the sex and group size of hunting cheetahs influences prey selection, with male coalitions taking the juveniles of larger prey, while single females preyed more heavily on smaller antelopes. Hunting larger prey is one adaptation male coalitions make to meet the increased food demands of group living. The three-male coalition averaged 79 kills per year and consumed approximately 1.4 kilograms of meat per cheetah per day. The researchers also observed that the coalition's hunting success was higher, but not significantly so, than that of the two female groups, but the frequency of hunting attempts per prey encountered was significantly higher in the female groups.

While in Etosha I saw 28 cheetah chases, about half of them successful, although it was not until the significance was brought home to me that I attached much importance to the fact that every one had involved a female hunter. Not until I had the opportunity to watch several hunts in the Kruger did I appreciate the difference in modus operandi between a single female and a band of brothers. That was first demonstrated to me around 4 o'clock one overcast afternoon on the edge of an open seepline, where a triumvirate of male cheetahs lounged flat on their sides, with only their heads raised. At the other end of the short-grass clearing a herd of wildebeest grazed unconcernedly and the cats seemed to pay them little heed. I had seen a cheetah pull down a tan wildebeest calf, but the youngest animal in this group was a yearling, too big for cheetahs, I felt certain. But suddenly the cheetahs were scrutinising the herd with professional interest. They stood up, their high bellies testifying that they had not eaten recently, and with that menacing, stiff-legged walk so characteristic of these cats they approached the wildebeest, which by now were becoming a little uneasy but still had not stampeded. I thought they might chase them for fun – surely they were not going to try to capture one of these oversized beasts? But the three cheetahs had already chosen their quarry and the next moment they launched into that incredible burst of acceleration that takes them from 0 to 95 kilometres per hour in just three seconds. After a short chase, two of them locked their sharp dew claws into the bucking yearling's hindquarters, anchoring it, while the third spotted fiend went for the throat, clamping the windpipe with a suffocating bite, the standard method of dispatching a victim. Then the wildebeest was down, its hooves flailing. Deadly teamwork, indeed!

But the important question, as far as cheetahs are concerned, is not what effect they have on prey populations but what the future of the cheetah itself is. They seem to have many factors in their favour, for instance they are highly successful hunters that produce large litters of cubs, and yet they are scarce. But they are also difficult to count and, though they quickly can become habituated to vehicles, ordinarily they are secretive and shy by nature, so there might be more of them than we are aware of. James Stevenson-Hamilton observed that 'although perhaps comparatively numerous within a given area, it is seldom met with, which is surprising considering that much of its hunting is done in the early morning and late afternoon'. Surprisingly perhaps, accurately counting cheetahs in the Kruger these days, while much more complex and scientific, is almost as difficult as it was 100 years ago. For example, in 2012 the EWT's final report on the Kruger Western

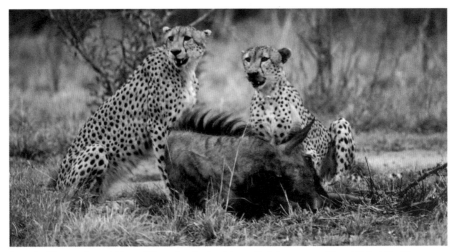

I watched in surprise as this coalition of male cheetahs pulled down a yearling wildebeest with consummate ease. Hunting larger prey is an adaptation male coalitions make to meet the increased food demands of group living.

Boundary project estimated cheetah numbers at 421 in total, with a range of between 369 and 545 animals. That tally is based on an estimate of 17 (with a range of 14 to 34) cheetahs in the northern region, an estimated 183 (with a range of 134 to 271) cheetahs in the central region, and an estimated 210 (with a range of 175 to 267) cheetahs in the southern region. 'The figures are a lot higher than for other surveys,' Kelly Marnewick, project co-ordinator and manager of the EWT's Carnivore Conservation Programme explained to me. 'That's because for the first time we ran mark-and-recapture analyses[3] on the data from the last photographic survey whereas earlier estimates were minimum counts from cheetahs ID'ed in photo surveys.' If the new estimates are correct, that means there are twice as many cheetahs in the Kruger as previously believed.

Despite the Kruger cheetahs' rarity, the population appears stable and healthy enough to survive competition with other predators.

Cheetahs are still spread over several hundreds of thousands of square kilometres in Africa, occurring widely in Namibia, Botswana, Tanzania and Kenya and more sporadically in Zimbabwe, Zambia, Mozambique, Ethiopia, Sudan, several Sahel states and South Africa's Limpopo province. Inevitably, though, there will be constant attrition in numbers and range as more and more land is taken for human use, and in the long term their future will depend on the continent's system of national parks and private reserves.

Despite the Kruger cheetahs' rarity, the population appears stable and healthy enough to survive competition with other predators. The difference between these highly adapted felids and other cats is personified by their hunting technique, which presumably developed in open savanna, so, if the park's revised policy regarding veld burning delivers on its promise to knock back areas of bush encroachment and re-establish patches of more open habitat such as existed in the not-so-distant past, it should give cheetahs a chance to extend their range, and in so doing boost their overall numbers.

---

1 About 40 per cent of adult male cheetahs live a solitary existence. These 'floaters' drift over a large home range but, lacking the strength-in-numbers advantages of territorial male coalitions, they often exhibit signs of stress and poor condition. In addition, they do not live as long as territorial male coalitions.

2 Cheetahs' preference for male impalas in the Kruger is paralleled by their preference for male Thomson's gazelle in Serengeti. Males are less vigilant, are found in smaller groups than females and often occupy the periphery of herds. As males are more expendable than females, their greater vulnerability to predation has the effect of lessening the impact of predation on prey populations.

3 Mark-and-recapture is a method commonly used in ecology to estimate population size. It is most valuable when a researcher fails to detect all individuals present within the population of interest every time he or she visits the study area. An example of this procedure: researchers capture animals alive and tag them. Then the animals are returned unharmed to their environment. Trapping of individuals from the population continues and data are taken on how many are captured with tags. A mathematical formula is then used to estimate population size.

11

Wild dog
running

Soon after sunrise ... I was surprised to hear an outburst
of rapid gunfire ahead of me. I came to Ben's Land Rover
abandoned in the track with three dead wild dogs lying
close beside it. Some moments later Ben and John
reappeared dragging two more dead dogs after them ...
Ben's sunlined face had a benign expression on it.
I believe of all natural things he hated only the
wild dogs for their ruthless ways with
weaker animals.

Laurens van der Post,
The Lost World of the Kalahari, 1958

They're called African hunting dogs, or simply wild dogs, and like wolves, whose pack-orientated social structure theirs closely resembles, they were for generations demonised by westernised commentators for their grisly efficiency in dispatching prey. 'The rapacious appetite of these foul creatures is staggering. I maintain these pests should be outlawed wherever found,' opined white hunter John Hunter, best known for shooting 1 000 rhinos in Kenya to make way for a short-lived groundnut scheme. 'It will be an excellent day for African game and its preservation when means can be devised for their complete extermination,' British foreign service officer and old-style game warden Reginald Charles Fulke Maugham harrumphed in tones of colonial disapproval. 'Fortunately, they are not as numerous as they were some years ago,' remarked A.C. White, publisher of Bloemfontein's *The Friend* newspaper, in a chapter titled 'The wild dog – most cruel of hunters' in his 1948 book *Call of the Bushveld*.

All this vitriol for an animal that has never attacked a human, or at least has not done so in the wild. 'I never knew one of them make the slightest attempt to revenge itself upon a human adversary, nor in fact do anything except try to escape,' recalled James Stevenson-Hamilton. 'There is no gleam of rage in the large brown eyes, such as is always apparent in those of cats in similar position; but rather the appealing and frightened look worn by a domestic dog when injured.' But even those, like Stevenson-Hamilton, who should have known better, joined the chorus. 'There is no other predatory animal in Africa responsible for so much disturbance of game as the hunting dog, and in proportion to his numbers there is none which deals out more wholesale destruction.' Such implacable hostility led inevitably to relentless persecution. Formerly widespread in South Africa, wild dogs had been exterminated everywhere in the country except for the Kruger Park and adjacent districts by 1920.

All this vitriol for an animal that has never attacked a human, or at least has not done so in the wild.

A distant cousin of the wolf and domestic dog, the wild dog split from the ancestor of other canids three to two million years ago and today is the sole member of a unique lineage. Though its shape follows the general canine body plan, it differs taxonomically from true dogs in having only four toes to each forefoot, lacking the vestigial dewclaw, or fifth toe, found in most canines. Once dismissed as a pariah, the wild dog, like the wolf, is acknowledged at last as a legitimate and integral part of its ecosystem. Now people are rallying to the cause of this beautiful and elusive predator and it is being rehabilitated in the public imagination. To hurry the process along, human allies are promoting a name change – the old one, it is said, conjures up images of a house pet gone bad. The new name, 'painted wolf', is a translation of its scientific designation, *Lycaon pictus*, and refers to its curious jigsaw pattern of black, white and sandy yellow coat markings that aptly have been called 'a furred version of combat fatigues' by the writer Natalie Angier. Apart from the fact that it is misleading, wildlife conservation biologist Greg Rasmussen dislikes the term 'wild dog' because it reinforces the animal's bad reputation, he believes. Founder and director of the Painted Dog Conservation project, he has studied them for over 20 years in Zimbabwe's Hwange National Park and worries that the old name fuels prejudice and 'is detrimental to conservation efforts'. As yet, 'painted dog', or 'painted wolf', is still to be fully embraced by the broader scientific community, which prefers 'African wild dog'.

Another way of converting people to their cause might be to emphasise the wild dog's highly evolved social etiquette. Pack members are for the most part gentle and considerate with one another. They practise close-knit family values, with both sexes helping to raise the pack's young. When a hunting party returns from a kill, pups and adult babysitters solicit food, which both sexes and all ages provide by regurgitating meat. In addition to feeding pups, non-breeding helpers take part in guarding and protecting them from lions, leopards and hyaenas. They rarely fight within a pack, even at kills. Juveniles are allowed to feed first, followed by the alpha pair, with all adults and yearlings eating together, unlike lions and hyaenas, where might is right. If strife should erupt, both animals involved assume an appeasement posture, which terminates the face-off. Their intense social harmony is reinforced by elaborate rituals involving tail wagging, high-pitched chittering, muzzle-to-muzzle contact and exuberant leaps and bounds. This social bonding is renewed whenever they wake up, just before a hunt and after returning from a kill.

> **Pack members are for the most part gentle and considerate with one another.**

They also assist injured pack mates. Greg Rasmussen tells of a dog that had its neck deeply gashed in a lion attack. A vet recommended euthanising it 'but the pack knew better', Rasmussen fondly relates. One of the dogs assumed the role of nurse, often licking the wound – saliva is a natural antiseptic, so licking aids healing. It also made sure the patient got enough food when the pack regurgitated part of the proceeds of the hunt. 'Three months later I saw the injured dog, its neck now healed, back in the pack and taking part in the hunt.' This communal spirit enhances the cohesiveness of the pack, which works to its advantage, as the loss of even a single individual could disrupt the efficiency of the hunt and the raising of large litters of dependent pups.

However, there are limits to this kindly attention. Wild dogs seem able to distinguish between injury and illness and, in contrast to the care accorded to wounded pack mates, diseased dogs invariably are abandoned without apparent remorse. When rabies took hold of a pack in Kenya's Masai Mara in 1991, sick individuals were attacked by as-yet-unaffected members; one was driven from the pack shortly before it died. Rabid dogs did not initiate fights but did bite in self-defence and in so doing probably transmitted the disease to other pack mates. Veterinarian Pieter Kat, who led a multi-disciplinary project to learn the reasons behind the collapse of the Serengeti-

Mara's population, speculated that the inability of sick dogs to respond normally in social interactions might have provoked aggression – an adult set upon by yearlings showed no evident signs of disease. Long-term monitoring revealed that these social carnivores formed a single breeding unit in the vast Serengeti-Mara ecosystem, with individuals capable of traversing its entire extent in search of mates. Ultimately, ' recurrent outbreaks of rabies, and possibly canine distemper, both almost certainly picked up originally from Maasai villagers' dogs, resulted in their local extinction.

The organised slaughter of wild dogs has ended – they became a protected species in the mid-1980s – yet, disturbingly, their numbers continue to decline. Wild dogs live at low population densities under the best of conditions, but over the last 50 years an ever-expanding human population has evicted them from 25 of their 39 former range countries. Moreover, 60 per cent of those survivors occur in populations known to cross international boundaries, with almost 70 per cent of their range traversing those borders. Habitat destruction and modification, loss of prey and direct persecution, as well as episodic exposure in some parts of Africa to infectious diseases carried by domestic dogs, have

Beyond park boundaries wild dogs encounter human threats such as roads, snares, poison and gun-toting farmers.

reduced them to highly fragmented population groups, dangerously isolated both genetically and geographically. Less than six per cent of the species' historical range still supports resident packs and most of those live in protected areas. But, even in parks, humans are responsible for more than 50 per cent of recorded adult mortality and that includes the Kruger's population. With numbers down to around 5 750 living in 1 000 packs, mainly in southeastern and southern Africa, wild dogs have become Africa's second-most endangered carnivore, after the Ethiopian wolf.

The South African *Red Data Book* has wild dogs listed as one of only three endangered terrestrial mammals in the country. Their legal status is 'specially protected' but that is not always enough to safeguard them. These inveterate travellers readily slip under fences surrounding protected areas like the Kruger – a survey revealed that more dogs survive outside of protected areas in South Africa than was thought possible, especially west of the greater Kruger; from 1996 to 2002 numbers fluctuated between 42 and 106. This exacerbates the challenges conservationists face in trying to protect them. Beyond park boundaries wild dogs encounter human threats such as roads, snares, poison and gun-toting farmers. Many farmers have an exaggerated notion of the impact wild dogs have on prey, but they will take domestic stock when natural prey is scarce, which highlights the importance of protecting wild prey. And when they develop a taste for livestock the damage can be dramatic; one pack killed 70 merino ewes and 67 lambs on a single Kenyan ranch in 1996. Some commercial game ranchers tolerate them, even consider them an asset, but most regard them as a threat to their livelihood for killing antelopes that could otherwise be hunted or sold. These ranchers often take the law into their own hands and reach for a rifle, even though it is illegal to kill wild dogs in South Africa without permission from the conservation authorities. But they know there is little chance of being prosecuted.

Wild dogs live a wide-ranging, fugitive existence, rarely spending two consecutive nights in the same location except during the three-month annual denning period, when pups are very young. Living on the move – up to 50 kilometres a day if prey is scarce – is an adaptation to finding patches unoccupied by their mortal enemies, lions and hyaenas, and because prey may become skittish if a pack remains in one place too long. A Serengeti study found that during denning their home range shrinks by about 90 per cent to between 50 and 260 square kilometres but expands to up to 2 000 square kilometres at other times. In the Kruger a pack used 80 square kilometres when denning but 885 square kilometres afterwards. Stevenson-Hamilton spoke of the species' 'restless habits and the vast areas which it unceasingly roams over ... The pack which formerly hunted the country between the Sabi and Crocodile Rivers in the Sabi Game Reserve, and which ranged over an area of some fifteen hundred square miles [3 885 square kilometres], well stocked with impala and reedbuck, consisted, before it had been artificially reduced in numbers, of between sixty and seventy individuals. A second pack, having a very wide range from the Sabi on the south to the Olifants River on the north, and from the foothills of the Drakensberg on the west, nearly to the Limpopo River on the east, was never quite so numerous, in spite of the wider area at its disposal.'

MOUNTAINEERING WITH WILD DOGS

Wild dogs reach their highest densities in woodland savanna but their habitat matrix encompasses open grasslands and mountain ranges and practically everything in between, except for rainforests and the driest deserts. In 1970 the explorer and author Wilfred Thesiger sighted them at 5 800 metres during his ascent of Kilimanjaro. 'This was at a time when the crater and slopes of Kibo carried far more snow than is often seen; a less probable place for wild dogs could scarcely be imagined and there was nothing to eat but ourselves ... There were five of them, standing about on the great southern glacier ... They were unmistakeable, round eared, inquisitive in demeanour, blotchy in colouring though looking almost black seen through snow glasses on a dazzling background of ice.' Thesiger's party came across the dogs' tracks leading into the crater itself, while the curious pack followed parallel to them along the glacier ridge. The mountaineers had encountered two characteristics typical of wild dogs. As they do wherever they are not persecuted, wild dogs show more curiosity than fear of humans if approached carefully. And they occupy enormous home ranges, far larger than would be predicted on the basis of their size and metabolic requirements.

Mark Broodryk

The Kruger is one of the few reserves in Africa large enough to contain the 200 to 300 individuals thought to be a rough minimum for long-term population persistence, without having to resort to intensive management. However, such a small population is at risk of genetic inbreeding and studies have shown that the Kruger's wild dogs do not show as much genetic diversity as other populations. For a variety of reasons, some of which conservationists are only now beginning to understand, their numbers have fluctuated widely over the past century. 'Wild dogs (animals which no one previously had troubled to hunt) were present in considerable numbers,' James Stevenson-Hamilton wrote of the first 20 years in the Sabi Game Reserve. The reserve's first ranger, Harry Wolhuter, also noted that wild dogs 'were a great deal more plentiful then than they are now. They used to congregate in packs of twenty to forty; and, as we regarded them as vermin to be reduced without mercy, they afforded us great sport.' Early ad hoc control policies that amounted to shooting on sight any predator rangers came across while on patrol consigned to death a minimum of 1 142 wild dogs between 1903 and 1927.

'In later years the wild dogs contracted some disease that killed them off in hundreds, so that even to this day they remain scarce throughout the Kruger National Park, and are very seldom seen,' Wolhuter recalled. Stevenson-Hamilton noted that 'from about 1920 onwards, hunting dogs in the Park suffered from some fatal disease, possibly *Rickettsia canis*, which is most destructive to domestic dogs. It first showed itself in the extreme north, where, in the year mentioned, nearly all domestic and many wild dogs died. About eight years later it appeared in the southern areas, and from about 1928 there was so steady a decrease of wild dogs in all the central and southern regions of the Park that by about 1935 none were to be found indigenous between Sabi and Olifants Rivers, and very few south of the former ... In the Sabi country, densely stocked with impala, none were noticed between 1931 and 1944, where formerly great packs used to roam.'

It first showed itself in the extreme north, where, in the year mentioned, nearly all domestic and many wild dogs died.

The deadly tick-borne rickettsial disease that almost wiped out wild dogs in the southern half of the park seems to have originated among domestic dogs used to track and bring to bay carnivores, including wild dogs. The only known tick vector for the strain of rickettsia responsible for the epidemic has not been found on free-living wild dogs, although they are invariably infested with ticks. Following the epidemic, all domestic dogs in the park were vaccinated, since when there have been no detectable disease-related declines in the Kruger's wild dog population. A study undertaken from 1990 to '93 into the health status and diseases of 10 wild dog packs in the Kruger's Southern District by the Veterinary Sciences faculty of the Medical University of Southern Africa concluded that 'disease could not be incriminated as an important cause of death', although new dangers may be threatening, as will be seen later in this chapter.

Intriguingly, the study also discovered that 80 per cent or more of the population was under four years of age, with very few dogs living longer than six years. That is surprisingly low, given that life spans in the wild in other parts of Africa can range up to 10 years and in captivity to 15 years. Poor survival among young wild dogs – in the Kruger only 16 per cent of newborns survive to adulthood at two years; in Selous the survival rate is nearly two-and-a-half times higher – is the main cause of the Kruger wild dogs' short life span.

In the wake of the rickettsia calamity, South Africa's last viable contiguous wild dog population began a slow recovery that by 1964 yielded an estimated 335 dogs, of which 120 occurred south of the Sabie River, 65 in the Central District and 150 north of the Olifants River. In 1988 a new census was launched by Anthony Maddock as part of a Natal University post doctoral project and supervised by SANParks' carnivore research fellow, Gus Mills, with support from the Endangered Wildlife Trust's Carnivore Conservation Group (now known as the Carnivore Conservation Programme). Maddock relied on each dog's unique coat pattern to identify individuals as well as to establish the composition and number of packs. He was greatly assisted by the nearly 2 000 images submitted by visitors in response to a wildly successful photographic competition, which sought to create awareness of the dogs' plight while counting them at the same time. To top it off, the census results were encouraging: a total of 357 dogs in 26 packs were identified, comprising 84 animals in seven packs south of the Sabie River; 115 in five packs in the Central District; and 158 in 14 packs in the Northern District. The average pack size was a healthy 14 dogs.

Subsequently the Endangered Wildlife Trust (EWT) and SANParks have run follow-up surveys every five years. As with the cheetah surveys, those analysing the photographic file are at pains to emphasise that the results represent a minimum count and actual numbers could be significantly higher. Even so, the 1995 results looked promising. A total of 434 individuals in 36 packs were photographed, with a bumper 250 dogs identified in the Northern District. But all that was about to change. In 2000 only 177 dogs in 25 packs were counted and the mean pack size had dropped to seven animals. The reduced pack size was itself cause for concern. Before wild dogs became endangered, larger packs were more common. Since mothers cannot raise pups without assistance, the pack, rather than the individual, is considered the basic unit. A pack may be as small as a pair or as many as 50 adults, yearlings and pups, but evidence suggests that reproductive success is positively correlated with larger pack size. Scott and Nancy Creel, who have studied wild dogs in Tanzania's Selous Game Reserve since 1993, found that the number of pups emerging from the den at about three weeks of age was related to pack size – the bigger the pack, the higher the pup survival rate. This is also true of the Kruger, where a study showed that packs smaller than five averaged 11 pups; packs of six to 10 averaged 13 pups; and packs greater than 10 averaged 20 pups.

Wild dogs almost always hunt as a pack, in contrast to other social carnivores like lions and hyaenas. In terms of kilograms killed per kilometres chased, each member achieves better foraging success hunting as part of a team – for one thing, they can pull down bigger prey. Combining teamwork, strategy and allegiance, a wild dog pack

Since mothers cannot raise pups without assistance, the pack, rather than the individual, is considered the basic unit.

reveals itself as a singular force of nature, one of the most efficient predatory units on Earth, with a success rate of 43 to 70 per cent. But it requires a minimum pack size to hunt at maximum efficiency. Hunting success is higher and energetically less costly in larger packs. Big packs reduce the distance chased per hunt, are often able to make more than one kill per hunt and can better defend kills against bigger predators. Even a small loss of food to thieves may have a big impact on the time they must hunt to achieve energy balance. Its very high energy requirements are the reason that, for its size, the wild dog eats more meat each day, around 3.5 kilograms, than any other carnivore. Mothers in larger packs usually give birth to larger litters as a direct result of obtaining more food than mothers in smaller packs. In small packs the loss of a single pup guard to the hunting party – which cannot contribute to feeding pups and also

Giggling nervously, a hyaena is harried by wild dogs frustrated at being shadowed by the scavenger while on a hunt. Wild dogs show aggression by holding their tails stiffly straight up.

requires regurgitated food itself – could reduce a pack's viability. If it drops below a critical size it may be caught in a downward spiral, low reproduction and survival further reducing its size, culminating in the pack's collapse. The Kruger's mean pack size is just four or five adults, compared with eight or nine adults in Selous and Botswana's Moremi Game Reserve, both of which have much lower pup mortality rates than the Kruger.

Wild dogs almost always hunt as a pack, in contrast to other social carnivores like lions and hyaenas.

Wild dog population dynamics are intrinsically linked to the pack, so it is worthwhile taking a closer look at that cooperative entity's complex and rather extraordinary social organisation. In the pack's simplest structure, all the adult males are related to each other and all the adult females to each other, but the males and females are not related. Packs form when single-sex groups, usually litter-mate siblings, break away from their natal pack and join a similar group of the opposite sex or team up with a pack that has lost residents of one sex, or launch a hostile takeover by evicting unrelated same-sex residents from a

The dominant female is usually the oldest and the only one assured of breeding.

functioning pack. Relations become more complicated when unrelated individuals are accepted into the group, and others emigrate to seek mating opportunities elsewhere, which is one reason why wild dog packs fluctuate in size far more than hyaena clans or lion prides.

Within a pack, there is a clear dominance hierarchy among females and another among males. The dominant female is usually the oldest and the only one assured of breeding. But, while most packs have a single breeding female, sometimes a second and even a third female will produce pups, particularly in large packs. In the Kruger, a second female was found to breed in nearly half the packs containing more than one bitch. At one den, Gus Mills recorded three lactating females sharing 28 pups. Litter sizes range from two to 21 pups, with an average of about 10; one fecund female, whose progress Mills was following, produced litters of 21, 18 and 13 pups, 52 altogether, in three successive years. The high fecundity of the Kruger's dogs – litters tend to be bigger in the Kruger than in Moremi or Selous – is nature's response to poor pup survival. But, if the alpha female is not amenable, she is usually able to inhibit another bitch from breeding. If not, she may kidnap a sister's pups and raise them as her own, or kill them, or discourage other pack members from feeding them. It is a tenuous existence for subordinates' offspring and in the Kruger less than 10 per cent of their pups survive to a year old. And, though alpha males usually monopolise mating, they may not sire all the pack's pups. Genetic studies in the Kruger revealed that 10 per cent of pups are not those of the dominant male and two out of 10 litters have multiple paternities, as occurs with other carnivores. All of which can produce a complex web of genetic relatedness within packs.

Most subordinate adults forego the right to mate and instead act as helpers, willingly investing the time and effort as all pack members are related to the puppies. Or so it was thought. In the 1990s, wildlife biologist John 'Tico' McNutt and his anthropologist wife, Lesley Boggs, discovered unexpected social behaviours after years spent tracking generations of wild dogs in Moremi. 'Cooperative breeding by wild dogs has been described as strongly kin-related,' says McNutt. 'Helpers were assumed to be invariably closely related to offspring.' However, their study has shown that this is not always the case. A minimum of 25 per cent of the packs in their study area contained non-breeding adults that cared for unrelated pups. McNutt believes that the benefits of adopting unrelated weaned pups pertains to increasing pack size 'and may indicate important mechanisms underlying adoption and the evolution of helping behaviour in wild dogs'. So vital is pack size that in the Kruger it features on a list of so-called thresholds of potential concern. That means that if the total number of packs in the park drops to 12, or to an average pack size of less than six animals, park management must decide if action needs to be taken.

Results for the 2005 census reinforced the bad news of five years earlier. The total minimum count had dropped to 140 dogs in 17 packs and this included those recorded in the private reserves on the western boundary. 'The continuing years of above average rainfall are believed to be the major reason for the low numbers,' Gus Mills, Ursula Buettner, Harriet Davies-Mostert and Johan du Toit reported after completing an investigation into the factors affecting the survival of juvenile wild dogs in the eight to 12 packs inhabiting the Kruger's 4 280-square-kilometre Southern District. By analysing rainfall data, the research team was able to show that the amount of rain that falls up to two years before pups are born could influence their survival by affecting their mothers' condition before birth. Most pups in the Kruger are born in early June, shortly after the onset of the dry season. At this time of the year, grass is usually shorter and shrubs smaller, allowing coursing hunters like wild dogs that chase their quarry for up to five kilometres at a steady 48 kilometres per hour to avoid obstacles like tree stumps and holes in the ground more readily. Less cover also makes it easier to detect lions, which actively seek out and kill wild dogs. Plus, with less greenery to eat, impalas and other prey lose condition, rendering them increasingly vulnerable to predation. The opposite is true after a couple of above-average rainy seasons, when high grass, thick bush and well-fed prey may last well into the dry months. So a drier cycle generally improves the dogs' nutritional well-being, in turn benefiting the pups' survival chances, particularly up to the age of six months but less so up to nine months. Once they are a year old, the link is broken and influences such as pack size affect survival. Although dry conditions do not ensure pup survival, the researchers hoped 'that several dry years will reverse the population trend'.

But the 2009 photographic count's minimum total population of 130 dogs in 19 packs indicated that overall average pack size had declined to seven. Just 11 dogs in four packs were photographed in the Northern District, down from the estimated 250 in 19 packs 14 years earlier. The latter figure was particularly distressing as until then the northern population had not fluctuated in the way the Southern District's had. 'As yet we don't know why the northern population has dropped so dramatically,' wild dog specialist Harriet Davies-Mostert told me. Currently chairperson of the Wild Dog Advisory Group (WAG), and head of science and research at the EWT, she spent four years from 2002 to 2006 in the field investigating pack dynamics, movement and dispersal rates of a pack of wild dogs reintroduced into Venetia Limpopo Nature Reserve on South Africa's northernmost border with Botswana and Zimbabwe for her D. Phil. from Oxford University. 'Several untested hypotheses have been put forward including increased lion predation, disease, increased edge effects outside park boundaries due to a growing human population, or a combination of the above.' Scientists like Davies-Mostert are well aware that effective conservation depends on correctly identifying the threats that cause decline or hinder recovery. 'If, for example, the decline is due to disease, we could vaccinate domestic dogs on the western boundary,' she says. 'Or if the small size of their population is limiting recovery, we could artificially boost numbers through translocation, as was done successfully in Hluhluwe-Imfolozi Park in the early 2000s. This year [2011] the EWT, in partnership with SANParks, is starting a five-year study to look at a number of factors we believe could be responsible.'

Although dry conditions do not ensure pup survival, the researchers hoped 'that several dry years will reverse the population trend'.

The enigma of what so severely limits game-park populations of this supremely efficient hunter and producer of bountiful litters of puppies has long puzzled conservationists. In striking contrast to lion and hyaena densities of approximately 100 per 1 000 square kilometres in the Kruger, wild dogs hover at a minimum density of just 17 per 1 000 square kilometres. Improving their long-term conservation status in the Kruger had become a pressing issue by the late 1990s when zoologist Martyn Gorman, from Aberdeen University's School of Biological Sciences, and Gus Mills submitted a paper that examined factors affecting wild dog distribution and density. Data for the study were collected from eight packs inhabiting the Southern District, which has the park's highest wild dog density. By fitting individuals with radio collars or with collar-mounted satellite transmitters or by implanting radio transmitters, they were able to locate them at least once a month and determine pack locations and composition.

A territorial wildebeest bull stands his ground (above). Unlike in other parts of Africa, Kruger wildebeest show little fear of wild dogs. An alpha wild dog (right) uses a stalking threat display to intimidate an assertive subordinate.

Until this study there had been much support in scientific circles for the 'resource dispersion' hypothesis, which predicted that wild carnivore populations are limited by food distribution. So an immediate priority was to establish the packs' food habits. It was discovered that impalas comprised nearly 75 per cent of kills and 80 per cent of the meat eaten by the Southern District's wild dogs. Kudu venison made up eight per cent of their diet, although in the Pretoriuskop region, where kudus are particularly plentiful, that jumped to 35 per cent of meat eaten and 15 per cent of kills. Duikers and steenbok each comprised nine per cent of kills, followed, at two per cent, by bushbucks and reedbucks.

Lean, long-legged and light-footed, wild dogs are built for endurance chases that depend on persistence, speed and stamina.

Thirty years earlier, in the 1960s, Tol Pienaar published findings that showed impalas made up a similar 80 per cent of prey killed by wild dogs. In the south, impalas comprised nearly 95 per cent of kills but in the Central and Northern districts both waterbucks and kudus had higher preference ratings, which measures kills in proportion to the prey species' population size. Other important prey included reedbuck, mountain reedbuck (at Malelane), bushbuck, nyala, duiker, steenbok, Sharpe's grysbok and ostrich. Young wildebeest, tsessebe, eland and even sable were taken during the calving season but adults were largely ignored. Pienaar also found that, in contrast to lions and even leopards, wild dogs killed large numbers of pregnant females and newborns during the lambing and calving seasons. In the dry season comparatively larger numbers of single territorial males or individuals from male herds were caught and during the rut exhausted or injured rams were often run down.

A fascinating 2003 study in Zimbabwe's Save Valley Conservancy undertaken by Alistair Pole, Iain Gordon and Martyn Gorman from Aberdeen University found 'that wild dogs selectively predate those individuals within a population that are in poorer condition'. Lean, long-legged and light-footed, wild dogs are built for endurance chases that depend on persistence, speed and stamina. To produce the food that supplies the energy to keep their bodies moving, the pack must hunt every morning and evening but, because their hunting method exacts very high energy costs, they live on an energetic knife-edge. One coping adaptation that plays a key role does so by storing a reserve of oxygen-carrying red-blood cells, which are released into the blood stream as the chase intensifies. The turbo-boost of oxygen prevents muscle fatigue, so the dogs can keep running as their quarry tires. But just as important to their success, as the biologists showed, is the tactic of cutting out the weakest animals.

As they scatter on sighting a hunting pack, many impalas employ a characteristic rocking-horse gait known to biologists as a 'pursuit deterrence'. The display signals that those impalas are in prime condition and too nimble to catch. It is the impalas that do not display that draw the pack's attention. By analysing the marrow fat levels in the leg bones of 242 impalas killed by wild dogs with those of 67 impalas randomly shot during the course of a year, the researchers were able to demonstrate that the robust impalas' fervent dance of defence really works. Low bone-marrow fat levels indicate animals in poor condition. The marrow levels in the culled impalas were relatively high and varied little throughout the year. The levels in wild dog kills, however, were generally lower, particularly in the wet season, indicating that impalas in poor condition were caught most often – a fine example of Darwin's survival of the fittest.

In their study, Mills and Gorman found that the density of wild dogs in the Kruger does not appear to be determined solely by the dispersion pattern of their prey.

The researchers were surprised to discover that 'there was a strong but inverse relationship between the number of impala in a pack's territory and the density of dogs in that territory ... This quite unexpected finding implies that wild dogs were at their most dense where there was least food.' Conversely, the dogs occurred at their lowest densities where impalas, their primary prey, were most abundant.

'If the dispersion pattern of food plays only a minor role in determining the density and distribution of wild dogs in KNP, what other factors might be more important?' Mills and Gorman wondered. By analysing their data regarding the type of habitat preferred by large predators, it emerged 'that wild dogs avoid those habitats chosen by lions regardless of the fact that they may contain high densities of their own prey'. Lions' favourite prey, wildebeest, buffaloes and zebras, are at their highest densities in combretum bushveld, acacia thickets and marula savanna, and these habitats are highly favoured by lions but avoided by wild dogs. The reason? Lion predation is an important cause of wild dog mortality. In the Kruger, lions account for nearly 40 per cent of pup mortality and around 45 per cent of natural adult deaths. With its herds of antelopes and zebras, the Kruger's central plains are a carnivore cafeteria, and it is for that very reason that wild dogs stay away. Mills and Gorman argue that this largely explains why wild dog density is lower in the Kruger, and possibly other areas, than would be predicted based on prey availability. Although wild dogs do not reach high densities anywhere, they are lowest where hyaenas and lions are most common.

Mills and Gorman note that the Kruger's wild dogs also tend to avoid habitats favoured by hyaenas, although not as ardently as they do those occupied by lions.

A tranquilliser dart finds its mark. This wild dog is destined to play a role in the Endangered Wildlife Trust's Kruger Rare Carnivore Programme, which is investigating the threats wild dogs and cheetahs face and the factors affecting their numbers and movements in the Greater Kruger ecosystem.

There are no records of hyaenas killing wild dogs in the Kruger and, although they often attend their kills – Tol Pienaar reports that eight wild dogs hunting along the Jock of the Bushveld Road in Malelane section were followed by five low-flying vultures, a hyaena with two half-grown pups and four jackals – they rarely deprive the dogs of food and appear to be more of an irritant than a significant limiting factor. The researchers point out that past management practices, especially the widespread installation of artificial waterholes, have favoured lions and hyaenas by encouraging the buildup of resident prey populations. They suggest

Kelly Marnewick

that 'if the major conservation objective of the KNP is to "maintain biodiversity in all its natural facets and fluxes", then a move toward a more natural distribution and availability of water may be to the benefit of smaller and less dominant carnivores, including the wild dog and cheetah'. By holding wild dogs at low densities through direct killing, competition at kills, loss of food and exclusion from areas of high prey density, interspecific competition plays a direct role in making them vulnerable to extinction.

Just how determined wild dogs are to raise pups in a lion-free environment was brought home to me during my early days in wildlife conservation when I was based in the mining town of Phalaborwa, close to the Kruger entrance gate. At the time there were two parallel border fences, about 500 metres apart, sealing off the park as comprehensively as possible from the town and neighbouring cattle country. Between the fences was a tangle of mopane scrub that supported a fair number of impalas, kudus, warthogs and steenbok, and whenever I had the time I would duck through the barbed wire and take long rambles along well-maintained game trails. One stifling morning some unseen animal gave a deep, harsh alarm bark and hurriedly retreated through the long grass towards a tall termite mound. I thought it might be a warthog heading back to its burrow and decided to climb the termitarium in the hope of catching a cooling breeze. While sitting there I noticed a lot of dog-like tracks and for a moment thought 'hyaena!' but rejected it almost immediately as I knew their track well and was just concluding that, in fact, I was sitting on top of a wild dog nursery when I heard a sudden movement behind me. I looked over my shoulder and there, almost within touching distance, stood a lone adult wild dog. For a long, suspended moment we stared into each other's eyes, then it gave another '*woof*', turned and trotted away. I quietly lowered myself to the burrow entrance it had just come out of and came face to face with a collection of pups that regarded me without the least sign of concern. I left quickly, not wanting to upset the domestic scene any more than I already had. As I headed home it occurred to me that the pack had come through the fence specifically to den in a place that lions would have difficulty accessing.

> For a long, suspended moment we stared into each other's eyes, then it gave another 'woof', turned and trotted away.

A decade later, in the mid-1980s, I spent a year at Sabi Sabi Private Game Reserve, part of the Sabi Sand complex, and was struck by the unusually high number of cheetahs and wild dogs. Not only were they regularly seen but nearly every female cheetah had cubs, ranging in age from those just out of the lair to nearly full-grown subadults – clearly a very healthy survival rate. The wild dog packs also had youngsters of various ages, including one pack of 22, of which almost half were juveniles. What was missing was a single functioning pride of lions. There were lions of both sexes, but they were all young nomads and, without the security of the pride, they had very little success in raising cubs. I guessed, although it was pure speculation, that perhaps commercial hunting on neighbouring properties had killed all the adult males and in the process caused the breakdown of pride structure. Whatever the truth of that hunch, the absence of territorial lions and the relatively few hyaenas had given the local wild dogs and cheetahs a window of opportunity, of which they were taking advantage.

Things at Sabi Sabi have changed dramatically in the interim. Both wild dogs and cheetahs are now few and far between, while lions and lion prides are flourishing. This situation is repeated throughout the private game reserves. In 2010, while in the Kruger for personal research, I met up with Jessica Watermeyer, a master's student at Rhodes University, and Grant Beverley, a project research coordinator, both contracted by the EWT to gather and analyse data on the population dynamics and dispersal habits of wild dogs and cheetahs operating beyond the Kruger's western boundary. They confirmed that, yes, lion numbers had increased dramatically, which is thought to be a major reason why wild dogs and cheetahs are doing so badly. The following year Jess e-mailed me to report that nine of the 12 pups born at Ngala Safari Lodge in Timbavati were missing, apparently killed by lions. Plus, the only surviving subadult from a pack that denned in Sabi Sand in 2010 had been killed by lions in early 2011.

There was worse news to come. From January to December 2010 about 30 domestic dogs in Sabi Sand were confirmed to have rabies. Although so far no wild dogs have tested positive, one was shot in Timbavati in 2009 as a precaution; the results returned negative. Carried across the park's western boundary by domestic dogs owned by subsistence farmers engaged in illegal hunting, the virus has become a pervasive threat in the region. The Serengeti experience grimly demonstrated that rabies is a virulent killer of wild dogs. Like Serengeti, the Kruger has a small population that is vulnerable to a knockout blow. SANParks' large-mammal ecologist Sam Ferreira worries, 'If disease breaks out there are not enough animals to serve as a buffer and allow immunity to develop effectively. This could lead to a dramatic decrease or even local extinction of this population.'

The dog on the left shows submission by licking the corners of a dominant dog's mouth. Unlike other canids, wild dogs have a passive hierarchy, with rank determined by body language, and submission emphasised over aggression.

As the world increasingly becomes a handmaiden to the human species, saving large carnivores like wild dogs has become one of the most difficult tests conservationists face. What happened to the wild dogs of the Lowveld is a case study of how a thriving species can get knocked down by multiple blows. Faced with disease and shrinking room to roam in their African home and pushed into marginal lands by stronger competitors, what options are left? It was always believed that, if free-ranging packs were to be viable, they required big, wild country and plenty of it. And that is a big part of the problem – they have run out of space.

In the absence of safe migration corridors along which wild dogs can move, forward-looking wild dog specialists in South Africa hit upon the idea of complementing the country's single population in the Kruger by managing separate subpopulations in several small, geographically isolated conservation areas as a single meta-population.

This highly technical concept involved reintroducing wild dogs into suitable reserves and, because dispersal, immigration and gene flow could not happen naturally, they would be mimicked by translocation. In other words, to maintain genetic diversity, these parks would swap breeding stock, much as zoos do.

Beginning in Hluhluwe-Imfolozi in 1980, 127 wild dogs were released into 12 reintroduction sites – including Madikwe, Marakele, Pilanesberg, Mkhuze, Venetia Limpopo and Tswalu Kalahari Reserve – on 18 separate occasions. Up to 2007 they produced 129 puppies. The high survival rates of the released dogs and their offspring, and the fact that pups were born at all release sites, signal the success of the operation so far, particularly in light of past failures in other African states. Those failures resulted mainly from human persecution but, because most South African game parks are fenced and regularly patrolled, wild dogs are at least somewhat prevented from straying and potentially falling foul of unfriendly neighbours. It makes all the difference. Harriet Davies-Mostert reports that the deaths of 71 per cent of radio-collared wild dogs (the least biased method of assessing mortality) in the meta-population between 1998 and 2007 were due to natural causes. But it is still a dangerous world out there for wild dogs and they will need a lot of human help for the foreseeable future if these inveterate wanderers are to survive in their natural element.

From January to December 2010 about 30 domestic dogs in Sabi Sand were confirmed to have rabies.

Wild dog behaviour during greeting ceremonies involves play-fighting and jumping over each other, accompanied by bird-like twittering sounds and high-pitched squeals. All this excitement helps build the pack's enthusiasm for the upcoming hunt.

12 The **hyaena's** song

**Nothing that enters the mouth
of a hyaena comes out again.**

Ndau proverb

Nigel J. Dennis/Images of Africa

The spotted hyaena has long had a sinister reputation, but it should be said at the outset that its true way of life has been obscured by the myths, superstitions and mystery that swirled around it. Modern research has gone a long way towards revising its bad image, including the African legend that this seeming abomination of creation is unable even to get its gender sorted out and changes sex from male to female at will. Beginning in the 1960s, fascinating field research in South and East Africa began to draw aside the veils of ignorance surrounding this much-maligned creature's basic biology.

It turns out that hyaenas are not hermaphrodites, but the real story is almost as fantastical as the legend. Female spotted hyaenas are unusual in the animal world in that they are heavier and more aggressive than males and are socially dominant. This linear dominance hierarchy is asserted almost every time there is any question of precedence. When they meet, males give way to females. Both sexes engage in territorial scent-marking expeditions, territorial defence and hunting, but females usually take the lead, and only females actively feed and protect cubs. Theirs is a fully matriarchal society, which arguably has taken female liberation a step beyond equality, in that somehow in her evolution the female hyaena has developed bizarre male-like genitals – it is difficult for humans to tell the sexes apart, except when a lactating mother has swollen nipples. A female's enlarged clitoris is similar in size, shape and erectile ability to the male's penis. In addition, the external labia are fused to form a pseudo-scrotum. Females urinate, mate and give birth through a urogenital canal in the clitoris that is twice the length of that of a similar-sized mammal, which has risky repercussions for young females giving birth for the first time.

> It turns out that hyaenas are not hermaphrodites, but the real story is almost as fantastical as the legend.

As the clitoris' opening is much narrower than the newborn's head, it takes time for the foetus to push through, but time is not on its side. The placenta is shorter than the birth canal and eventually becomes detached, which starves the cub of oxygen and many are stillborn when delivery takes too long. Moreover, giving birth is so traumatic for new would-be mothers that nine to 18 per cent of them die in labour. For those that survive, subsequent births are easier once the clitoris opening is torn. So, given the high costs, how and why did this curious quirk of nature develop?

The direction in which reproductive organs develop begins in the foetus and is determined by the hormones secreted. Female hyaenas produce high levels of androgen, a steroid hormone that controls the development of masculine characteristics. As to the advantage that this offers, one theory suggests that dominant females are able to guard against potentially cannibalistic males eating their offspring. Another proposes that sexual mimicry is the outcome of selection for female dominance and all the benefits that accrue to high rank holders within the rigidly enforced clan hierarchy.

The latter hypothesis notes that in this openly competitive society, high-ranking females have priority at carcasses, which provides increased reproductive success in comparison with low-ranking females. The cubs of high-status females eat better, grow faster and bigger and achieve higher rank, which is passed on from mother to daughter and comes with privileges denied the lower classes. In the struggle to gain a foothold on the highest rungs of the social ladder, siblings are genetically programmed to fight from their first moments to establish a rank that they will keep for the rest of their lives.

The number of infants in a litter is typically two, occasionally one and rarely three. Unusually for carnivores, they are born with their eyes open and canine teeth fully erupted. As the second cub emerges, the first attacks it by taking hold of the skin on its neck or back and shaking it furiously. No sooner is the new arrival free of the placenta than it fights back. Fighting may continue for hours or days until dominance is established. When the subordinate ceases defending itself, aggression diminishes but the dominant cub continues to threaten and attack. Mothers will intervene when they can but often they cannot, as the den's tunnels are too narrow to admit an adult. When feeding time comes around, the cubs emerge from the burrow to suckle above ground.

The subordinate cub grows more slowly, probably the result of having second choice of teat and because of frequent interruptions; twins' weights can differ by as much as 30 to 50 per cent. So fierce are the battles that 25 per cent of newborn cubs may fall victim to siblicide, especially in female–female litters. Killing a competitor means the winner has exclusive access to mother's milk, greatly improving its chances of surviving the dangerous first year – only 50 to 60 per cent of cubs do so, the rest being lost to siblicide, infanticide by adult clan members, starvation, predation and burrow cave-ins.

Social politics among clan members is very important in hyaena society, with individuals regularly forging alliances and coalitions. Its complex clan life probably

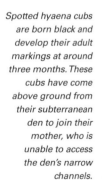
Spotted hyaena cubs are born black and develop their adult markings at around three months. These cubs have come above ground from their subterranean den to join their mother, who is unable to access the den's narrow channels.

accounts for the hyaena's social intelligence, which is on a par with some primate species. Studies indicate that the relative amount of frontal cortex in their brains not used for motor control is higher than in other carnivores. Field research in the Kruger has shown that clans occupy territories of 25 to 150 square kilometres, which are clearly delineated by scent-marking stations where clan members deposit anal-gland secretions onto grass stalks – for hyaenas, scent talks – and defecate at prominent communal latrines, especially in border regions. Kruger hyaenas spend one-fifth of their activity time on territorial patrols. Though members range over a wide area, they demarcate and aggressively defend only the central part of their total range against incursions from other clans. When scent-marked borders are violated, adjacent clans engage in fierce, noisy battles to reinforce boundaries.

Breakthroughs in scientific cognisance notwithstanding, legends linger. Some have only to hear the hyaena's eerie vocalisations to sense it is in league with the devil. Nervous listeners imagine the mischief these shuffling, lurking night stalkers might be up to as they give voice to perhaps the most evocative sound in the African bush – a loud, haunted '*whoo-oop*' that begins low, rises to a falsetto scream and ends with a deep, soft growl. There is also the famous maniacal laugh plus a cacophonous repertoire of other weirdly human-sounding whines, giggles, shrieks, gurgles, yells and chuckles. A pack on a kill or in a territorial fight sounds like hell's own choir. Then

Until the middle of the last century several tribes, including the Maasai, laid out their dead for hyaenas to dispose of.

there is the hyaena's association with death. Until the middle of the last century several tribes, including the Maasai, laid out their dead for hyaenas to dispose of. These master thieves soon became adept body-snatchers around villages, regardless of whether the bodies were dead or alive. All that, plus the belief that they are hermaphrodites, only added to their aura of evil.

Field research helped alter the hyaena's stereotypical image but its reputation remained unredeemed well into the 20th century. In *Green Hills of Africa*, an account of a month on safari in Serengeti and nearby Lake Manyara district in 1933, Ernest Hemingway, who prided himself on his sportsmanship, regaled his readers with a savage description of his dealings with a creature he treated as the dirty joke of the natural world:

'Highly humorous was the hyena obscenely loping, full belly dragging, at daylight on the plain, who, shot from the stern, skittered on into speed to tumble end over end. Mirth provoking was the hyena that stopped out of range by an alkali lake to look back and, hit in the chest, went over on his back, his four feet and his full belly in the air. Nothing could be more jolly than the hyena coming suddenly wedge-headed and stinking out of high grass by a *donga*, hit at ten yards, who raced his tail in three narrowing, scampering circles until he died... We shot thirty-five hyena out of the lot that follow the wildebeest migration to keep after the cows that are about to calve and wish we had ammunition to kill a hundred.'

Hemingway got it right when he observed that Serengeti's hyaenas shadow the migratory wildebeest. In the dry season, when their principal prey, wildebeest, Thomson's gazelles and zebras, depart the open plains for the woodlands, some hyaenas become

FOLKLORE, MYTHOLOGY, WITCHCRAFT AND HYAENAS

In his wonderfully satisfying book *The Tree Where Man Was Born*, author
and naturalist Peter Matthiessen writes: 'Many tales are told in many parts of
Africa of hyena spirits in human form who are detected by some such sign
as a mouth in the back of the head. A werewolf hyena is often an old witch
woman … The Bantu of Tanzania know of those who ride hyenas in the night.
Peasants are more witch-ridden than hunters and nomads, and among the
Mbugwe, tillers of sorghum and millet who settled on the bare mud flats south
of Lake Manyara as a protection against Maasai raids, more than half the adult
population are considered witches who control all the hyenas or "night cattle"
in the region, and sometimes lions into the bargain.'

nomadic, following their prey. However, mothers with cubs too young to accompany
them are forced to commute on long hunting expeditions of up to 140 kilometres on
a round trip, spending between 46 and 62 per cent of their whole year shuttling back
and forth between the herds and their cubs, while travelling a total of some 2 800 to
3 700 kilometres per year. Once they have fed they hurry back to the den, but they risk
being absent for as long as three or four days. Ordinarily a mother suckles her cubs twice
a day, in the early morning and evening; her high calcium diet may explain her ability to
suckle for 14 to 18 months while producing the richest milk of any terrestrial carnivore.
But when she is away the cubs get nothing to eat.

Spotted hyaena mothers do not share in the care of offspring, which means that
females do not suckle cubs other than their own. Nor do they carry food back for them
and, unlike wild dogs, hyaenas do not regurgitate meat for their young. That they
have not adopted a more helpful system towards cubs seemed odd to zoologist Hans
Kruuk, who began studying them in Serengeti in 1964 and later in Ngorongoro Crater,
but in all probability it is yet another example of the jockeying for position within the
clan's pecking order. Though cubs show remarkable resilience – they can survive for as
long as nine days without food – Kruuk often saw Serengeti cubs in a pitiful condition
and once found three that had starved to death. As most cubs die in one of the den's
underground tunnels, he could only wonder how many succumbed this way each
year. It is tempting to think that, had Hemingway known that by so casually pulling
the trigger he was potentially condemning young cubs to a slow death, he might have
desisted. Or perhaps he would have chalked it up as a bonus. With its slouching gait,
scruffy appearance, misshapen symmetry and ghoulish grin, the hyaena is not an easy
animal to admire or sympathise with.

The reason so few facts were known about hyaenas for so long is that they are
mostly active after dark, when they take advantage of their superior night vision to
do their hunting. Not until intrepid field researchers and wildlife cinematographers
ventured forth after sunset into the action-packed night was the hyaena revealed as a
highly successful hunter in its own right. It was a long time coming, given that as far

back as the 1880s British East African colonial commissioner and wildlife artist Harry Johnston had noted 'the spotted hyaena is a much more predatory animal than one generally imagines. Not only does it steal sheep and calves from the herds, but it even carries off children and will often attack wounded or weakly men'.

The way a hyaena obtains its food powerfully affects its role in the network of savanna relationships. It is the most abundant large carnivore in the Kruger – there are an estimated 2 700 with densities ranging from three to 20 hyaenas per 100 square kilometres – so an understanding of its ecology is essential when considering the role of predation in the lives or, more important to hyaena needs, the deaths of the prey populations.

Although they prefer fresh meat, hyaenas can and will eat every piece of an animal – bones, horns, hooves and even teeth are digested within 24 hours thanks to their highly acidic stomach juices. They share qualities with a pit bull, a dog that is all skull and maw, bred to bite. Vice-like jaws, massive and immensely strong, together with a short and broad muzzle, thick neck and rounded skull have superbly fashioned hyaenas for the task of biting. The immense power of their neck muscles and forequarters is best appreciated as they tear chunks off a carcass or hoist a whole impala carcass well off the ground. Heavily constructed large back teeth (carnassials) in their upper and lower jaws slice like shears through stubborn tendons and thick hide. They splinter bones to extract the rich marrow or crush them into digestible fragments – even buffalo thigh bones are not immune. I once saw a lion gnaw on a terrapin for an hour before giving up; a hyaena took over and with a single crunch cracked the carapace the way a parrot cracks a nut – pop!

Hyaenas are anything but fastidious eaters. They eat meat in the final stages of putrefaction and feed on the carcasses of predators such as lions and leopards and sometimes other hyaenas. They will

Night stalkers at work. Brought to bay, this exhausted kudu cow turns to face her tormentors, a pair of hyaenas who have pursued her relentlessly.

gobble down lion and wild dog dung, probably because of the high protein content. They dine on animals that have died of anthrax and foot-and-mouth disease without experiencing any ill-effects, and may be a factor in preventing the spread of the diseases. (On the other hand, the late Kenyan professional hunter Syd Downey claimed that they will not touch an animal that has died of rinderpest or been killed by a poisoned arrow.) Hair is practically the only animal product they cannot digest and they solve that problem by disgorging hairballs. Only inorganic matter is passed in faeces, which turn chalk white when dry due to the high mineral content – almost pure calcium mixed with guard hairs, which is handy for researchers wanting to identify what kind of beasts they have been eating. On the African savanna, bits and pieces of most wild animals enter a hyaena's mouth sooner or later.

These hyaenas reveal their lighter side while playing amicably in a pool on a hot day. Hyaenas also cache food in shallow pools to keep it safe from jackals and vultures.

During his 1939 hyaena study in eastern Tanzania's Masai Steppe, Harrison Matthews recorded: 'The spotted hyaena is primarily a scavenger, but often pulls down game on its own account. Several individuals often combine in hunting … In seeking food its movements are largely determined by the wanderings of herds of game and of nomadic bands of Masai and their cattle.' But it was not until the late 1950s and early '60s that Pretoria University zoology professor Fritz Eloff, with invaluable help from local Bushman trackers in the Kalahari Gemsbok National Park (now part of the Kgalagadi Transfrontier Park), was able to announce that the spotted hyaenas of the Kalahari are true hunters 'and scavenging seems to be the exception, and not the other way around'.

Eloff confessed that he had never witnessed a hyaena kill but his trackers were able 'to reconstruct the whole event from the spoor prints and other signs left in the sand'. The most abundant large antelope, the gemsbok, appeared to be the desert hyaena's main quarry although it is also the hyaena's most dangerous adversary. His party came across a dead hyaena with a wound in its belly, which may have been caused by a gemsbok's sharp horns. The park warden, Elias Le Riche, recalled three separate cases of a hyaena being killed by a gemsbok. Eloff also noted that 'in spite of its lazy, cumbersome appearance, the hyaena can not only travel fast [up to 65 kilometres per hour] but has great staying powers'. A ranger tracked a pack that pursued a gemsbok for 23 kilometres before overtaking and killing it. Eloff personally followed the spoor of hyaenas that travelled 80 kilometres overnight from their den and back in order to feast on a few goats penned near the warden's house. He discovered that the hyaenas of the southern Kalahari 'maraud in packs like the African hunting dog'. The largest number he found together was 11 but according to Le Riche packs of up to 30 take part in hunts and on one occasion more than 50 were seen together at Kwang waterhole in the Nossob River. 'They were not found at a kill and were probably out hunting,' the professor surmised.

When Eloff's findings were published in 1964 they were widely thought to be an exception to the rule. Ten years later his Kalahari observations were confirmed when Gus Mills began his career with SANParks and spent the next 34 years studying the large carnivores of the Kgalagadi and Kruger parks. Mills' first project was in the Kalahari researching the comparative behavioural ecology of brown and spotted hyaenas. From 1979 to 1982 he used direct observations, analysed found carcasses and tracked spoor to establish the feeding habits and prey selection of the area's spotted hyaenas. Of the 346 carcasses he examined, wildebeest and gemsbok made up 67 per cent of kills and 63 per cent of carcasses fed on. Juveniles contributed 58 per cent of the kills, with gemsbok calves alone comprising nearly 30 per cent. Mills noted that just 36 per cent of the carcasses had been scavenged. In other words, the spotted hyaenas of the Kalahari hunted most of the food they consumed, concentrating their hunting on vulnerable animals.

In Serengeti, Hans Kruuk calculated that there were 500 prey animals for every hyaena but in Ngorongoro that dropped to 40 prey animals for each hyaena. Such a high degree of predation pressure ensures that very few Crater antelopes or zebras grow old. Hyaenas also exact a heavy toll on the annual crop of Ngorongoro's newborn wildebeest calves, although the slaughter varies from herd to herd. The closed ranks of a big herd reduce losses by hiding and shielding calves, whereas hyaenas pick off all or nearly all of the calves in a small herd. Those calves that survive are soon strong enough to keep up with the herd, whereupon the Crater hyaenas turn their attention back to the adults, concentrating on the sick, lame and old. Victims are often selected when hyaenas test a herd by loping through it, to see if a weakened member falls behind or exhibits some subtle flaw that may be imperceptible to the human eye.

Though Crater hyaenas undoubtedly have a major impact on their main prey, to the point that Crater wildebeest die at a younger age and have a faster population turnover than in neighbouring Serengeti, wildebeest equally are controlling the hyaenas. The Crater hyaena population is much denser than in Serengeti. Like the wildebeest, the hyaenas also have a faster turnover rate and adults die at earlier ages, but in their case it is because there is scarcely enough food for them all. It transpires that herbivore numbers in Ngorongoro are limited by the amount of grass available in any one year, with hyaenas taking those wildebeest weakened by starvation when overgrazing threatens, thus preventing the grasslands from being ravaged. Once again, all is in flux, all comes full circle: rainfall determines grass growth, which decides how many wildebeest and zebras there are, which regulates the hyaena population by creating more or less competition.

He discovered that the hyaenas of the southern Kalahari 'maraud in packs like the African hunting dog'.

The Ngorongoro situation is the way it is because the prey population does not migrate. By contrast, in Serengeti, hyaenas have to make a great effort to connect with their food supply at certain times of the year, which may explain why their numbers are relatively low compared with prey biomass, and why they have a comparatively small impact on prey numbers. Typically they hunt alone 75 per cent of the time for small prey such as Thomson's gazelle, or in small groups of two to five, but they are flexible and larger packs cooperate to bring down bigger prey. Kruuk noted that a lone hyaena hunting wildebeest calves in Serengeti has a 15 per cent success rate, which increases to 23 per cent for a pair and 31 per cent for three or more hunters. A study in adjoining Masai Mara National Reserve found that adding a second hunter increases the success rate by 19 per cent and a third hunter by a further 20 per cent. On average, 30 to 35 per cent of all hyaena hunts end in kills.

Hyaenas generally tend to hunt whichever prey species are seasonally abundant. In the Mara, more than 80 per cent of their kills are topis (the northern tsessebe) and Thomson's gazelles, but they switch to wildebeest and zebras for four months of the year when the migration arrives. Changes in prey abundance in Ngorongoro between the 1960s and '90s led to increased hyaena predation of buffalo calves and adult wildebeest.

In the Kruger it had been recognised as early as the 1960s that hyaenas were more resourceful and formidable predators than their reputation suggested, although 20 years earlier James Stevenson-Hamilton had echoed the universally held view of them as 'subsisting principally upon carrion and bones'. He believed that the hyaena's 'lack of speed and his natural tendencies [meaning cowardice] prevent him from being a game-killer in the same sense as the hunting dog or the leopard'. That is not so but he uncharacteristically misconstrued several aspects of hyaena behaviour, perhaps because he was unable to witness nocturnal activities and hopefully not because he gave way to personal prejudice towards a creature he regarded as a 'wily robber' and 'cowardly animal'. Despite his professed disdain for hyaenas, Stevenson-Hamilton reported 'instances in the Kruger National Park of several spotted hyaenas having combined to attack and kill even full-grown larger antelopes which they have in some manner succeeded in cornering'.

When assembling his 1969 landmark profile of predator–prey relationships in the Kruger, Tol Pienaar ruefully acknowledged the shortcomings inherent in counting carcasses to determine what hyaenas are hunting: 'The remains of prey animals killed by spotted hyaenas are rarely found in view of the complete manner in which the carcass is devoured.' Hyaenas generally consume almost 100 per cent of a carcass while other predators leave 25 to 35 per cent of theirs as wastage, some of which is also eaten by hyaenas. Pienaar supplied an example of the problem confronting him: 'A full-grown impala was recently caught by a few spotted hyaenas on the lawn in front of the research block at Skukuza. So completely was the carcass consumed that a few fragments of bone and a smudge of blood and intestinal contents were the only traces left to tell of the tragedy.' In their 2008 analysis of predator–prey size relationships in the Kruger's large-mammal food web, Norman Owen-Smith and Gus Mills suggest that even if half the food obtained by hyaenas comes from scavenging rather than their own kills, fewer than five per cent of hyaena kills are found.

On average, 30 to 35 per cent of all hyaena hunts end in kills.

Of the Kruger's five largest carnivores, hyaenas have the widest diet. In a 1990 paper detailing the results of fieldwork conducted between June 1982 and September 1984 that examined the diet of the Kruger's hyaenas, Pretoria University's Joh Henschel and John Skinner listed an astonishing diversity of items on their menu, including spiders and insects, barbel, frogs, snakes, tortoises, owl eggs, doves, mice, aardvarks, pangolins and porcupines, although 12 ungulate species represented 45 per cent of all items the hyaenas fed on and 94 per cent of the meat they ate. The researchers also examined factors that could influence diet, such as prey abundance, species size, causes of mortality, food availability and social relationships among hyaena clan members. To do so they radio-collared 11 of the 17 members of the Mavumbye clan living along the Mavumbye River north of Satara rest camp, and observed them for nearly 3 700 hours as they went about their affairs. Hyaena scats were collected and analysed at six other sites near Pretoriuskop, Lower Sabie, Orpen, Olifants, Shingwedzi and Pafuri for comparison.

Henschel and Skinner found that, although Kruger hyaenas frequently scavenge carcasses of large ungulates, particularly buffalo, more than half of the meat they eat is from their own kills. The most important prey species overall in the study was impala, which supplied 33 per cent of what they ate, and buffalo (22 per cent), followed sequentially by wildebeest, zebra, kudu and warthog. The study coincided with the prolonged 1982/3 drought, and the researchers noted that the high importance ratings of impala, kudu and warthog in hyaena diets suggest that they selectively hunt these species when they become weakened by drought. In contrast, buffalo meat was mostly scavenged from drought victims and lion kills.

Between December 1974 and July 1978, Butch Smuts examined the stomach contents of 167 hyaenas culled in the Central District and found that they fed mainly on impalas, zebras and wildebeest. During the lambing season, some hyaenas hunted impalas almost exclusively; their diets comprised nearly 90 per cent impala meat, of which over 90 per cent was made up of lambs. Smuts believed that the Kruger hyaenas also hunt zebra foals and wildebeest calves for themselves but rarely take large ungulate adults, instead scavenging them from lion kills. In this regard their behaviour is similar to that of other hyaenas living in dense habitats, and in contrast to the pack-hunting methods often used by hyaenas living in open grasslands like Ngorongoro. Indirect evidence for this assumption came from 386 nights of casual observation, during which time the largest foraging group of hyaenas he saw was three, with singles being most common.

Research into the ecology of the spotted hyaena in the woodlands of eastern Hwange National Park by Julia Salnicki and Marion Teichmann from the Zimbabwe-based Hyaena Research & Conservation Project has added an unexpected name to the list of animals hunted by hyaenas. 'Our results indicate that hyaenas, when in a group of more than seven, can successfully hunt elephant calves even when adult elephants are present.' Towards the end of the dry season in September/November 1999, the scientists studied a clan of 19 adult and subadult hyaenas by following radio-collared individuals, usually at night, using a spotlight, or at sunrise and sunset. On five occasions they saw them feeding on or killing an elephant calf. Given Hwange's high elephant population, estimated at over 31 000, the researchers note that 'it is not unreasonable to expect that spotted hyaenas would take advantage of this seasonally abundant prey' when elephants gather around windmill-pumped pans, the only available surface water in the dry season. The one occasion they witnessed hyaenas killing a calf, the cow was emaciated, with ribs and pelvic girdle

Some people think there's something infinitely creepy about hyaenas, but they do have endearing qualities, especially the cubs, with their fluffy coats and eyes full of youthful curiosity.

protruding, and the newborn calf was frail and struggled to keep up with its mother. Hyaenas from another clan were observed killing a further four baby elephants; in all nine instances, except for a five-year-old, the calves were only a few days old.

It is conceivable that in future a similar situation could arise in the Kruger when conditions become stressful. Severe droughts leading to malnutrition could trigger increased lion and hyaena predation of infant elephants as well as reduced fertility in female elephants and so help stabilise the surging elephant population. It happened with the Kruger's buffalo population and now natural attrition has replaced the discredited cull. Salnicki and Teichmann point out that many elephants are in poor condition towards the end of the dry season and were particularly so in 1999 because of the reduced quantity and quality of forage, due to poor rains the previous wet season.

Salnicki and Teichmann noted that, although Hwange hyaenas usually forage alone or in groups of two to five, when hunting elephant calves, pack size jumps to between seven and 10 adults. Hans Kruuk also recorded that, when hyaenas in Ngorongoro deliberately set out to hunt bigger prey, specifically zebras, they formed big packs of up to 30 animals. Before a zebra hunt, Kruuk observed clan members meeting and performing what seemed like an infinite number of greeting ceremonies. Once the socialising was over, the pack headed off in the alert posture, their whisk-broom tails flared and upraised, with females usually taking the lead. They ignored herds of wildebeest along the way and when they came across a family group of zebras they began a slow, long-distance chase. The protective stallion tried to bite encroaching

hyaenas and lashed out with his front hooves, so a successful hunt required that he be outflanked. When that happened, the vulnerable target zebra was further slowed by bites to the tail, legs and loins and as it visibly tired the pack closed in rapidly – the more hyaenas, the speedier the end.

Although hyaenas are hunters, they are also opportunists, and will not turn up their nose at an easy meal. The proportion of time hyaenas devote

Hyaenas invariably hunt alone for smaller prey such as impalas (top). An experienced solitary hyaena can even pull down animals as large as this adult wildebeest (above left). The bloody mask of the consummate hunter and scavenger (above right).

to hunting as opposed to scavenging varies according to local environmental conditions. Where prey is plentiful and other predators, especially lions, outnumber hyaenas, they may live primarily as scavengers, provided they are not too numerous themselves; where interactions between lions and hyaenas are few or when scavenging is unrewarding, such as during the wet season, they hunt to a much greater extent. In Ngorongoro in the early '70s when Hans Kruuk undertook his pioneering study, the Crater's 70 lions obtained practically all their food by appropriating 20 per cent of the kills made by the 400 hyaenas, which make their living almost exclusively as hunters. In

Before a zebra hunt, Kruuk observed clan members meeting and performing what seemed like an infinite number of greeting ceremonies.

essence, Crater hyaenas were responsible for selecting prey for both themselves and the lions. Kruuk found that Serengeti hyaenas, on the other hand, scavenge about one third of their food and in turn are robbed of about five per cent of their kills, mainly by lions.

This behaviour – lions obtaining food by robbing hyaenas of their kills – is seldom observed in the Kruger, however. Here, hyaenas scavenge far more from lions than vice versa and may be more reliant on scavenging from lion kills than in most other African parks. So though hyaenas are the Kruger's most abundant large predator, with a biomass equal to that of lions, because they scavenge around half of what they eat, their impact on prey populations is significantly lower than that of lions, except perhaps in the case of impalas. Hyaena society in the Kruger is less organised, with less pack hunting and more solitary foraging than in Ngorongoro, for example. That may explain why Kruger hyaenas rarely kill adult wildebeest or zebra weighing three to four times their own adult weight of 45 to 70 kilograms, instead restricting their hunting to prey smaller than 150 kilograms.

Hyaenas sometimes turn the tables on lions by driving them off a kill. With hair erect and tails held perpendicular, all the while voicing a harsh, menacing growl known as a 'low', they launch intimidating concerted rushes towards the feeding big cats. If there are no adult male lions present and if the hyaenas outnumber the female and subadult lions by four to one, they have a good chance of displacing them. In his 1963 review of the distribution and status of the Kruger's large mammals, Tol Pienaar noted that 'hyaenas will take incredible risks in snatching portions of carcasses killed by lions and often pay with their lives for such rashness … Considerable numbers of spotted hyaenas are killed annually by lions when the latter are molested at kills, but they are rarely eaten by the lions or by other scavengers. Even vultures are apparently loath to feed on hyaena carcasses.'

In an intriguing variation on the customarily hostile relations between lions and hyaenas, I was told an anecdote by a safari operator about a Kruger lioness that lived on her own and the unconventional arrangement she reached with two hyaenas. The trio was first spotted amicably sharing a wildebeest kill that the lioness had made. In the weeks that followed, the three unlikely companions were seen on several more occasions eating together on prey provided by the lioness. It was an extraordinary association but one that proved mutually beneficial to the three participants. The hyaenas got an easy meal but, in a sense, so did the lioness. If she had driven them off, which she could have done, the hyaenas would have called up their clan comrades to help dislodge her. The lioness would have lost out, but the two hyaenas would have ended up with a lot less to eat. Unlike wild dogs, in hyaena society it is every animal for itself, so the hyaenas were tolerated at the kill in exchange for their silence.

For both Kruger's hyaenas and lions, scavenging seems largely a seasonal affair. It is particularly profitable during dry-season droughts when the remains of weakened buffaloes killed by lions can constitute up to 40 per cent of the hyaena's total diet. Their ability to smell carrion four kilometres away and hear the sounds of predators killing prey or contesting a carcass over 10 kilometres away has adapted hyaenas well for their role as scavengers, as has their willingness to eat almost any flesh in any state that comes their way.

Their proficiency at making the most of a meal means that, as predators, more hyaenas can subsist on fewer prey animals than their competitors can and as scavengers they can extract nourishment from what other predators leave behind. Unsure of when next they will eat, hyaenas gorge themselves whenever they can. Hans Kruuk watched 38 hyaenas eat an entire adult zebra in 15 minutes. Disposing of so much food in so little time is a hyaena speciality. An adult Kruger hyaena eats on average around four kilograms of meat per day but is quite capable of bolting 18 kilograms – one third of its own body weight – at a single sitting, far more proportionately than a lion can manage. Ruthlessly applied social etiquette requires that dominant females claim priority access to carcasses so they can eat and quickly return to the communal den to suckle their cubs. Hyaenas that rank low in the clan hierarchy learn to eat fast and eat alone.

Unlike wild dogs, in hyaena society it is every animal for itself, so the hyaenas were tolerated at the kill in exchange for their silence.

Although it is now the Kruger's most abundant large carnivore, the park's hyaena population has exhibited periodic fluctuations in numbers in the past. They were intensively hunted, trapped and even poisoned in the early years and, according to Tol Pienaar, 'by 1925 their numbers were reduced almost to extinction. Some epidemic disease, later becoming endemic in the population, may also have played a role here, as their numbers showed a gradual incline during the 1930s despite persistent control measures.' He noted that, even after the carnivore control policy was terminated in 1960, hyaenas remained relatively scarce in certain regions, whereas they increased exponentially in places like Kingfisherspruit and Tshokwane in the Central District and the Malelane area in the Southern District. 'The population in the far northern part of the Park also experienced an inexplicable decline in numbers during the early 1950's, but has recovered its former status over recent years.' Today they are most abundant in the Central and Southern districts – although Butch Smuts reported a conspicuous absence of hyaenas in the relatively open savanna country east of Crocodile Bridge in the Lower Sabie region and speculated that their distribution was dependent on impala distribution – and least numerous in the Northern District.

It was not until the 1980s that it was fully appreciated just how much the unforeseen and often far-reaching consequences of management actions such as predator control can disrupt the balance between competing carnivores. A perfect example came to light in the 1970s following the lion and hyaena cull in the Central District (see Chapter 3, page 58 and Chapter 8, page 130). Although the lion population bounced back rapidly, the hyaena population had still not fully recovered seven years later. Hyaena researcher Joh Henschel suggested that hyaenas were slow to recolonise areas that had been cleared by control due to competition with lions in combination with the hyaena's distinctive social system. Because their numbers had been reduced, it seems females were unable to synchronise litters and establish a communal den. That led to unusually high cub mortality. The cubs that survived were too few to compensate for adult deaths, most of which were caused by lions. In light of the potentially unpredictable outcomes, Henschel emphasised the need for caution before implementing such high-impact management options as culling.

When visitors to the Kruger talk about hyaenas they are of course referring to the spotted hyaena – it is the only hyaena species found there. But that was not always the case. In the 1940s James Stevenson-Hamilton reported that the slightly smaller brown hyaena 'has been found to exist throughout [the Kruger], though nowhere numerous'. In the 1960s Tol Pienaar considered them 'rare in the Kruger Park and the total population probably does not number more than 150. Of these, the larger proportion inhabits the western areas of the northern district. South of the Olifants River brown hyaenas are very rarely encountered and their impact on the prey community is insignificant.'

> Hyaenas that rank low in the clan hierarchy learn to eat fast and eat alone.

The brown hyaena is a shy and inconspicuous, predominantly nocturnal scavenger that lives in small social groups of up to nine adults and subadults but always forages alone. With its long, shaggy coat of brown to black hair set off by a white ruff around the neck and shoulders, it is a striking-looking, handsome animal. It is thought of as a creature of arid country, including waterless realms like the Namib Desert where it is able to obtain all the moisture it needs from wild fruits such as tsamma melons. But it also lives in open woodland savannas and though seldom seen is still quite common in South Africa's Limpopo province, including the Messina district, adjacent to the northern Kruger, where it favours rocky, mountainous areas with bush cover to lie up in during the day.

The first time Stevenson-Hamilton came across the species in the Sabi Game Reserve was when a male that had been taking young goats from an African kraal was caught in a trap. A month later a female was trapped in a deep ravine near the same place. Then in the winter of 1941, a den occupied by a family of brown hyaenas was discovered on the northern bank of the Sabie River behind a screen of thick bush and reeds. It had apparently been used by the family for some years as 'the vicinity was littered with bones, and it was quite evident that most, if not all the animals had been seized alive and killed by these hyaenas. This was to me rather a remarkable discovery, since hyaenas, as a tribe, have never been regarded as primary hunters. In the present instance there was no doubt about the matter. The heads of fourteen full-grown impala rams, all quite recently killed, the skulls of several baboons, and of two chitas [sic] (one of them a full-grown animal), remains of guinea fowls, and a large tree snake ("boomslang"), partly chewed, were among the exhibits.'

Despite his certainty that 'these hyaenas must have developed a sound hunting technique', Stevenson-Hamilton had misinterpreted the evidence. Twenty years later the real scenario still remained an enigma and Tol Pienaar conceded that 'very little is known about the habits of these nocturnal predators ... It would have been most interesting to observe how the brown hyaenas succeeded in capturing prey ... Unfortunately this has never been witnessed yet and the mystery remains unsolved.'

It was not until Gus Mills embarked on his classic multi-year field study of the brown hyaena in the southern Kalahari in the 1970s and '80s that the true scientific facts came to light.

To prosper, every creature requires a measure of safety from its enemies and a place within a healthy community.

The brown hyaena is 'a poor hunter', Mills concluded. 'Hunting is unspecialized and opportunistic ... a chase-and-grab effort at any small animal that it encounters.' Of the 128 hunts he observed, only six (five per cent) were successful. The animals most often hunted were springhares, springbok lambs, bat-eared foxes and ground-nesting birds such as korhaans. Instead, the brown hyaena makes its living 'primarily as a scavenger of a wide range of vertebrate remains ... and relies more on scavenging than any of the other mammalian carnivores.' It supplements its diet with fruits, insects and birds' eggs. How could Stevenson-Hamilton have got it so wrong? By making an incorrect assumption: the remains of prey animals scattered around the Sabie River den had not been killed by the hyaenas themselves, except probably for the boomslang and guinea fowls. Unlike spotted hyaenas, brown hyaenas frequently bring food back to the den for their young to eat. In the Kalahari, Mills observed one brown hyaena carry a 7.5-kilogram carcass 15 kilometres. What Stevenson-Hamilton saw were other predators' leftovers that the brown hyaenas had scavenged and brought home.

Sadly, it has been at least 60 years since the last brown hyaena breeding record was obtained in the Kruger. Very occasionally vagrants that have crossed into the park from the west are fleetingly glimpsed but no evidence of breeding exists. Because of their low profile, Kruger's brown hyaenas slipped into local extinction without anyone really noticing. And the cause of their disappearance? The most likely explanation is that the species was so thoroughly outcompeted by the spotted hyaena that it could no longer sustain itself in the Kruger Park.

In their hyaena status survey and conservation action plan for the IUCN/Species Survival Commission's Hyaena Specialist Group, Heribert Hofer from the Leibniz Institute in Berlin and Gus Mills noted that 'the spotted hyaena is dominant to the brown hyaena and in certain areas deprives it of a significant amount of food. This may have a detrimental effect on brown hyaena numbers and may even effect its distribution, as where the spotted hyaena is common the brown hyaena is usually absent or very rare.'

While driving around the Kalahari, Gus Mills saw 'brown hyaenas four times more frequently in areas where there were few spotted hyaenas than in the area of spotted hyaena dens'. He also observed that in a one-on-one contest a spotted hyaena was able to appropriate a carcass from a brown hyaena on every occasion. 'As with lions and wild dogs in Kruger, it appears that a larger and more dominant species has a negative influence on the distribution and numbers of a smaller rival,' he concluded. With that knowledge and in hindsight, the clues to the brown hyaena's disappearance from the Kruger fall into place.

The vagrants that now and then cross into the park come from areas where spotted hyaenas have been eliminated because of their stock-raiding reputation, while the much more elusive brown hyaenas are often overlooked (and anyway their impact on domestic stock is usually small). The family of brown hyaenas that took up residence on the Sabie River may have been exploiting a window of opportunity created by low spotted hyaena numbers in the wake of virulent predator control, together with an epidemic. As it was, two years after the original den was discovered, the brown hyaenas were forced to move to a new site on the Sabie, closer to the Sand River junction, when several lions began digging up the old system of warrens to get at the meat they could smell underground.

But the knockout blow came with the proliferation of boreholes sunk in the Kruger from the 1930s to the 1970s, which led to an increase in the density of resident herbivores that in turn led to a buildup of lion and spotted hyaena numbers in parts of the park where previously they had been absent, scarce or only seasonal visitors. While increasing prey density benefits the biggest carnivores, it can have dangerously adverse consequences for weaker competitors. When two related species compete for similar resources, the larger species usually displaces the smaller and may force its population to such low densities that it becomes unviable. Though it has not been scientifically proven, that appears to be exactly what happened to the last of the Kruger's brown hyaenas.

To prosper, every creature requires a measure of safety from its enemies and a place within a healthy community. It is a lesson the brown hyaena's disappearance reinforces:

The brown hyaena is slightly smaller than its spotted cousin and always forages alone. Never common in Kruger, their last breeding record was 60 years ago. It appears that they were displaced by spotted hyaenas and lions after the proliferation of artificial water points opened up areas where previously the bigger carnivores were rare or absent.

successful conservation requires protection of both species and the processes that maintain ecosystems. Biodiversity has become both a major objective and the currency of conservation in the modern era. Whether the Kruger can maintain its spectacular biological diversity, which includes many of the megafauna that roamed Earth in the last geologic period, depends as much on knowing how to manage biological communities as knowing how to minimise human impact. Modern conservation biologists are learning how to manage remnant ecosystems like the Greater Kruger – which despite its size has become an island in a sea of human development – so that they function almost as if they were intact. All life is an accident of fate shaped by many forces, some random, some chaotic, but to lose a world where elephants roam free and the spotted hyaena's song coyly calls in the night would be to lose something infinitely precious.

Index